The Politics of Law and Order

Street Crime and Public Policy

Stuart A. Scheingold

with new Foreword by Malcolm M. Feeley

Classics of Law & Society Series

Quid Pro Books

New Orleans, Louisiana

The Politics of Law and Order

Street Crime and Public Policy

Previously published in 1984 by Longman Inc., New York, New York (now Pearson Education, Inc.).

Published in the 2016 hardback *Classics of Law & Society* edition by Quid Pro Books.

ISBN 9781610277983 (cloth)

Quid Pro, LLC
5860 Citrus Blvd., Suite D-101
New Orleans, Louisiana 70123
www.quidprobooks.com

qp

Publisher's Cataloging-in-Publication

Scheingold, Stuart A.

 The politics of law and order: street crime and public policy / by Stuart A. Scheingold.

   p. cm.

 Includes index.

 Includes 2010 foreword by Malcolm M. Feeley.

 Series: *Classics of Law & Society.*

ISBN: 1610270363 (paperback edition, 2010)
ISBN: 1610277988 (hardback edition, 2016)
ISBN: 1610270371 (Kindle edition, 2010)
ISBN: 0582284155 (original hardback edition, 1984)
ISBN: 0582284163 (original paperback edition, 1984)

1. Crime and criminals—United States. 2. Crime and criminals—Government policy—United States. 3. Criminal justice. Administration of—Political aspects—United States. 4. Social conflict—Philosophy. 5. Social values. I. Title. II. Series

HV6789.S32 2010   364'.973   2010–16212

THIS BOOK IS FOR LEE

*I can only hope
that it is worthy of her*

Contents

[Pages in brackets refer to the original pagination of the 1984 edition. These page numbers are inserted into this edition's text using brackets, for continuity of citations, references and syllabi.]

Foreword to the 2010 Classics of Law & Society Edition i

Foreword (1984) v

About the Author vii

Preface ix

Part I. Crime

    1. Perspectives on Crime 1

Part II. The Public

    2. The Politicization of Crime 33

    3. Crime, Culture, and Political Conflict 57

Part III. Criminal Process

    4. Traditional Policing 91

    5. The Politics of Police Reform 113

    6. Equity in the Criminal Courts 145

    7. The Politics of Criminal Court Reform 171

Part IV. Criminal Justice

    8. Beyond the Politics of Law and Order 199

    9. The Politics of the Criminal Process 221

Index 229

Foreword
to the 2010 *Classics of Law & Society* Edition

The Politics of Law and Order: Street Crime and Public Policy was originally published in 1984. It was brilliant then and it is brilliant today, over twenty-five years later. Indeed, it is amazing to see how perspicacious Stuart Scheingold's reflections were. He hit the nail on the head in just about every stroke. His observations are as pertinent today as they were when the book was first published. This is little short of amazing since he was writing in the very early stages of the long build-up to the War on Crime. Yet, his analysis is robust and mature, written with the confidence of a historian who has ample perspective and writes from hindsight.

This leads to the question, how is it that Scheingold could write with such authority about what was in effect breaking news? The answer, I think, is that he had already developed a powerful theoretical framework through which to see and understand the world of public policy. His construction of that framework evolved slowly and was fully mature by the time he wrote *The Politics of Law and Order.* He developed it in the 1960s, as he reflected on the long history of the failed promise of American constitutional rights, and it came to fruition in his classic essay, *The Politics of Rights*, published in 1974. *The Politics of Law and Order* is an elaboration and extension and adaptation of a powerful and well-developed framework. It was written at the height of Scheingold's intellectual power. The book is eloquent testimony to the power of *theory*, as distinct from reporting, and from standard social science empiricism. It resonates powerfully with the insights of political psychology and social theory. Scheingold stands alongside the best of the social scientists walking in the footsteps of Durkheim and Weber.

Scheingold's many insights into the tragic nature of American crime policy are also singular when seen in another light—in comparison to those whose work he wrote about, and in comparison to others who later wrote on the same topic. In this book, Scheingold examines "mainstream" thinking about crime of the times, and contrasts it to Marxist and other conflict theories of crime. In all this, he anchors these examinations in cultural analysis and social theory in ways that bring out the unarticulated premises of these various conventional ways of thinking. Thus his analysis of crime and crime policy is linked to deep cultural imperatives in American political culture.

It is this approach that produces such a timely and timeless analysis at one and the same time. Scheingold's book can profitably be read when reflecting on the current penchant for American states to continue to spend millions of dollars to execute prisoners even as their cities are laying off thousands of police officers. And his analysis can also be read profitably by those exploring the peculiar history of the American approach to law and order.

His book can also be compared to others which have written in the same vein. Since publication of *The Politics of Law and Order* in 1984, a veritable library on America's crime problems has been produced. Much of this literature is topical and ephemeral: charting the ups and downs of crime and imprisonment rates, showing that punishment and crime have little to do with each other, and revealing scandal, abuse, disparity, and more in the criminal process—despite many pledges to overcome them. Similarly, there is a small handful of theoretically informed work on American crime and crime policy. The works of David Garland, Jonathan Simon, and Loïc Wacquant in the United States, as well as Nicola Lacey, Dario Melossi, Richard Sparks, and Lucy Zedner in the UK and on the Continent, immediately come to mind. Of course there are many others. This work is splendid—at its best stunning. However, all of its authors owe an enormous debt to Scheingold, and his *The Politics of Law and Order*, as well as his earlier masterpiece, *The Politics of Rights*. In many ways both acknowledged and unacknowledged, these works are direct descendants of Scheingold's pioneering work. He was there first, a decade or more before the others. In many respects, the works that that followed *The Politics* volumes are variations and footnotes on his themes. He is the giant among this lot.

So, it is particularly appropriate that *The Politics of Law and Order* be made available to a new generation of readers. It is important for what it says—and how it says it—about American crime and crime policy, as well as American political culture. It speaks truth to power today as much as it did when it was first published. It speaks to an enduring feature of American social life in much the same way that the works of Louis Hart and Richard Hofstadter did. And for those interested in the history of ideas or the sociology of the professions, this book is one of the foundations—the foundation—on which the most sophisticated social theoretical analyses of crime policy in late modernity are based. It is the Ur text as it were. If one wants to do a thorough history of ideas in this area, he or she must start with this book.

Of course few ideas spring from nowhere or only one source, and Scheingold's theoretical framework has its own genealogy. He wrote in the tradition of his colleagues, Murray Edelman (*The Symbolic Uses of Power*) and Lance Bennett (*The Politics of Illusion*), each of them descendants of Durkheim in sociology, Harold Lasswell in political psychology, and Clifford Geertz in anthropology, as well as the rich tradition of European social theory.

No single book springs forth alone and fully formed. Still, if one is looking for the foundational text in the cultural understanding of the politics of law and order in late twentieth century America, and perhaps beyond, this book has to be one of the starting points.

Malcolm M. Feeley
CLAIRE SANDERS CLEMENTS DEAN'S PROFESSOR
JURISPRUDENCE AND SOCIAL POLICY PROGRAM
BOALT HALL SCHOOL OF LAW
UNIVERSITY OF CALIFORNIA AT BERKELEY
December, 2010

iv

Foreword
to the Original Edition

In 1974, Stuart Scheingold published *The Politics of Rights*, a book which explored the nature and impact of public interest litigation on the political process in the United States. The thesis of that book was that law has two lives whose impact is experienced and must be understood on two quite different levels. There is, Scheingold wrote, "the concrete institutional existence of the law" which is familiar to us. But, he continued, law "also has a symbolic life; it resides in the minds of Americans." He then went on to explore the significance of the symbolic form of law, demonstrating how law conditions perceptions, establishes expectations and develops standards for legitimacy of policies, in short how it affects the context in which politics is conducted in the United States.

In *The Politics of Law and Order*, Scheingold builds on and extends this earlier work, merging his cultural-symbolic perspective with conflict theory in criminology. The result is a penetrating examination of crime and crime policy in North America. He begins by examining the appeals and shortcomings of both mainstream and radical commentators on criminal justice, showing how their common-sense assumptions are oversimplified and their policy prescriptions flawed. Most of these discussions of crime policy, he argues, suffer because they do not take into account the symbolic nature and consequences of crime policy and because they fail to recognize the complexity of the phenomena of crime. In contrast he maintains that his perspective provides a richer and more insightful means for understanding the criminal process and for developing policies about crime.

Having presented this framework and distinguished it from others' views, Scheingold then employs it in his examination of the criminal justice issues confronting the public, the police, prosecutors, and judges. The results of this examination are illuminating and often fly in the face of conventional wisdom. For instance, while liberal observers of the criminal process are nearly united in their desire to restrict, structure and limit official discretion, Scheingold unabashedly embraces policies that would significantly expand it.

This book should appeal to a wide and diverse audience. Social theorists will be fascinated by Scheingold's effort to merge cultural-symbolic analysis with conflict theory. Criminal justice policy analysts will find many of their cherished notions challenged and be forced to reconsider their most comfortable assumptions as they confront Scheingold's novel new ideas. Students seeking an overview of the criminal justice system, will find a lucid critique of major perspectives on crime, and an incisive and original discussion of the central problems of the criminal process. Ultimately, whether or not one agrees with Scheingold's central thesis, *The Politics of Law and Order* will force all its serious readers to rethink many of their long-held views on crime and the nature of the criminal process.

Malcolm M. Feeley
PROFESSOR
MADISON, WISCONSIN
1984

About the Author

Stuart A. Scheingold (1931–2010) taught generations of students as a Professor of Political Science at the University of Washington, and was an internationally recognized scholar on topics as diverse as street crime, the myth and reality of legal rights, punishment, political integration, activist lawyers, and political fiction. He wrote or edited 15 books and numerous articles and essays. His 1974 book *The Politics of Rights: Lawyers, Public Policy, and Political Change* is considered an essential part of socio-legal study. "He was quite simply one of the world's leading commentators on law and politics," notes Amherst College's Austin Sarat.

Dr. Scheingold received his Ph.D. from Berkeley and taught at the University of Wisconsin and the University of California at Davis before joining the Washington faculty in 1969. He was previously a Social Science Research Council Fellow and a Research Associate at the Center for International Affairs of Harvard University. His published writings include *The Rule of Law in European Integration: The Path of the Schuman Plan* (1965, and 2011 edition by Quid Pro Books), *The Law in Political Integration: The Evolution and Integrative Implications of Regional Legal Processes in the European Community* (1971, and 2010 edition by QP), and *Europe's Would-Be Polity: Patterns of Change in the European Community* (with Leon N. Lindberg, 1970). He was also a contributor to and coeditor (with Lindberg) of *Regional Integration: Theory and Research* (1971). He published *The Politics of Street Crime: Criminal Process and Cultural Obsession* in 1991. Later, he coauthored with Sarat an acclaimed series on cause lawyering, and most recently he published *The Political Novel: Re-Imagining the Twentieth Century* (Continuum, 2010).

In 2001, the Law & Society Association awarded Dr. Scheingold the Harry J. Kalven Jr. Prize for distinguished contributions to socio-legal scholarship, observing that "his intellectual legacy is both broad and deep." Three years later, the American Political Science Association presented him with the Law and Courts Lifetime Achievement Award. In 2009, the University of Washington established the Stuart A. Scheingold Professorship of Social Justice in his honor.

Preface

Beginning in the mid-1960s, crime, especially street crime, became a political issue of considerable importance at both the local and the national levels. How are we to explain the sudden emergence of crime as a political issue? What consequences have followed from this politicization of crime?

At first glance, the answers to these questions seem obvious enough. Crime became a political issue because of popular dissatisfaction with a rising crime rate. Certainly crime began increasing at an alarming rate at roughly the same time that the fear of crime began to spread through the society. The results of politicization also seem obvious: the government declared war on crime, federal monies were channeled through the states to local law enforcement agencies, and by about 1973 the crime rate had leveled off. Read in this way, the last two decades can be interpreted as a textbook example of responsive government.

On closer inspection, the politicization of crime turns out to be a much more complicated story. It is true that the fear of crime was rising along with the crime rate during the late 1960s and early 1970s, but the calls for law and order which symbolized the public's reaction to crime reflected concerns transcending crime as such. During that period, the country was also convulsed by protests against racial injustice, poverty, and the war in Vietnam. Particularly as these protests spilled over into the streets, public anxieties about social order began to increase. Calls for law and order were, then, integrally linked to an unsettling sense of rapid and unwelcome social change as well as to the crime rate.

The story of politicization is further complicated by the fact that politicization and the crime rate have not really moved in parallel paths. To take just one example, one would have never known as the 1982 elections approached that crime had leveled off in the mid-1970s—much less that there were signs after 1980 of an actual decrease in crime. Tom Wicker, hardly one to play up the public's anxiety about crime, interpreted the opinion data in the summer of 1982 as revealing "a picture of a nation in fear."[1] And politicians on both the right and left were inclined to see crime as a promising issue—"the issue" according to Rep. Geraldine Ferraro.[2]

Finally, there is little or no reason to believe that the crime picture has improved because of the additional resources made available to law enforcement officials or because of get-tough policies which are associated with the calls for law and order.[3] If the crime wave is actually receding, it probably has more to do with demographic changes than with policy changes.

> The fact of the matter is that crime often increases or decreases for wholly mysterious or uncontrollable reasons—like the number of male youths in the population. The number of murders in New York recently fell 14.4 percent, for instance, but no one knows exactly why. And it is to the everlasting credit of the police chief there, Robert J. McGuire, that when asked to account for the wonderful new numbers, he simply said he could not.[4]

This view, expressed by columnist Richard Cohen, tends to be shared by criminologists and by many police executives in addition to Chief McGuire.

The essential point is that the "politics of law and order," the subject of this book, turn out to be a good deal more puzzling on careful analysis than seems to be the case on first glance. The key to the puzzle, as I see it, is the realization that crime control, the ostensible objective of the politics of law and order, frequently takes a back seat to the scramble for power and position among politicians and among participants in criminal process as well. Politicians in search of an issue have good reason to believe that campaigning on crime is good politics—at least if one takes a get-tough stand. Law enforcement officials are also well served by the fear of crime, since the result is frequently that more resources are directed to the agencies of criminal process.

This more complex view of the politics of law and order leads us back to slightly different versions of the two questions posed initially. We are led to wonder, in the first place, just how, when, and why the public is so easily aroused and so punitively inclined on the crime issue? Politicians who choose to campaign on crime may find that they have a tiger by the tail. "If you are a politician," columnist Cohen tells us, "there is nothing quite as bad as being called 'soft on crime.'"[5] We are, in the second place, led to wonder whether politicization has much of an impact on operative policy. Crime control is, after all, only the ostensible objective of the politics of law and order, and nobody really knows how to control crime anyway. Consequently, there is reason to suspect that, for better or worse, get-tough political promises may not actually be kept.

These two questions are the primary foci of this book. My point of departure is, briefly put, that the politics of law and order has a life of its own which is quite independent of crime and criminal victimization. The case which I can make for this controversial point of view is incomplete and circumstantial, because there is a shortage of directly relevant empirical research. Still, in systematically calling attention to the symbolic dimensions of the politics of law and order, I am doing no more than applying to criminal process a perspective which has proven useful for analyzing other political problems. It, of course, remains to be seen whether my interpretation will stand up to empirical inquiry and, indeed, I have already undertaken such research myself. If this book does no more than prompt further research, it will have served an important purpose. I also hope, however, that the book will make a contribution of its own by providing a plausible and coherent account of the politics of criminal process.

This book has been a very long time in the making and I fear that I shall not be able to recall all of the people who have helped me along the way. To anyone who has contributed and whom I fail to mention, I offer my profound apologies and the consolation of not being associated with this rather unorthodox look at crime and criminal process. Of course, those who are mentioned do not share in the responsibility for my sins. All too often, I have failed to heed their advice.

Since the empirical follow-up which I have already begun is so inextricably linked to this book, I must first acknowledge my debt to the Law and Social Science Program of the National Science Foundation for financial assistance and to its estimable director, Dr. Felice Levine, for the encouragement that has made it so much easier to push ahead. Several of my colleagues at the University of Washington and elsewhere have read major portions of this manuscript and commented in great detail including Dan Lev, Lance Bennett, Malcolm Feeley, David Olson, Sandy Muir, Erza Stotland, and Marvin Zetterbaum. Others who have provided helpful critiques of one or another portions of the manuscript are Craig Carr, Lief Carter, Bob Erwin, Erika Fairchild, Herman Goldstein, Ed Greenberg, Bill Haltom, Greg Hill, Herb Jacob, Hubert Locke, David Neubauer, Jon Pool, Charles Silberman, and Marlie Wasserman. Nor should I forget the Thursday cabal and especially Malcolm Griffith with whom I developed my ideas for the use of popular fiction. As usual, my students had to persevere through all the stages of this project and they contributed more than they will ever realize. Working with Longman Inc. has turned out to be a real pleasure thanks to cooperative and efficient people like David Estrin, Joan Matthews, and most of all, Irv Rockwood, who has been patient, gracious, and sensible through waves of delay and equivocation on my part. I have dedicated this book to the most important person in my life. She has borne the heaviest burdens of this project and she alone has made it all worthwhile.

Stuart A. Scheingold
1984

NOTES to the Preface

1. *The New York Times*, 9 July 1982.

2. Ibid., 16 March 1982.

3. Elliott Currie, "Fighting Crime," *Working Papers Magazine* 9, no. 4 (July/August 1982): 16–25.

4. *The Washington Post*, 11 July 1982.

5. *Loc. cit.*

Part I

Crime

{Page 3}

1

Perspectives on Crime

CRIME AND COMMON SENSE

Among the most vexing aspects of crime in America is its capacity to survive all the policy assaults mounted against it. Why is it that we cannot keep crime within manageable limits? Street crime, which is the principal concern of this book, is a crude and reprehensible activity conducted by people who, for the most part, are without talent or training. Arrayed against these outcasts is a veritable army of trained professionals backed by committed political leaders and an aroused public. Common sense tells us that it should be no contest, and so when crime continues to flourish we become frustrated and angry.

The objective of this book is not to provide a solution to the problem of crime but to demonstrate how misleading our common-sense understandings are. Lurking beneath the surface is a complexity that makes crime an intractable problem. Once we understand the full extent of the problem, we shall be less beguiled by the easy answers offered by politicians, journalists, and some criminal justice professionals. Our preoccupation with easy answers leads us toward scapegoats and allows us to fall prey to demagogic politicians. While there may be no solutions to the crime problem, there are better and worse ways of responding to it. We shall be able to make the better choices only when we are able to transcend the cops-and-robbers images that tend to dominate our thinking about crime.

Common sense suggests that society has established rules that must be followed if we are to live together in reasonable harmony. Some of these rules

1

are merely conventions. For example, it is not important whether {4} people drive on the right or the left side of the road—only that a choice be made and that we abide by it. Other rules are important in their own right because they prohibit behavior that we deem intrinsically wrong, such as rape or murder or robbery. But whether rules are rooted in moral imperatives or are designed simply to promote predictable social interaction, violations call for condemnation. Society cannot function if it is constantly jeopardized by behavior that puts lives, safety, or property at risk.

Mainstream American responses to crime are drawn from this common-sense perspective. The focus is on criminals and on preventing them from committing crimes. There are, however, rather sharp differences between liberals and conservatives on how this can best be done. Liberals are inclined to trace criminal behavior to social causes, such as poverty and racism. As a result, liberals look to policies that will reduce social inequities and increase opportunities. Conservatives think that there are fundamental differences between criminals and the rest of us. That is, criminals suffer from some basic character defect and must be segregated from society or at least dealt with in a restrictive fashion. Society must, in short, make it difficult and costly to commit crimes in order to compensate for the criminal's lack of social conscience, self-control or both. Whereas liberals favor the carrot, conservatives prefer the stick.

But we should not exaggerate the differences between conservatives and liberals. In actual practice, society tends to pursue liberal and conservative policies simultaneously—albeit with discernible drifts in one direction or the other. These days, conservative forces seem to be in control; fifteen to twenty years ago, liberal programs predominated.

One reason why the society can accommodate to these shifts and even to a continuing mélange of liberal and conservative policies is that the differences between liberal and conservative thinking are not nearly so great as appears at first glance. Both views share a belief in the legitimacy of basic rules. Both liberals and conservatives agree that whether criminals are seen as victims of circumstances or deficient human beings, they have violated the social contract and must either be brought into the mainstream or excluded from it. Neither liberals nor conservatives raise fundamental questions about the viability or desirability of mainstream American life.

Nevertheless, radically different understandings of crime in America exist. Marxism provides the most coherent and theoretically sound alternative to the mainstream view. According to Marxists, capitalism is criminogenic, and the real criminals are the capitalists. Crime is a by-product of capitalism, and the only effective way of ridding society of crime is to do away with capitalism and embrace socialism. Mainstream and Marxist views are, in a sense, mirror images. "One group would resocialize, or even liquidate, the poor, while the other would resocialize, or even liquidate, the rich."[1] {5}

2

One either is or is not a Marxist. Someone who does not share Marxists premises cannot accept Marxist analyses and Marxist prescriptions. Yet, non-Marxists can learn a good deal about the causes and consequences of crime from Marxists. By effectively calling into question virtually every common-sense assumption about crime in America, Marxists allow us to step back from our preconceptions, take a fresh look at crime, and see things that had previously gone unnoticed. Regardless of whether we accept Marxism, then, it serves an important critical function.

Less apocalyptic critiques of the mainstream are provided by conflict theorists, who remind us of the political nature of criminal law and criminal process. Disputes between liberals and conservatives are ample evidence of the essentially conflictual character of law-enforcement policy making. It therefore stands to reason, the conflict theorists tell us, that the rules of the game in criminal process, like other authoritative rules in the society, are products of political decisions rather than moral or functional imperatives. Thus it is necessary to remain sensitive to differentials in political power and alternative value structures in order to fully understand the nature and consequences of crime. Criminality must be understood much as a status conferred by the political order.

Like the Marxist perspective conflict theory calls into question the harmonious mainstream social vision. Unlike the Marxist perspective, conflict theory leaves open the possibility that conflict is not necessarily a terminal social disease. Nor, from this perspective, does conflict preclude some basic agreements among us on social values and social functions. Conflict theory provides the appropriately skeptical frame of reference required to escape the misleading confines of the common sense-view of crime. The remainder of this chapter explores in more detail each of the three perspectives, and in so doing, makes a case for conflict theory as the most useful frame of reference.

THE MAINSTREAM

The mainstream is not so much a single school of thought as a way of characterizing the full range of commonly accepted American criminological wisdom. The work of James Q. Wilson typifies mainstream thinking in two important ways: (1) Wilson has fashioned a moderate position between reform-minded liberals and hard-line conservatives; and (2) Wilson's active and cogent presentation of the moderate mainstream position has made him an influential figure in policy debates.[2] For both reasons, this section relies heavily on Wilson's work in discussing mainstream views.

With some justification, Wilson sees his thinking as midway between that of liberals and conservatives.[3] Unlike liberals, Wilson is not reluctant {6} to put the blame for crime squarely on the shoulders of criminals. He is very impatient with liberal inclinations to look to social welfare policies as the primary tool for coping with crime and sees punishment as the necessary centerpiece of an effective crime-control policy. In contrast to conservatives, however, Wilson is sensitive to calls for social reform. More fundaméntally, he does not share the hard-liners' belief that crime control can be achieved by increasing penalties and reducing the legal protections available to defendants.

While there is, therefore, a certain evenhandedness to Wilson's position, he is more a moderate conservative than a true centrist. He shares most of the conservative assumptions about the causes and consequences of crime. He also partakes of the conservative faith in punishment. He distinguishes himself from hard-line conservatives primarily by having developed a more balanced and better-informed critique of criminal process. In this way, Wilson has been able to stake out a responsible conservative position that is widely respected in policy circles.[4]

Moderate Conservatism

Crime is, for Wilson, first and foremost a traumatic event in which predatory strangers victimize decent citizens. "Unless otherwise stated or clearly implied, the word 'crime' when used alone in this book refers to predatory crime for gain, the most common forms of which are robbery, burglary, larceny, and auto theft."[5] Thus Wilson sees street crime as the central problem to be faced by those responsible for coping with crime. Wilson is not unaware of less coercive forms of crime; he simply feels that they pose less of a threat to society.

> This book deals neither with "white-collar crimes" nor, except for
> heroin addiction, with so-called "victimless crimes." Partly, this
> reflects my conviction, which I believe is the conviction of most
> citizens, that predatory street crime is a far more serious matter
> than consumer fraud, antitrust violations, prostitution, or gamb-
> ling, because predatory crime...makes difficult or impossible the
> maintenance of meaningful human communities.[6]

Wilson's main concern is with the disruptive social consequences of the increase in street crime since the mid-1960s.

Wilson does not labor under the illusion that crime can be eliminated. He simply wishes to keep crime within tolerable limits, which he feels have been exceeded in recent years. These days, according to Wilson, crime impinges on our freedom, our security, and our peace of mind. More explicitly, Wilson discerns two distinct ways in which crime restricts "the formation and the maintenance of community."[7] As the tide of crime rises, we are faced with the alternatives of fleeing to an island of suburban safety {7} or adapting to an environment of fear. But whether we grit our teeth or pack our bags, street crime and human community work at cross purposes to one another.

Flight, according to Wilson, tends to be the preferred solution for those who can afford to move. Thus, flight drains the community of its most stable elements, its "human infrastructure."[8] The people who leave are those least likely to cause crime and most likely to participate in the kinds of networks that discourage crime. Nevertheless, these inner-city groups do not fit in well in the suburbs, which they tend to destabilize.

> With the more affluent having departed and the community-maintenance functions they once served now undermanned, the rates of predatory crime in inner-city areas rose. At the same time, because some of those persons who moved out. white and black, were not yet by the standards of their new communities fully middle class, the reported rates of crime in these areas also went up.[9]

In this way, flight tends to decrease the resistance to crime in the cities while increasing its likelihood in the suburbs.

The problem would not be solved by somehow stemming the flow of inner-city emigrants because the crime that tempts people to leave severely diminishes the quality of their lives.

> By disrupting the delicate nexus of ties, formal and informal, by which we are linked with our neighbors, crime atomizes society and makes its members mere individual calculators estimating their own advantage, especially their own chances for survival amidst their fellows.[10]

Wilson does not specify exactly what he means by this, but the basic argument seems reasonably clear. We can either curtail normal activities so as to reduce the hazards of urban life or we can try to lead a relatively normal life while courting injury and property loss. Either way, we are forced to live with a fear that drains pleasure from our lives and plants seeds of distrust of those around us.

With crime looming over us so ominously, it may seem odd at first glance that Wilson is not really interested in figuring out the causes of crime. That is because he feels that causal analysis tends to get in the way of effective policy making.

> [U]ltimate causes cannot be the object of policy efforts precisely because, being ultimate, they cannot be changed. For example, criminologists have shown beyond doubt that men commit more crimes than women and younger men more (of certain kinds) than older ones. It is a theoretically important and scientifically correct observation. Yet it means little for policy makers concerned with crime prevention, since men cannot be changed into women or made to skip over adolescent years.[11] {8}

In other words, some things cannot be changed, and policy makers must work with "what is variable or contingent."[12] Moreover, the kinds of changes suggested by research into the causes of crime "lead into the realm of the subjective and familial, where both the efficacy and propriety of policy are most in doubt.[13]

> McCord and McCord, for example, draw the lesson from the Cambridge-Sommerville study that the true causes of delinquency are found in "the absence of parental affection" coupled with family conflict, inconsistent discipline, and rebellious parents. They are quite possibly correct; indeed if I may speak on the bases of my own wholly unscientific observation, I am quite confident they are correct. But what of it? What agency do we create, what budget do we allocate, that will supply the missing "parental affection" and restore to the child consistent discipline supported by a stable and loving family.[14]

Clearly, insofar as Wilson is concerned, the scale, the intrusiveness, and the speculative character of such undertakings make them undependable and dangerous.

Wilson's own proposals are more modest, but they are at least loosely connected to causal analysis. He is obviously attracted to Cloward and Ohlin's theory that "each individual occupies a position in both legitimate and illegitimate opportunity structures," but is concerned that they fail to pursue this theory to its logical conclusion, namely, a focus on "the costs and benefits of illegitimate as opposed to legitimate opportunities."[15] This path leads Wilson toward deterrence and behavior modification.

> Criminals may be willing to run greater risks (or they may have a weaker sense of morality) than the average citizen, but if the expected cost of crime goes up without a corresponding increase in the expected benefits, then the would-be criminal—unless he or she is among that small fraction of criminals who are utterly irrational—engages in less crime, just as the average citizen will be less likely to take a job as a day laborer if the earnings from that occupation, relative to those from other occupations, go down.[16]

The solution to the problem of crime is therefore rather simple—at least in theory: increase the risks of crime by a more consistent policy of punishing criminals and "increase the rewards of alternative sources of income" by, for example, job programs for unemployed teenagers, who are our most crime-prone age group.[17]

In Wilson's view this moderate approach places him between the hard-liners and the liberals. The hard-liners are too punitive, and the liberals are too preoccupied with the social roots of crime. Wilson accepts the importance of punishment, but in measured doses. He is willing to acknowledge an underlying social malaise as the real source of our current crime problem, but he sees this malaise as largely beyond the reach of public policy. In any case, he perceives both conservatives and liberals as {9} naive in their understandings of the nature and consequences of crime and simplistic in their response to it. By sketching the contrasts between Wilson and those to his right and left, then, we can get a better sense of the full range of mainstream positions and Wilson's place therein.

Hard-Line Conservatism

Those on the right are inclined to see crime in terms of individual moral responsibility and thus tend to raise the stakes of the moral game by dwelling on more lurid and reprehensible crimes. Criminals are perceived as free to choose between abiding by the law and committing crimes. In choosing to prey on others, they clearly demonstrate that they are defective human beings. Accordingly, it is futile to appeal to them on grounds of reason or morality. Force is the only appropriate response to criminality. Nor should criminals be accorded their legal and constitutional rights; these are for upstanding citizens, not for sociopaths. It is particularly objectionable when such rights protect criminals from prosecution and punishment because the result is to jeopardize the law-abiding. The due process reforms of the U.S. Supreme Court under Chief Justice Earl Warren are prime targets of hard-liners, who believe that these reforms have made it more difficult to apprehend and convict criminals. With little to fear from law enforcement, criminals simply follow their predatory instincts.

Wilson's views are less stark. He is fully prepared to assess moral blame but is not obsessed by villains, nor does he dwell on those crimes that are most shocking to our sensibilities. He sees crime as symptomatic of a general breakdown of society: dropping out of school, drug addiction, the family in decline, and too much reliance on welfare.[18] "[T]he social bonds—the ties of family, of neighborhood, of mutual forbearance and civility—seem to have come asunder."[19] In the background of Wilson's analysis of crime is a sense of fundamental moral decay, a feeling that we are failing to transmit a moral message to significant portions of the society.

With this more subtle sense of crime, it is not surprising that Wilson finds it simplistic of the hard-liners to believe that the answer to crime is to allow the police to crack down hard on criminals and similarly simplistic to blame the increase in crime on the Warren Court.

> Conservatives, exaggerating the crime increase, blamed it on a "soft" Supreme Court and a "permissive" attorney general on the apparent assumption — never defended, and in fact indefensible — that the Supreme Court and the attorney general could effectively manage the day-to-day behavior of the local police, and that

> the level of police effectiveness was directly related to the level of crime.[20] {10}

In other words, if crime is indicative of a breakdown in the civic order, it is hardly reasonable to look to the police for a solution. Wilson is therefore very skeptical about the capacity of the police to prevent crime.[21] He is similarly reluctant to attribute the increase in crime to Warren Court decisions that limit police methods of interrogation.

> Most persons arrested for the more common serious crimes, such as burglary and robbery, have been arrested under circumstances such that no confession is required, no searches need be conducted, and scarcely any police interrogation occurs. Often they are caught right in the act of robbing or burgling. Frequently there are witnesses to testify or stolen property that can be identified. Many—I should say most—of those arrested...are eager to talk in order to see whether, by confession to other crimes or implicating other persons, they can lighten the charges against them.[22]

For Wilson, in short, a simple unleashing of the police is not a sensible way to respond to crime.

Because Wilson is sensitive to the combination of circumstances that lead individuals to crime, he is less inclined than the hard-liners to deny defendants the protection of the law and more willing to think of them as rational human beings. Whatever their moral shortcomings, they are entitled to "hearings and trials under strict standards of due process...where the issue of guilt is in doubt."[23] Moreover, because most criminals are rational, indiscriminate increases in criminal penalties are likely to be self-defeating. In the first place, penalties deter crime only if criminals believe that they will be caught and that, once caught, the penalties will be imposed. Clearly, the harshness of the sanction does not increase the likelihood of being caught, and according to Wilson, "the more severe the penalty, the more unlikely that it will be imposed."

> The more severe the sentence, the greater the bargaining power of the accused, and the greater likelihood he will be charged with a lesser offense. Extremely long mandatory minimum sentences do not always strengthen the hand of society; they often strengthen the hand of the criminal instead.[24]

Second, because criminals do reason and calculate, they are most likely to be influenced by a well-thought-out combination of carrots and sticks that leads them away from crime. This means providing job options for the unemployed and a schedule of penalties calibrated primarily to the seriousness of the offense and the offender's prior record. Research on deterrence, moreover, tells Wilson that certainty of punishment is more important than severity, and he therefore advocates some "deprivation of liberty" for all "nontrivial offenses."[25] For Wilson, punitive solutions are necessary, but they are not sufficient.

Wilson is thus able in a number of ways to distinguish his moderate views from hard-liners to his right, but he never really indicates who these archconservatives are. Nor am I aware of any systematic presentations of {11} the true right-wing position. Ernest van den Haag takes a position somewhat to the right of Wilson—but not much. Van den Haag puts more emphasis on the severity of punishment and has more faith in the police.[26] He also finds the exclusionary rule much more objectionable than does Wilson.

> What is wrong is that the judiciary has so weakened the position
> of prosecutors that they must habitually agree to inappropriate
> punishment because they cannot hope to do better by trial.[27]

The differences between Wilson and van den Haag are marginal, however. Most important, van den Haag is no more inclined than Wilson to think of the criminal as beyond the reach of policies that appeal to calculations of costs and benefits. In other words, van den Haag and Wilson agree that while criminals do not respond to moral suasion, they do respond to pleasure and pain. Among responsible commentators, then, Wilson's position seems distinctly conservative or neoconservative—as he is frequently characterized.[28] It remains true, nonetheless, that Wilson is more moderate and certainly in closer touch with the realities of criminal process than those who indulge in vitriolic denunciations of courts and are frequently heard from in the media or in law-and-order political campaigns.

Liberal Variations

To the left of the mainstream are the liberals, who are Wilson's primary target. The liberal view is most comprehensively presented in *The Challenge of Crime in a Free Society*, a report prepared by a special commission appointed by President Lyndon B. Johnson to look into the problems of crime in America.[29] The commission conducted a variety of studies on the causes, incidence, and consequences of crime—including some path-breaking research on victimization and public attitudes toward crime. Two basic themes run through this report. The first, essentially social, is that crime is associated with poverty and its correlates: weakened family structures, inadequate slum schools, limited job opportunities, and the like. The primary solution to these problems, according to the commission, are social programs of the kind undertaken in President Johnson's "war on poverty."[30] The commission's second concern is institutional: upgrading the police, the criminal courts, and the correctional system. Here the focus is on better-trained personnel, more efficient procedures, and humane treatment of offenders.[31]

The Challenge of Crime in a Free Society reflects mainstream thinking in the sense that neither society's values nor its institutions are called into serious question. Yet a distinctly liberal note is struck in tracing crime to {12} society's failure to live up to its social and institutional ideals. The first problem is that America is, according to the liberal perspective, no longer a land of opportunity for many of its people. Social programs are a way of providing the resources that can enable disadvantaged Americans to make a decent life for themselves. Similarly, rehabilitation is the way that criminals can be psychologically and vocationally adapted to mainstream American life. Liberals also object to the failure of the institutions of criminal process to live up to constitutional standards—whether because of shortages of funds, training, or accountability. Accordingly, the objective is to reform these institutions, principally by imposing strict due process standards upon them.

Liberals thus agree on the need for thoroughgoing reform, but there is an underlying tension within the reformist core of liberal mainstream views. Social and institutional reforms are compatible in principle, but not always in practice. There is, in the first place, the simple question of priorities. Given scarce resources, where is the emphasis to be put? More fundamentally, rehabilitative programs that must be tailored to differences among individual offenders tend to run at cross purposes to concerns with equality before the law. Liberals, like conservatives, are therefore divided among themselves, and these divisions surface particularly sharply on issues pertaining to the criminal courts which are considered in Chapters 6 and 7.

Wilson is clearly at odds with the social reform theme. He devotes an entire chapter to a rejection of the linkage between poverty and crime. The crime rate, he points out, "soared" during the 1960s, "this country('s)...longest sustained period of prosperity since World War II."[32] Criminal behavior is not, for Wilson, simply a sign of material deprivation. "During the 1960's," he tells us, "we were becoming two societies—one affluent and worried, the other pathological and predatory."[33] Street criminals are not simply victims of circumstances, they are morally deficient. As such, they are beyond the reach of ameliorative programs of the sort favored by liberals. For similar reasons, Wilson scoffs at rehabilitation.

> Today we smile in amusement at the naivete of those early prison reformers who imagined that religious instruction while in solitary confinement would lead to moral regeneration. How they would now smile at us at our presumption that conversations with a psychiatrist or a return to the community could achieve the same end. We have learned how difficult it is by governmental means to improve the educational attainments of children or to restore stability and affection to the family, and in these cases we are often working with willing subjects in moments of admitted need. Criminal rehabilitation requires producing equiv-

alent changes in unwilling subjects under conditions of duress or indifferences.[34]

A moral chasm separates street criminals from the rest of us, as Wilson sees things, and it is futile for the government to try to bridge it. {13}

On institutional issues, Wilson and the liberals are much closer together. Wilson believes, as do the due process liberals, that the criminal courts are essentially out of control. They are, according to Wilson, slow, erratic, and lenient.[35] Due process liberals would take issue with Wilson on the question of leniency. They are, however, at least as unhappy as Wilson with the law's delays and with the arbitrary behavior they detect among judges and other criminal process professionals. Accordingly, a consensus of sorts seem to have emerged in recent years, aimed at a more evenhanded enforcement of criminal statutes and at the imposition of sentences that correspond to the seriousness of the offense.[36]

A Last Look at the Mainstream

For the time being, this agreement on limiting discretion in criminal process seems to have muted the substantial differences between liberals and conservatives. It remains to be seen whether agreement on what is, after all, a fairly narrow point of principle can be transformed into a firm alliance on operative policy. Tensions will rise when the issue of leniency surfaces. Moreover, should liberals transfer their concerns with discretion to the police, conflicts are bound to arise because Wilson and other mainstream conservatives are inclined to give the police considerable leeway. Most significantly, how long will liberals be satisfied with a crime-control program that ignores problems of social inequity? For the time being, however, there is a good deal of agreement within the mainstream, and Wilson's neoconservatism is clearly ascendant.

MARXIST VIEWS

Mainstream and Marxist views have relatively little in common beyond an agreement that the incidence of street crime has risen precipitously in recent years. Marxists trace crime to its roots in the prevailing social order: to modes of production; to relationships among workers, managers, and owners; and to the structures of political authority. In so doing, Marxists are led to an understanding that differs radically from mainstream ideas concerning the causes of crime, the nature and varieties of criminal behavior, and the consequences of criminality for the society.

At the heart of differences between Marxists and the mainstream are sharply contrasting social visions. The mainstream posits an essentially harmonious and consensual society with criminals striking one of the few discordant notes. Marxists look at the same setting and see a society irreconcilably divided among classes, which are defined by the division of labor in the economic system. Relationships among classes are hostile {14} because of the dynamics of the capitalist order, which poses class against class in what is seen as literally a life-and-death struggle.

Different understandings of crime flow directly from these contrasting ideas of the social order. Marxists believe that each class has its own interests and values. The most powerful class, the capitalists who control the means of production, are able to write their interests and values into the criminal code. To violate the criminal code is not, therefore, to strike out against some underlying consensus but to behave in a manner that runs counter to the interests and values of a particular class, the capitalists. Crime is thus drained of its moral connotations; it becomes a simple expression of class antagonism. Similarly, increases in crime indicate a sharpening of those antagonisms. Whereas mainstream commentators view increased crime with trepidation, Marxists welcome such increases as precursors of a social revolution.

Before going on to examine Marxist views in some detail, a discussion of sources is in order. Marx and Engels make only passing reference to crime, so there is no really authoritative Marxist theory of crime—even in a rudimentary sense.[37] Nevertheless, given the breadth and depth of Marxism, crime, like other social phenomena, is amenable to Marxist analysis, which is increasingly employed for such work.[38] One scholar who works from Marxist principles, Richard Quinney, has developed a comprehensive and coherent theory of crime. Although there is considerable dispute about Quinney's view of what a Marxist theory of crime entails, the broad contours of his theory provide a reliable guide to Marxist understandings of crime. The discussion that follows, therefore, is drawn exclusively from Quinney.[39]

Crime and Class Conflict

According to Marxism, most of society's problems can be traced to profit, which is the engine of capitalism. Profits are derived primarily from surplus value, which can be crudely defined as the productivity of workers over and above what is paid to them.[40] In other words, workers add value to the things they produce by transforming raw materials into semifinished products and semifinished products into, for example, consumer goods. The capitalist's profit is largely determined by how much of that extra value can be retained. Accordingly, the relationship between worker and capitalist is inherently antagonistic—a struggle between levels of profit and standards of living.

It is not only labor that adds value to products, however, it is machinery as well. Increasing the use of machinery tends to make production more efficient, thus enabling capitalists to increase their profits. But once again profits result in class conflict because machinery tends to displace workers, resulting in unemployment. To make matters worse for {15} the working class and better for the capitalists, unemployment tends to lower wages because with more workers chasing fewer jobs, workers are willing to sell their labor more cheaply.

The basic struggle, then, is between the capitalist and working classes. For purposes of this presentation, it is not necessary to pursue further subdivisions within the class structure, but the underlying dynamic of the class struggle is directly relevant. As the scale of production increases, so too does the concentration of ownership. The result is that the capitalist class becomes ever smaller. Current estimates, according to Quinney, indicate that 1.5 percent of the population are in the capitalist class; another 18.5 percent are in privileged positions as managers of capitalist enterprises or as professionals, such as doctors and lawyers. This leaves approximately 80 percent of society in the working class.[41]

To begin to appreciate the relevance of class conflict to crime, it is necessary to look more closely at the working class. Some workers fare much better than others do in their struggle with capitalists. The more skills workers have, the more bargaining power they can bring to bear, and the less likely they are to end up among the unemployed. Employment for those without skills is much more contingent, and unskilled workers tend to constitute a permanent pool of underemployed and unemployed. There is a long-term tendency for this pool to grow larger and deeper as machinery replaces workers. More specifically, Quinney distinguishes between the "reserve army" and the "pauperized poor" estimated, respectively, at 15 and 25 percent of the population.[42] The reserve army is, according to Marxist economist Harry Braverman, comprised of "the unemployed; the sporadically employed; the part-time employed; the mass of women who, as houseworkers, form a reserve for the 'female occupations'; the armies of migrant labor, both agricultural and industrial; the black population with its extraordinarily high rates of unemployment; and the foreign reserves of labor."[43] Beyond these marginal workers is a "pauperized mass" without "any chance of ever being fully or even partly employed. No longer able to search for jobs, they are forced on to the welfare rolls."[44] Capitalist society, in other words, produces a profoundly disadvantaged and ever larger underclass.

The basic connection between crime and the class struggle is clear enough. Capitalism forces substantial portions of the population into such degrading circumstances that criminal activity becomes an altogether reasonable response. It is in this sense that Marxists deem capitalism criminogenic.

The Nature of Crime

Crime is, from the Marxist point of view, essentially an adaptation to capitalism, but the picture is more complex than appears at first glance. {16} There are many such criminal adaptations, and they are not confined to the underclass, although that group is the primary source of street crime. Skilled workers, those with privileged status as managers or professionals, and even members of the ruling class commit crimes. Each stratum tends to commit its own kind of crime, appropriate, we might say, to its station in life.

Most surprising in this line of argument is the idea that the capitalist class commits crimes. Is it not inconsistent with Marxist premises that capitalists should, as a class, break the law? After all, the law, according to the Marxist perspective, reflects the interests and values of the capitalist class. Why should they have to break laws designed to serve their purposes?

There are, according to Quinney, three kinds of crime committed by, or in the name of, the capitalist class: economic crimes, political crimes, and social crimes. The last is an informal category comprised of social injuries—"sexism, racism, and economic exploitation"—that are 'integral" to capitalism but are not legally defined as crime.[45] More conventionally criminal are white-collar crimes, such as price-fixing, pollution, and fraud, which are designed "to protect and further capital accumulation."[46] Laws against such activity are established in the interest of the capitalist class. That is to say, these laws are directed at some of the self-destructive tendencies of capitalist competition. Nevertheless, individual capitalists are tempted to violate these laws to serve their short-term self-interest. This explains the apparent paradox of capitalists violating their own rules. Finally, the state commits two kinds of crime: (1) crimes such as Watergate, which are designed to preserve the power of a particular administration or particular individuals; and (2) "crimes of control" committed against those who are perceived as enemies of society—be they street criminals, subversives, or agents of foreign powers.[47]

Crimes committed by the less privileged classes in the society are primarily crimes of accommodation. "Predatory crimes" such as burglary, robbery, and drug dealing are committed for monetary gain and are easily explained by the impoverished condition of the underemployed, the unemployed, and the unemployable. In contrast, personal crimes such as murder, assault, and rape cannot be explained by monetary motivations. According to Quinney, these are crimes of rage and frustration, committed by people "brutalized by the conditions of capitalism."[48] Life at the bottom is so hard, such a constant struggle for survival, that people simply turn on those around them—lashing out blindly and irrationally.* Personal {17} crimes in particular

---

* For a novelist's insight into personal crime, consider the reflections of Bigger Thomas, the poor young black man in Richard Wright's *Native Son*, New York: Harper & Row, 1966. "He closed his eyes, longing for a sleep that would not come. During the last two days and nights he had lived so fast and hard that it was an effort to keep it all real in his mind. So close had danger and death come that he could not feel it was he who had undergone it all. And, yet, out of it all, over and above all that had happened, impalpable but real, there remained to him a queer sense of power. *He* had done this. *He* had brought all this about.

are, so Quinney tells us, "usually directed against members of the same class."[49]

The working class does not always settle for accommodation to capitalism. Sometimes it resists. As Quinney sees it, generally speaking it is the underclasses that accommodate, while those who are more secure within the work force resist. This resistance takes the form of what French socialist André Gorz refers to as "clandestine acts of sabotage against a product."[50] These acts of resistance are not necessarily conscious but flow from the tedious and dehumanizing character of labor in a capitalist society.[51] The conditions of labor in advanced capitalism, even for those gainfully employed, are so dull and demeaning that workers lash out against the forces of production. Whether conscious or unconscious, crimes of resistance are symptomatic of opposition to the prevailing order.

The contrast between Marxist and mainstream perspectives on the nature of crime are abundantly clear. According to the Marxist view, society is not divided between criminals and the law-abiding, as mainstream commentators would have us believe, but among different sorts of criminals. When the underclasses turn to crime, they take to the streets—primarily because they do not have the skill or social access for more sophisticated forms of crime. Conversely, why would the privileged classes engage in anything as dangerous and as basically unremunerative as mugging when they can become white-collar criminals? And if street criminals are more violent, it is because their lives are so dehumanized.[52]

The Consequences of Crime

Both Marxists and mainstream commentators appreciate the social costs of crime—the suffering of victims, the anguish of friends and relatives, and the widespread fear. But that is about as far as the agreement goes. Whereas those in the mainstream see crime as the cause of this social disorganization, to the Marxist the problem is capitalism. Crime from the Marxist perspective is not the cause but a symptom. As capitalism breaks down, it spawns an army of displaced persons, who turn to crime out of desperation. Moreover, while Marxists may see crime as deplorable in the {18} short run, a burgeoning

---

In all of his life these two murders were the most meaningful things that had ever happened to him. He was living, truly and deeply, no matter what others might think, looking at him with their blind eyes. Never had he had the chance to live out the consequences of his actions; never had his will been so free as in this night and day of fear and murder and flight.

He had killed twice, but in a true sense it was not the first time he had ever killed. He had killed many times before, but only during the last two days had this impulse assumed the form of actual killing. Blind anger had come often and he had either gone behind his curtain or wall, or had quarreled and fought" (224–25; italics in the original).

crime rate is a welcome sign of the coming socialist revolution. Criminals can be transformed into revolutionaries once they come to understand that the true cause of their oppression is the capitalist economic order.

Of course, the state has resources for dealing with worker disaffection, but Quinney offers a plausible scenario for the progressive diminution of these resources as a result of the problems generated in the advanced stages of capitalism. Rising unemployment is the key to the revolutionary dynamic. Unemployment is an integral part of the capitalist order because it helps keep wages and prices down. Unemployment is not an unmixed blessing because of the dissatisfaction it sows among workers. Traditionally, capitalism has dealt with unemployment in three distinct ways. The first step is to head off disaffection by imposing a capitalist consciousness on the working class. Capitalist consciousness is anchored in individualism and leads people to think of unemployment as a personal failing rather than an integral element of the capitalist system. Second, the state provides social services to alleviate the pain and problems of poverty resulting from unemployment. Against those who prove immune to these instruments of "pacification" and turn to crime or to revolutionary political activity, the state employs coercion.[53]

While these techniques have proven effective so far, Quinney argues that capitalism in its advanced stages will create so much surplus population that the control schemes will prove inadequate. Once conditions get bad enough, legitimation and social services will be insufficient to hold down the crime rate.

> By its very nature, the welfare state generates more problems than it can solve. It cannot integrate the displaced population produced by the late capitalist mode of production. More state control and repression become necessary.[54]

As people become aware that they are part of an ever increasing underclass of the permanently unemployable, they will, first, cease blaming themselves and begin to understand that the system is at fault. Moreover, as the surplus population increases, the demands for welfare will become so great that a fiscal crisis will develop. The basic indicators of the crisis are inflation and tax revolt, resulting in a reduction in welfare benefits and more restiveness within the working class.[55] Disaffection and desperation will lead to ever increasing crime, which the state will attempt to control with repression, and this use of coercion against larger and larger portions of the population will rob the state of its remaining vestiges of legitimacy.

Quinney views the recent increases in crime in this hopeful context. He sees the crime-control commitment the federal government made in the early 1970s as an indication that repression is under way. Somewhat paradoxically, he points out, crime control has spawned its own employment boomlet as people have been put to work producing and utilizing the {19} instruments of crime control. In the long run, however, the costs of policing and incarceration will simply add to the fiscal problems of the state.[56] In any case, from a Marxist perspective, the increase in crime is a necessary step along the road to revolution. Criminals are not perceived as revolutionaries, but once they are taught to understand the underlying dynamics of capitalism, they can be expected to progress from crimes of accommodation to crimes of resistance and finally, with the proper instruction and leadership, to revolutionary action.[57]

CONFLICT, CRIME AND POLITICS

Mainstream and Marxist perspectives, despite the important insights they provide into the nature and consequences of crime, are each unsatisfactory in fundamental ways. Marxism links crime to capitalism and thus turns our attention to sharp cleavages in the society. But Marxism overstates and oversimplifies these cleavages. First, we are divided not only along class lines but also by race, sex, religion, roles, and so on. These multiple and crosscutting divisions generate overlapping loyalties in most of us. Society is more a collage than a mosaic, and this imagery calls into question the Marxist picture of mutually exclusive classes at war with one another. Second, as mainstream analysts point out, there is surely a powerful and enduring consensus against predatory criminal behavior. Mainstream commentators, however, ignore the divisions that coexist in combination with a least-common-denominator sense of social order. If Marxists exaggerate cleavages in society, mainstream analysts exaggerate social and moral harmony.

A satisfactory approach to crime must accommodate, in appropriate measure, both our agreements and our diversity. And it must, of course, explain the relevance of these social factors to crime. The conflict school of criminology provides such a frame of reference.[58] According to conflict criminologists, divisions in society give rise to multiple patterns of values and interests. Rich people and poor people, blacks and whites, and lawyers and police officers tend to see the world in different ways. What is attractive and advantageous for one segment of society is often bad news for another. The more influential segments are able to shape the rules of society to conform closely to their values and interests. Certain groups are particularly well placed to decide which patterns of behavior will be deemed legitimate and which will be deemed criminal. Accordingly, social conflict and the politicization of that conflict are keys to understanding the nature and consequences of crime.

Before going on to examine the conflict perspective more carefully, let us look briefly at the problematic features of Marxist and Mainstream views. {20}

Thinking about Marxism

Richard Quinney would have us believe that capitalism is *the* cause of crime and that we need look no further than class conflict to explain exploitation, hostility, and strife in society. In attributing crime exclusively to class conflict and capitalism, this view runs counter to both history and sociology. Class is just one of the lines of cleavage that divide us from one another. It seems inappropriately reductionist to think of differences of race, sex, ethnicity, and social role as merely derivative of class. And if these other differences are important in their own right, they must somehow be incorporated into our understanding of crime. Moreover, crime predates capitalism, and it is hard to believe that it will be extinguished by socialism. Finally, is there not, as mainstreamers believe, some basic level of civility that is necessary for a society to function effectively? If so, it does not seem reasonable to think of laws against murder, rape, and armed robbery as creations of the ruling class with the essential purpose of preserving existing distributions of political power.

Societies have always been united, and forever will be united, by a consensus against manifestly predatory behavior. Exclusive attention to class conflict and capitalism is therefore misleading in at least two important ways: important elements of social cleavage are concealed, as is an equally significant unifying theme. Quinney not only provides a suspect image of post-revolutionary futures but tends to oversimplify the present as well.[*]

---

[*] The shortcomings I ascribe to Marxism may be attributable to Quinney's particular interpretation. In "Delinquency and the Age Structure of Society" (see note 38), Greenberg argues that Marxist theory provides the best frame of reference for understanding the ambiguities of social conflict that are of special concern to me. "The conflict model...fails to specify the lines along which conflicts appear, and where cooperation can be located.... [A]ny society has elements of both consensus and dissensus, cooperation and conflict.... Historical materialism provides the conceptual tools for investigation *the degree* of conflict present in a society and the forms it takes" (215). Greenberg substantiates his case for Marxism by dealing with class in a flexible and dynamic fashion that sheds considerable light on the ostensible Marxists paradox of delinquency among juveniles from economically advantaged backgrounds. "[J]uveniles in an advanced capitalist economy have a common, if temporary, relationship to the means of production, characterized by exclusion during a period of mandatory training for entry into the labor force. In Marxian terms, this means that juveniles can no more be assigned the class of their parents than housewives can be assigned the class of their husbands" (216). The problem with all this is that the more subtle Marxism of Greenberg and Isaac Balbus, for example, has not been incorporated into a comprehensive analysis of crime and criminal process. Only Quinney has shouldered this burden.

Thinking about the Mainstream

The most problematic aspect of the mainstream argument is its vision of a harmonious society united around a moral consensus formalized in the {21} criminal code. It is an easy step from this starting point to Wilson's inclination to see those who violate the law as morally deficient, and indeed to assume that a rising crime rate is attributable to a decline in moral standards among some segments of the society. The message on the other side of this coin is that poverty does not make a significant contribution to the growth of crime.

It may well be true that poverty does not cause crime in the sense that poor people are somehow predestined to become criminals. Obviously many individuals are both poor and law-abiding, but logically and empirically the probabilities are that people may turn to crime when legitimate opportunities are closed off—as they tend to be for poor people. Wilson's presentation suggests as much. Although crime and prosperity rose together during the 1960s, as Wilson points out, this prosperity was not uniformly distributed. Wilson attributes the crime wave that began in the 1960s to teenage males, and it is precisely this group that experienced rising unemployment while the rest of the country was prospering. Minority teenagers were particularly hard hit.[59]

The easy moralizing of the mainstream seems equally wide of the mark. If the criminal code reflects a natural moral order that binds society together, how are we to account for the destabilizing impact of urban emigration, reported by Wilson and discussed earlier?[60] As Wilson sees it, emigration robs cities of their most stable and law-abiding people. Yet it is to the arrival of these model citizens that Wilson attributes the increase in suburban crime.[61] Those who were the backbone of their urban communities become the carriers of crime to the suburbs. Apparently there is less agreement on right and wrong in this society than mainstream analysis suggests.

The Politicization of Social Conflict

Conflict criminology is based on a social vision that avoids the pitfalls of mainstream and Marxist views.[62] The underlying premise of conflict criminology is that individuals differ from one another in a variety of ways that affect the goals they choose as well as their chances of reaching those goals. People are born into different circumstances and endowed with a wide variety of talents and handicaps, and people tend to be thrown into competition for the scarce resources that society makes available. The competition goes on among individuals and among groups that band together because of things they have in common. People may unite because their life chances are similar as a result of their jobs, race, or sex. Unity may also develop around a shared sense of right and wrong based on ethnicity, social class, or religious training. Organization and struggle tend to reinforce the interests and values shared within groups and to distance them from their competitors. {22}

Given this perspective, crime can be seen as the politicization of social conflict. Systems of stratification develop as conflict becomes routinized and certain segments of society gain the upper hand. Crudely speaking, these advantages may be exploited economically, politically, or both—in the work place or in the political arena. Conflict in the work place is over wages, profits, and working conditions. Political conflict is over the rules of the game, with the politically powerful establishing rules that favor their interests and values. Those who fail to conform are, by definition, criminals. As Quinney puts it:[*]

> By formulating criminal law (including legislative statutes, ad-
> ministrative rulings, and judicial decisions), some segments of
> society protect and perpetuate their own interests. Criminal de-
> finitions exist, therefore, because some segments of society are in
> conflict with others. By formulating criminal definitions these
> segments are able to control the behavior of persons in other
> segments. It follows that *the greater the conflict in interests be-*
> *tween segments of a society, the greater the probability that the*
> *power segments will formulate criminal definitions.*[63]

For this reason, Quinney argues that *"crime is created."*[64] It is not only in defining crime but also in applying the rules that stratification is relevant. *"The probability that criminal definitions will be applied varies according to the extent to which the behaviors of the powerless conflict with the interests of the power segments."*[65]

To make this a little more concrete, let us consider some examples drawn directly from the criminal law. Does not the politicization of crime best explain the odd contours of criminal law controlling gambling, drug use, and sexual behavior? How else are we to understand the passage of these laws and the patterns of inclusion and exclusion? Horse racing is generally legal, but numbers gambling is considered criminal. Alcohol and Valium may be used legally, while the use of marijuana and cocaine is prohibited. It can hardly be argued that these distinctions reflect some natural moral order. Clearly, some segments are imposing their values on others—perhaps to demonstrate symbolically their superior status or perhaps to protect vested economic interests. Symbolic uses of the criminal law seem to have been paramount in the creation of Prohibition.[66] Conversely, horse racing interests would be likely to suffer to the extent that other forms of gambling were legalized.

But it is not only in matters of so-called victimless crime that conflict criminology is helpful. Laws protecting persons and property are the high ground of criminal law, but even they are framed in ways that reflect social

---

[*] While it may seem odd to refer to Quinney as a conflict criminologist, he has in fact gone through a number of stages in his intellectual development. *The Social Reality of Crime* (see note 58) is a superb application of conflict criminology to all phases of the criminal process.

conflict as well as generally accepted values. If the purpose of laws against {23} murder is to protect human life, how are we to explain the failure to treat industrial accidents—even those involving gross negligence—as criminal matters? Jeffrey Reiman poses this question in contrasting newspaper coverage of two events, each of which resulted in substantial loss of human life: 26 miners killed in a coal mine explosion and the shooting deaths of 6 persons in what the newspaper termed a "mass murder."

> Why do 26 dead miners amount to a "disaster," and 6 dead sub-urbanites a "mass murder"? "Murder" suggests a murderer, while "disaster" suggests the work of impersonal forces. But if over 1000 safety violations had been found in the mine—three the day before the first explosion—was no one responsible for failing to eliminate the hazards? Was no one responsible for *preventing* the hazards? And if someone could have prevented the hazards and did not, does that person not bear responsibility for the deaths of 26 men? Is he less evil because he did not want them to die although he chose to leave them in jeopardy? Is he not a murderer, perhaps even a *mass* murderer?[67]

Reiman goes on to show that there is much less loss of human life from crime than from industrial accidents, unnecessary surgery, environmental pollution, and poverty, none of which are treated as criminal matters.[68] Similarly, if laws against robbery and burglary are to protect property, why are so many questionable business practices either accepted or treated as civil matters even when the upshot of these practices is to deprive some people of their property and enrich others? It is, for example, apparently standard practice for defense contractors to overcharge the government; if the over charges are discovered, it simply requires repayment. Not only are such matters rarely treated as criminal but neither interest nor punitive damage is assessed.[*]

Mainstream thinking suggests that the distinction between civil and criminal liability is rooted in two different kinds of harmful acts—that the distinction is, in fact, moral. Conflict criminology holds that social stratification is the key to understanding the difference between civil liability and criminal liability. Generally speaking, criminal liability obtains when the harm is direct and intentional. Thus, street crime is criminal because it involves knowingly harmful activity by one person against another. But civil liability applies to industrial accidents which are by-products of decisions to minimize costs—say, by not meeting safety standards. Reiman tellingly explains why this distinction, as a moral matter, does not stand up to careful scrutiny.

---

[*] In testimony before the Joint Economic Committee of the U.S. Congress, Admiral Hyman Rickover recently called attention to the need to criminalize cost overrun abuses by defense contractors. Reprinted as "Advice from Admiral Rickover," in the *New York Review of Books* (18 March 1982): 12–14.

Most murders, we know, are committed in the heat of some garden-variety passion like rage or jealousy.... Such a person is clearly a murderer.... But is {24} this person more evil than our executive who chooses not to pay for safety equipment?

The one who kills in a heated argument kills from passion. What he does he probably would not do in a cooler moment.... [T]he passion killer's action does not show general disdain for the lives of his fellows.... Our absentee killer intended harm to no one in particular, but he knew his acts were likely to harm someone.... His act is done, not out of passion, but out of cool reckoning. And precisely here his evil shows. In his willingness to jeopardize the lives of unspecified others who pose him no real or imaginary threat in order to make a few dollars, he shows his general disdain for all his fellow human beings.[69]

If we do not deploy the criminal law equally against comparably harmful acts, it is because of the way we as a society construe those acts, not because of their intrinsic differences. And our constructions reflect the interests and values of the more influential segments of the society—as, for example, entrepreneurial groups whose activities would be severely circumscribed by the imposition of strict criminal liability for industrial accidents or environmental pollution.

Enforcement is equally problematic. Assault may seem like a serious and threatening crime. Often it is. But assault with a deadly weapon may, in fact, signify no more than a tavern brawl fought with bottles; often "the victim" is simply the loser, who decides to invoke criminal sanctions. More generally, since total enforcement of criminal statutes is impossible, choices must be made about where to employ limited numbers of personnel, and it is reasonable to believe that these choices frequently reflect political priorities. Does it not, finally, go without saying that defendants who can afford high-priced legal representation are likely to fare better in the criminal court systems?

Morality and Criminality

Conflict criminology obviously leads to great skepticism about the moral quality of our criminal laws. "[T]here is," as Austin Turk put it, "no absolute standard of rightness/wrongness which can be articulated and applied...."[70] While perhaps overstating the basic point, this formulation provides a much needed corrective to the moral posturing of the mainstream. The emergence and application of rules of criminality has much more to do with competing values and interests than most of us realize. Like Marxism, conflict criminology turns our attention away from moral imperatives and the natural order of society. Unlike Marxism, conflict criminology alerts us to a complex tangle of values and interest that does not preclude some least-common-denominator agreement.[*]

One way to get a better sense of the problematic quality of moral {25} judgments based on the concept of criminality is to look carefully at the choices made by criminals. Even Wilson concedes that the best way to understand criminal activity is to think in terms of differential opportunity structures.[71] According to this way of looking at crime, there are both legitimate and illegitimate opportunity structures, and people tend to choose between them on the basis of a cost-benefit calculation. As Charles Silberman's work makes clear, stratification, rather than moral deficiencies, tends to push the urban poor toward illegitimate opportunity structures in general and violent street crime in particular.[†]

At least two fundamental features of urban poverty in particular are conducive to crime. Consider, first, the life chances of poor people:

> [P]oor children grow up in a world in which people work hard and long, for painfully meager rewards. It is a world, too, in which parents and relatives are at the mercy of forces they cannot control—a world in which illness, an accident, a recession, an employer's business reverses, or a foreman's whim can mean the loss of a job and a long period of unemployment, and in which a bureaucrat's arbitrary ruling can mean denial or loss of welfare benefits and, thereby, of food, clothing, fuel, or shelter.[72]

This contingent existence seems to generate a sense of hopelessness among the poor, which Silberman contrasts to the "sense of entitlement" discovered by psychiatrist Robert Coles in his interviews with upper-class children. "If you really work for the rewards, you'll get them," a youngster told Coles.[73] Whereas children from wealthy families grow up thinking of themselves as "masters of their fate," poor children, as Silberman sees it, believe that they are "servants" of theirs. Success is associated with "luck" rather than hard work.[74] Moreover, among the meager opportunities available, crime is the most accessible. As one ex-offender put it to Silberman, "If it had been doctors and lawyers who drove up and parked in front of the bars in their catylacks, I'd be a doctor today. But it wasn't; it was the men who were into

---

[*] In "Analyzing Official Deviance" (see note 58), Turk points out that agreement is the exception and the occasion for asking questions rather than a given to be taken for granted. "Even if universal agreement should be found...conflict theory leads one to ask *how* such a fascinating unanimity...has been arrived at in a world of diversity, *what* or *who* sustains it, and *what* or *who* could or will alter it. No empirical basis for moral absolutism is to be found" (83–84; italics in the original).

[†] Wilson can combine the theory of differential opportunity structures with moral pronouncements only because he takes for granted the moral superiority of legitimate opportunities.

things, the pimps, the hustlers and the numbers guys."[75] Different role models are not sufficient to change things. Poor people are also much less likely to have the intellectual, cultural, and financial resources to enter the legal and medical professions.

Can we, moreover, accept at face value the particular moral opprobrium that the mainstream attaches to street crime? Although it is true that {26} violent street crime is frightening and reprehensible, it does not necessarily follow that street criminals are more morally blameworthy than the corrupt politicians for whom Wilson expresses a grudging admiration. "I am rather tolerant of some forms of civic corruption (if a good mayor can stay in office and govern effectively only by making a few deals with highway contractors and insurance agents, I do not get overly alarmed).... "[76] Like other white-collar criminals, corrupt politicians are simply tapping illegitimate opportunities best suited to their capabilities and their positions in society. Strongarm robbery is for those who are unable to engage in less dangerous and more rewarding forms of crime. In what sense does this distinction provide a basis for making a moral judgment?

Even the violence itself—however abhorrent it may be—must be understood in a broader context. Silberman argues that while the level of violent crime among blacks is increasing, this increase does not reflect lower standards of morality but a refusal to continue sublimating frustrations and aggressions induced by centuries of deprivation. Silberman discusses a variety of these sublimating devices. "The great achievement of the toasts, as of the blues, the dozens, and black folklore in general, has been to deaden the pain felt by black Americans, especially black men, and to transform their rage into a source of entertainment."[77] Silberman sees that all this is changing and that violence is the understandable result. "The process no longer works, black adolescents and young men have begun to act out the violence and aggression that, in the past, has been contained and sublimated in fantasy and myth. It is this shift from the mythic to the real—from toasting, signifying, and playing the dozens to committing robbery, murder, rape, and assault—that underlies the explosive increase in criminal violence on the part of black offenders."[78] Whether or not this approach constitutes an adequate explanation of violent crime, it does cast further doubt on mainstream moralizing.

My reservations about the mainstream position are clearly and poignantly illustrated by the story of basketball star Isiah Thomas, as told by the gifted *New York Times* reporter Ira Berkow.

> It was Draft Day in the ghetto. That's what everyone called it. On
> a few days each year, chieftains of the notorious Vice Lords street
> gang appeared at certain homes on the West Side of Chicago to
> take recruits.
>
> On this summer night in 1966, 25 Vice Lord chiefs stopped in
> front of the home of Mary Thomas. She had nine children, seven

of them boys, ranging from Lord Henry, 15 years old, to Isiah, 5. The Thomases lived on the first floor of a two story red brick building on Congress Street, facing the Eisenhower Expressway.

One of the Lords rang the bell. Mary Thomas, wearing glasses, answered the door. She saw behind him the rest of his gang, all wearing gold tarns and black capes and some had guns in their waist bands that glinted under the street lamps. {27}

"We want your boys," the gang leader told her. "They can't walk around here and not be in no gang."

She looked him in the eye. "There's only one gang around here, and that's the Thomas gang," she said, "and I lead that."

"If you don't bring those boys out, we'll get 'em in the streets," he said.

She shut the door. The gang members waited. She walked through the living room where the rest of the family sat. Isiah, frightened, watched her go into the bedroom and return with a sawed-off shotgun. She opened the front door.

She pointed the gun at the caped figure before her. "Get off my porch," she said, "or I'll blow you 'cross the Expressway."

He stepped back, and slowly he and his gang disappeared into the night. Isiah Thomas never joined a gang, and was protected from the ravages of street life—the dope, the drinking, the stealing, the killings—by his mother and his brothers, even those who eventually succumbed to the streets. Two of his brothers became heroin addicts, one was a pimp, a couple would be jailed and one became a Vice Lords chief.[79]

Thus, even a rather stable family with a strong commitment to conventional values may not be sufficient to neutralize the effects of poverty. Most of the Thomas children eventually succumbed to the temptations and opportunities of street life. Isiah escaped—but just barely, as the article makes abundantly clear. Education tended to distance Isiah from his culture and his family, which, while essentially and vitally supportive, did at times question his loyalty. Lord Henry, with apparently comparable talent, never made it through high school.

For those at the bottom of society to achieve success through legitimate channels requires combinations of talent, determination, and good fortune far beyond what is demanded from those with more advantages. Rather than condemn as morally deficient people who are unable to rise above the obstacles of poverty, perhaps we would be better advised to marvel at those who are not overpowered by the burden they must bear. It takes truly heroic efforts to surmount the problems of poverty; yet Wilson would have us think of poor people who fail to make such efforts as morally wanting.

So far I have presented three different ways of looking at crime and criminal process. Each offers important insights, but my contention is that conflict criminology provides the best understanding of this society's response to crime over the past couple of decades. According to the conflict perspective, criminal law and its enforcement are neither the simple imposition of ruling-class justice, as Marxists would have us believe, nor the necessary bedrock of social order, as the mainstream argues. Conflict criminology encourages us to think instead in terms of the values {28} and interests affected by the way society defines crime and reacts to it.

This book uses conflict criminology to explore the punitive political climate that began to develop in the United States in the middle 1960s and the impact of law-and-order attitudes on operative policy in the criminal justice system. A subsidiary aspect of this inquiry contrasts the explanatory power of conflict criminology with that of the Marxist and Mainstream views. The principal advantage of thinking about crime as the politicization of social conflict is a heightened sensitivity to the complexity and controversiality of crime-control policy making. In the abstract everyone may agree that crime control is a desirable goal. Like our commitments to liberty and equality, however, the ostensible consensus on crime quickly disintegrates in the give and take of policy making. At each step along the way, from the formation of public opinion concerning crime to crime-control strategies carried out by the police and the criminal courts, a clash of interests and values shapes the course of events.

To begin, we explore the politics of law and order with special attention focused on the fear of crime. Mainstream analysts would have us believe that law-and-order attitudes are a direct outgrowth of a heightened fear of crime engendered by rising crime rates. Empirical research raises serious questions about this mainstream thinking. The Marxist position is that the politics of law and order is purely the product of political manipulation by ruling elites. Conflict criminology offers a more complex scenario. While increased fear and punitive policy preferences are derived partly from victimization, the fear of crime really tends to take on a life of its own. The fear of crime has become a social enterprise that provides entrepreneurs with political and pecuniary profit. Moreover, like all salable commodities, the fear of crime offers gratifications to its consumers—to us, the American public. All these matters are taken up in Part 2.

As to actual policy making, the impact of a law-and-order political climate turns out to be less intense and more problematic than is suggested by either mainstream or Marxist thinking. Law-and-order impulses tend to be refracted by the political and bureaucratic forces that control the course of criminal process. Politicians, police managers, rank-and-file police officers, prosecutors, judges, and all other participants in criminal process have their own particular concerns; and each policy decision has an impact on the status, power, and material well-being of these officials, as well as on the general public. Law-and-order impulses survive only to the extent that they are compatible with perceptions of more influential decision makers—and even then only in a watered-down and compromised form.

All of this may seem like the triumph of the particular over the public, and in some measure it is. The politics of policy making in criminal process, as elsewhere, is very much a politics of self-interest. But conflict criminology alerts us to some broader dimensions of these clashes over crime-control policy. There are genuine differences of opinion about what constitutes a {29} sensible strategy for coping with crime. Even within the relatively narrow confines of the mainstream, there are sharply different perceptions concerning the causes of crime and how best to deal with its consequences. These disagreements cannot be attributed entirely to narrow calculations of self-interest. At the heart of the policy differences lie alternative conceptions of human nature and social justice. These value conflicts are compounded by several realities of criminal process. Like the proverbial blind men and the elephant, each participant experiences only a limited portion of the entire process. The beat patrol officer, the judge, and the big-city mayor all experience crime in different ways. Analogous differences divide central-city residents from suburbanites. Disagreement is inherent in value differences and diverse understandings of crime, as well as in self-interest.

The underlying message of conflict criminology is that the problems of policy making in criminal process cannot be written off as the result of corruption, inefficiency, duplicity, or stupidity among policy makers. No doubt all these obstacles to effective policy making can be found throughout criminal process, and efforts should be made to uncover and correct such deficiencies. But turning the rascals out will only bring us face to face with the more fundamental problems that are the subject of this book. To understand these problems is not to discover solutions for them. Indeed, as has been suggested, the problems of criminal process may be largely insoluble. Nonetheless, the final section of this book focuses on policy—in particular on policies that seem consistent with the insights of conflict criminology.

NOTES

1. Harold E. Pepinsky, "A Radical Alternative to 'Radical' Criminology," in *Radical Criminology: The Coming Crisis*, ed. James A. Inciardi (Beverly Hills, Calif.: Sage, 1980), 300.

2. The most comprehensive presentation of Wilson's views is to be found in the widely circulated collection of his essays, James Q. Wilson, *Thinking About Crime* (New York: Vintage, 1977). A new edition was scheduled for publication in late 1983, after this book went to press.

3. Ibid., xiii-xv.

4. While Wilson is the most prominent and far-ranging spokesperson for moderate conservatism, the work of other outstanding scholars is basically compatible with Wilson's. See, for example, critiques by Carl Klockars, Jackson Toby, and Ronald Akers of the Marxist and conflict schools of criminology: Carl B. Klockars, "The Contemporary Crises of Marxist Criminology," in Inciardi, *Radical Criminology*, 92–123; Jackson Toby, "The New Criminology Is the Old Baloney," in ibid., 124–32; and Ronald L. Akers, "Further Critical Thoughts on Marxist Criminology: Comments on Turk, Toby, and Klockars," in ibid., 133–38. Several books considered subsequently work from premises {30} of moderate mainstream conservatism, although not all these scholars would agree with this characterization of their work. See William K. Muir, Jr., *Police: Streetcorner Politicians* (Chicago: University of Chicago Press, 1977); Andrew von Hirsch, *Doing Justice: Report of the Committee for the Study of Incarceration* (New York: Hill & Wang, 1976); and Martin A. Levin, *Urban Politics and the Criminal Courts* (Chicago: University of Chicago Press, 1977).

5. Wilson, *Thinking About Crime*, xx.

6. Ibid.

7. Ibid., 23.

8. Ibid., 42.

9. Ibid., 43.

10. Ibid., 23.

11. Ibid., 55.

12. Ibid., 64.

13. Ibid., 58.

14. Ibid., 57–58.

15. Ibid., 63.

16. Ibid., 197.

17. Ibid., 199.

18. Ibid., 5–18.

19. Ibid., 13.

20. Ibid., 5.

21. Ibid., Chap. 5.

22. Ibid., xii.

23. Ibid., 201.

24. Ibid.

25. Ibid., 194–204.

26. Ernest van den Haag, *Punishing Criminals: Concerning a Very Old and Painful Question* (New York: Basic, 1975), Chap. 15.

27. Ernest van den Haag, "Crime or Punishment," *National Review*, 2 March 1979, 289.

28. Peter Steinfels, *The Neoconservatives: The Man Who Are Changing America's Politics* (New York: Simon and Schuster, 1980), 55.

29. President's Commission on Law Enforcement and Administration of Justice, *The Challenge of Crime in a Free Society* (New York: Avon, 1968). See also Ramsey Clark, *Crime in America: Observations on Its Nature, Causes, Prevention and Control* (New York: Simon and Schuster, 1970).

30. President's Commission, *Challenge of Crime*, Chap. 3.

31. Ibid., Chaps. 3–6.

32. Wilson, *Thinking About Crime*, 4.

33. Ibid., 5.

34. Ibid., 190.

35. Ibid., Chap. 8.

36. Von Hirsch, *Doing Justice*.

37. Ian Taylor, Paul Walton, and Jock Young, *The New Criminology: For a Social Theory of Deviance* (New York: Harper & Row, 1973), Chap. 7.

38. Isaac Balbus, *The Dialectics of Legal Repression: Black Rebels Before the American Criminal Courts* (New Brunswick, N.J.: Transaction, 1977); David {31} F. Greenberg, "Delinquency and the Age Structure of Society." *Contemporary Crises* 1 (April 1977): 189–233; David M. Gordon, "Class, and the Economics of Crime," in *Whose Law? What Order?* ed. William J. Chambliss and Milton Mankoff (New York: Wiley, 1976), 193–214; E. P. Thompson, *Whigs and Hunters; The Origin of the Black Act* (New York: Pantheon, 1975).

39. Richard Quinney, *Class, State and Crime*, 2nd. ed. (New York: Longman, 1980). For a discussion of Marxist criminology in general and Quinney's work in particular, see David O. Friedrichs, "Radical Criminology in the United States: An Interpretive Understanding," in Inciardi, *Radical Criminology*, 35–60; Milton Mankoff, "A Tower of Babel: Marxists Criminologists and Their Critics," in ibid., 139–48; Steven Spitzer, "'Left-Wing' Criminology—An Infantile Disorder?" in ibid., 169–90; and Harold E. Pepinsky, "A Radical Alternative," in ibid., 299–315. While I have reservations about Quinney's first efforts at a Marxist analysis of crime, *Critique of Legal Order: Crime Control in Capitalist Society* (Boston: Little Brown and Company, 1974), the more recent book upon which I rely, *Class State and Crime*, is a serious and reasonable, albeit rather cursory, application of Marxist principles to crime in the contemporary United States.

40. Quinney, *Class, State and Crime*, 59.

41. Ibid., 86.

42. Ibid.

43. Quoted in ibid., 80

44. Ibid.

45. Ibid., 58–59.

46. Ibid., 58.

47. Ibid.

48. Ibid., 61.

49. Ibid.

50. Ibid.

51. Ibid.

52. Gordon, "Class and the Economics of Crime," 202–3.

53. Quinney, *Class, State, and Crime*, 52–57.

54. Ibid., 93.

55. James O'Connor, *The Fiscal Crisis of the State* (New York: St. Martin's, 1973).

56. Quinney, *Class, State, and Crime*, Chap. 4.

57. Ibid., 64–66.

58. Austin T. Turk, *Criminality and the Legal Order* (Chicago: Rand McNally, 1969); and idem, "Analyzing Official Deviance: For Nonpartisan Conflict Analysis in Criminology," in Inciardi, *Radical Criminology*, 78–91; and Richard Quinney, *The Social Reality of Crime* (Boston: Little, Brown, 1970). On Quinney's transformation from conflict theory to Marxism see Friedrichs, "Radical Criminology."

59. Wilson, *Thinking About Crime*, 11–19. Wilson acknowledges this linkage between crime and unemployment and recommends government programs to provide employment opportunities for teenagers. But antipoverty programs are clearly not central to Wilson's crime control strategies. Why else devote his first chapter to rejecting poverty as a cause of crime? See ibid., Chap. 1.

60. See Note 9. {32}

61. Wilson, *Thinking About Crime*, 42–43.

62. While there really is no single definitive version of conflict criminology, my presentation sticks pretty close to the ten "working premises" offered by Austin Turk: "(1) individuals diverge in their understandings and commitments. (2) Divergence leads, under specifiable conditions, to conflict. (3) Each conflicting party tries to promote his or her own understandings and commitments. (4) The result is a more or less conscious struggle over the distribution of available resources, and therefore life chances. (5) People with similar understandings and commitments tend to join forces, and people who stay together tend to develop similar understandings and commitments. (6) Continuing conflicts tend to become routinized in the form of stratification systems. (7) Such systems (at least at the intergroup level) are characterized by economic exploitation sustained by political domination in all forms, from the most clearly violent to the most subtly ideological. (8) The relative power of conflicting parties determines their hierarchal position; changes in position reflect only changes in the distribution of power. (9) Convergence in understanding commitments is generated by the (not necessarily voluntary) sharing of experience in dealing with 'insiders,' 'outsiders,' and the natural environment. (10) The relationship between divergence and covergence in human understandings and commitments is a dialectical one, ergo the *basic* social process or dynamic is one of conflict" Turk, "Analyzing Official Deviance," 82–83; italics in the original. For a similar list, see Franklin P. Williams, III, "Conflict Theory and Differential Processing: An Analysis of the Recent Literature," in Inciardi, *Radical Criminology*, 215. I go somewhat beyond conflict criminology by using Murray Edelman's ideas on the symbolic dimensions of politics in order to better understand the politicization process. See his *The Symbolic Uses of Politics* (Urbana, Ill.: University of Illinois Press, 1967); *Politics and Symbolic Action: Mass Arousal and Quiescence* (Chicago: Markham, 1971); and *Political Language: Words That Succeed and Policies That Fail* (New York: Academic Press, 1977).

63. Quinney, *The Social Reality of Crime*, 17; italics in the original.

64. Ibid., 15; italics in the original.

65. Ibid., 18; italics in the original.

66. Joseph R. Gusfield, *Symbolic Crusade: Status Politics and the American Temperance Movement* (Urbana, Ill.: University of Illinois Press, 1969).

67. Jeffrey H. Reiman, *The Rich Get Richer and the Poor Get Prison: Ideology, Class, and Criminal Justice* (New York: Wiley, 1979), 45–46; italics in the original.

68. Ibid., 65–86.

69. Ibid., 60–61.

70. Turk, "Analyzing Official Deviance," 83; italics in the original.

71. Richard A. Cloward and Lloyd E. Ohlin, *Delinquency and Opportunity*, (New York: Free Press, 1960).

72. Charles E. Silberman, *Criminal Violence, Criminal Justice* (New York: Random House, 1978), 88.

73. Ibid.

74. Ibid., 88–89.

75. Ibid., 90–91. {33}

76. Wilson, *Thinking About Crime*, xix. Wilson goes on to express his disapproval of corruption in law enforcement.

77. Silberman, *Criminal Violence, Criminal Justice*, 152.

78. Ibid.

79. *New York Times*, 27 April 1981.

Part II

The Public

2

The Politicization of Crime

There is widespread agreement that crime has exercised a marked and largely conservative influence on American political life over the last twenty years. Public anxiety about crime has generated a climate of fear that has come to play a part in election campaigns as politicians promise to "crack down" on crime.[1] Operative policy has turned in a more punitive direction. While there would be relatively little dispute over this general picture, it is another matter when we come to explain how these developments are related to one another or even to assess the extent of this conservative drift.

In the mainstream view, these developments have amounted to an example of democracy at work. A precipitous increase in street crime has generated demands from an aroused public to which our political leaders have been forced to respond. Campaign promises and subsequent efforts to implement measures to reduce crime have been seen as an index of political responsiveness.

Marxists think about politicization in starkly different terms: as a cynical manipulation of the public by the ruling class. Simply put, Marxists believe that political leaders are making scapegoats of criminals in an effort to divert attention from the decline of capitalism, which is the real source of the rising crime rate. This interpretation leads to the conclusion that politicization serves primarily as a pretext for repression, a way of justifying a crackdown on troublemakers whether their objectives are criminal or political.

Neither of these views tends to stand up very well to close empirical scrutiny. The available data reveal some strange twists and turns. The {38} various indicators of anxiety do not change at comparable rates, nor do they move in quite the same direction. While it can be safely said that public anxiety about crime has increased since the mid-1960s, there has not been anything like the steadily building crescendo of public concern suggested by the mainstream and Marxist interpretations. Nor do the implied relationships among victimization, fear, and punitive values appear in the data.

This chapter presents in more detail the mainstream and Marxist explanations of politicization and uses the available data on public attitudes to indicate the inadequacies of each of them. This is preparatory to a presentation of my own views, which are based on a cultural interpretation of politicization.

The data indicate that neither fear nor punitive attitudes are directly associated with increases in the crime rate, thus suggesting that our response to crime may have less to do with the actual impact of crime on our lives than with the symbolic importance of crime in American culture. This leads to an understanding of politicization, drawn directly from conflict theory, that is neither purely manipulative nor clearly democratic. According to this way of thinking, politicians seize an opportunity to exploit public predispositions in order to gain political office. Politicization, in other words, has more to do with gaining and retaining public office than with policy making, which calls for the careful manipulation of bureaucratic and legislative resources. It follows from this discontinuity between politicization and policy making that the impact of the politics of law and order on operative policy is likely to be a good deal more uncertain than is implied by either the mainstream or the Marxist view of things.

LAW-AND-ORDER ATTITUDES

Abundant data lend credence to the widely shared sense of the last couple of decades as an era of law and order. Nevertheless, a careful consideration of those data reveals some significant variations and ambiguities in the empirical picture. The American public did display a heightened anxiety about crime, but increases in fear seem a good deal less dramatic than we have been led to believe. Similarly, data on the political salience of crime may be read in ways that cast doubt on the status of crime as an inescapable political issue. Finally, while there is an unmistakably punitive side to the public's policy preferences, an undercurrent of moderation is also apparent. These data suggest that a complex story lurks beneath the surface themes of law and order. {39}

The Fear of Crime

The empirical indicators reveal an appreciable increase in the fear of crime—on the order of 10 percent since the baseline year of 1965. Most of these data are based on measures of fear very much like that used by the Gallup poll: "Is there any area right around here—that is, within a mile— where you would be afraid to walk alone at night?" The poll patterns shown in Table 2.1 are pretty much the same as those disclosed in other surveys.

TABLE 2.1   Respondents Reporting Fear of Walking Alone at Night, 1965, 1967, 1968, 1973, 1976, 1979 and 1982

Question: "Is there any area right around here—that is, within a mile—where you would be afraid to walk alone at night?"

Year	Percent Reporting Fear
1982	48
1979	42
1976	45
1973	41
1968	35
1967	31
1965	34

SOURCE: Constructed from *Sourcebook of Criminal Justice Statistics 1978* (Washington. D.C.: Law Enforcement Assistance Administration, 1979), 288; *The Gallup Poll: Public Opinion 1935– 1971*, 2 vols. (New York: Random House, 1972); *The Gallup Opinion Index*, Report no. 172 (November 1979); *The Gallup Report*, Report no. 200 (May 1982).

> Since 1965 Gallup, Harris, and other polling organizations have been quizzing people about their personal reactions to crime.... While the way these questions were worded affected the exact figures they obtained, the evidence suggests that levels of fear of crime rose significantly between 1965 and the mid 1970's, and that since then they have remained stationary.[2]

The findings all point to the same tendency: an initial decade of increasing but not runaway fear, with anxiety then stabilizing at the peak levels. But even a moment's reflection on this pattern raises a good many questions.

What are we to make of the 1965 baseline? It could be argued, on the one hand, that a 10 percent increase in fear is actually rather modest and that the plateau of the mid-1970s indicates that the public has pretty much adjusted to crime. On the other hand, to have more than 40 percent of the American public afraid of walking in their own neighborhoods at night is indicative of great anxiety and probably symptomatic of even greater fears {40} of, for example, nighttime ventures outside the neighborhood for shopping or entertainment. As to the recent plateau, it could be read less as an adjustment to crime than as a reflection of the parallel leveling off of crime itself.

Without pre-1965 data, there is no way to choose among these views. Fear may have reached and maintained unprecedented levels, or perhaps the last two decades are simply part of some historical pattern of ebb and flow. Substantial fear of crime may be something that Americans have lived with off and on since frontier days.

When we move from the general to the particular, it becomes immediately clear that fear is not distributed uniformly throughout the {41} population. As Table 2.2 (see next page) indicates, women, nonwhites, and older people are a good deal more fearful than are other Americans. Fear also seems to vary inversely with income and directly with city size.[3] Thus, heightened anxiety about crime is largely an urban phenomenon that disproportionately affects disadvantaged groups in the society.

At first glance, there seems to be a common-sense way of explaining these patterns of fear. According to the data, discernible relationships exist between the fear of crime and victimization. As pointed out, the overall rate of crime and the levels of fear have risen and stabilized in rough parallel since 1965 (see Figure 2.1). The linkage can be traced more precisely in the victimization surveys, which provide the best indications of how crime is distributed geographically and demographically.[4] While victims in general are not more fearful than nonvictims, those victimized by crimes involving personal contact and violence—such as rape, robbery, and mugging—express heightened levels of fear.[5] It also seems to follow that the greater fear among nonwhites, lower-income groups, and those living in urban areas is a result of the greater victimization of these groups.[6] There are, however, a great many discrepancies, which indicate that the {42} relationship between victimization and fear cannot be taken for granted. Not all groups that, according to victimization figures, should be more fearful are in fact more frightened, and vice versa.

> While Blacks and the poor do register higher levels of concern about crime, so do women and the elderly, groups which...generally enjoy low rates of victimization.[7]

Similarly, young males, who are among the most victimized group, tend to be the least frightened.[8] Moreover, correlations between fear and the more

TABLE 2.2   Fear of Crime among Major Population Groups in Chicago, Phila-delphia, and San Francisco, 1977

Question: "How safe do you feel, or would you feel, being out alone in your neighborhood at night? Very safe, reasonably safe, somewhat unsafe, or very unsafe?"

Demographic Group	Percentage "Very Unsafe"	(N)
Sex		
Males	6.4	(643)
Females	22.8	(693)
Age		
18–20	7.1	(71)
21–26	6.3	(256)
27–32	6.3	(263)
33–39	9.3	(174)
40–49	10.6	(149)
50–59	22.2	(152)
60 plus	40.7	(179)
Family Income		
Under $6,000	27.4	(215)
$6–10,000	17.0	(203)
$10–15,000	10.2	(255)
$15–20,000	6.5	(184)
$20–25,000	7.0	(81)
25,000 plus	10.9	(95)
Race		
Whites	12.6	(857)
Blacks	20.1	(368)

SOURCE: Wesley G. Skogan and Michael G. Maxfield, *Coping with Crime: Individual and Neighborhood Reactions* (Beverly Hills, Calif.: Sage, 1981), 75.

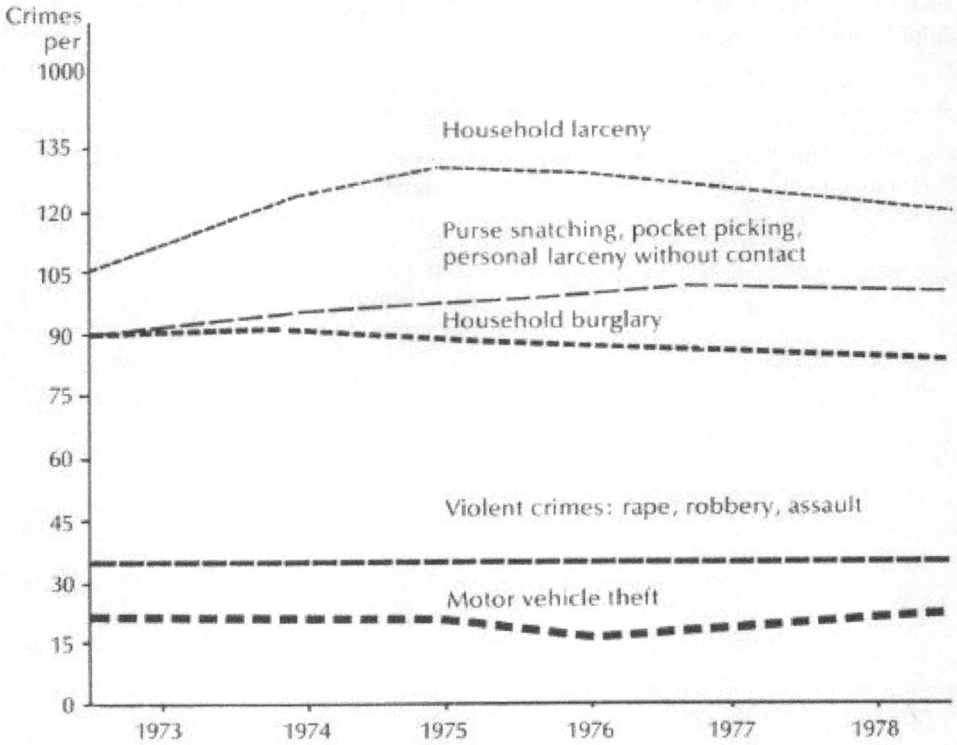

FIGURE 2.1 Criminal Victimization in the United States, by Crime: Trends from 1973–1978. (Source: *Criminal Victimization in the U.S. 1973–78 Trends*, Bureau of Justice Statistics, Washington, D.C., December 1980.)

frightening kinds of victimization are not particularly strong and are apparently confined to the elderly. "For other age groups, the differences are small or nonexistent."[9] Finally, serious crimes are relatively rare events. Only about 6 percent of the respondents in the victimization studies were recent victims of personal crimes, and of these only about 3 percent reported injury—with less than 2 percent seeking medical treatment.[10] This compares with the more than 30 percent of the respondents who expressed concerns about their safety.[11] These figures lead Skogan and Maxfield to conclude that "[t]he frequency of victimization is thus quite disproportionate to the number of persons in these cities who indicated that they were fearful of personal attack in their neighborhoods."[12] While there is clearly some association between victimization and fear, direct victimization provides only a partial explanation of the heightened anxiety about crime in society.[13]

It is apparently indirect, or vicarious, victimization that best explains the level of fear in society, although there is some dispute among researchers about just where the public learns to fear crime. On the basis of their long-term study of prime-time violence on television, George Gerbner and Larry Gross believe that our attitudes about crime are shaped by cradle-to-grave viewing habits.[14] Skogan and Maxfield's study of neighborhoods in San Francisco, Chicago, and Philadelphia leads them to reject the media, but not the vicarious victimization, hypothesis.[15] According to their data, the best predictors of heightened levels of fear are discussions with those who have been victimized, particularly with victims who are, demographically speaking, very much like themselves.[16]

For the time being, the differences between the two studies are less important than their agreement that vicarious victimization provides misleading images about crime.* As Skogan and Maxfield put it:

> [P]ersonal neighborhood communication networks substantially magnify the apparent volume of local violence.... Like media coverage of crime, the {43} processes which lead victims' stories of their experience to "get around" seem to accentuate the apparent volume of personal as opposed to property crime.[17]

Both studies indicate that vicarious victimization, whether as a result of television or conversations with victims, focuses attention on crimes against women and the elderly.[18] When taken together with the special vulnerability of these two groups, the data help us understand why women and the elderly tend to be especially fearful despite relatively low rates of victimization.[19] It also seems reasonable to believe that stories underscoring violence against frail and defenseless members of society put the general public in a vindictive frame of mind. These essentially cultural dimensions of public attitudes about crime are considered at greater length in the next chapter. At this point, suffice it to say that the more carefully we look, the clearer it becomes that the fear of crime reflects important misunderstandings about the nature of crime in America.

Political Salience

The data on political salience are neither so complex nor so puzzling as those on the fear of crime, but there is an intriguing variation between the

---

* It is also true, incidentally, that both explanations help us understand why fear is so much greater than victimization. Obviously television reaches into virtually everyone's life. Rather less obviously, Skogan and Maxfield (see note 2) found that "two-thirds of our respondents knew a victim of a serious crime" (161).

two different indicators of salience. One measure is based on open-ended questions and the other on forced-choice questions. The findings are that crime, relative to other political issues that concern Americans, is strikingly more salient when measured by forced-choice than by open-ended questions. These data suggest that the concern of Americans with crime is more latent than active—that crime is less a part of their everyday pressing concerns than something simmering beneath the surface.

Gallup has been using an open-ended test of salience for a good many years. Respondents are asked, "What do you think is the most important issue facing this country today?" There are really two or three points to be made about the responses to these questions, as reported in Table 2.3.

Surely this is the most volatile of all the indicators of law-and-order attitudes. It is difficult to know what to make of the ups (1968, 1969, 1973, and 1977) and the downs (1970, 1974, 1975, and 1978 to date). There is no apparent correlation with overall rates of victimization and fear, which, it will be recalled, leveled off together in the mid-1970s. It is clear that the downs outnumber the ups, which are probably inflated, in any case, by inclusion of such related concerns as lawlessness, juvenile delinquency, and immorality. Although it is difficult to generalize from such variable findings, two conclusions seem fully warranted. Crime, when measured by open-ended indicators, was not an issue of overriding importance throughout the period; it did surface with sharp insistence from time to time.

The picture provided by forced-choice questions is that crime is much more consistently important to Americans. When asked by the Roper {44} Center about spending on a variety of issues, the public, as is clear from Table 2.4, has very consistently been more willing to increase the financial commitment to "halting the country's rising crime rate" than to any other issue included. The response to these forced-choice questions shows none of the volatility associated with the open-ended Gallup questions—varying only 5 percentage points over the seven years for which there are data and being the preferred funding option in every year except 1973 when crime was a close second to spending on drug addiction programs. One time only surveys in 1977–78 by the Department of Housing and Urban Development and in 1981 by ABC News and the *Washington Post* tend to reinforce the primacy of crime when measured by forced-choice questions.[20] Of course, it is one thing to ask people about spending and another to broach the issue of salience directly. After all, there are some problems, such as inflation, for which the funding response is simply not relevant. Roper, for example, does not mention either unemployment or inflation—nor does the ABC News—*Washington Post* survey. The HUD survey does include unemployment, which is the third most important problem to urban and suburban residents but the most important problem to town and rural respondents.[21] Still, the contrast between responses to open-ended and forced-choice questions remains striking in terms both of the increased consistency and salience under forced-choice circumstances.

TABLE 2.3 The Political Salience of Crime in the United States, 1968–1980, Open-Ended Questions

Question: "What do you think is the most important issue facing the country today?" Percentage (and rank order) of those responding "crime" or crime combined with such related matters as "lawlessness," "law enforcement," "juvenile delinquency," and "immorality."

1968	1969	1970	1971	1972	1973	1974
29 (2)	17 (2)	5 (5)	7 (4)	10 (3)	17 (2)	4 (3)

1975	1976	1977	1978	1979	1980
5 (5)	8 (3)	15 (4)	3 (5)	8 (2)	2 (8)

SOURCE: Compiled from *The Gallup Poll: Public Opinion 1935–1971*, 2 vols. (New York: Random House, 1972); *The Gallup Poll: Public Opinion 1972–1977*, 2 vols. (Wilmington, Delaware: Scholarly Resources, 1978); *The Gallup Opinion Index*, Report no. 157 (August 1978), Report no. 172 (November 1979), Report no. 181 (September 1980).

Taken together, these findings signal a powerful current of suggestibility within the public when it comes to crime. According to the open-ended data, crime is occasionally an issue of great immediacy to Americans—something that comes spontaneously to mind—but most of the time other things (probably economic matters or questions of war and peace) weigh {45} much more heavily on people's minds. The response to forced-choice questions, however, indicates concern about crime is easily aroused and implies that crime can be rather easily politicized.

Punitive Values

Several indicators reveal a clearly punitive drift in American values over the last couple of decades. Support for capital punishment has increased {46} consistently throughout the period, as can be readily observed in Table 2.5. A growth in punitive sentiments is also indicated by responses to questions concerning the harshness of courts. As Figure 2.2 makes clear, an ever larger portion of the public seems to believe that the courts are not harsh enough. Not surprisingly, this trend is paralleled by a decreasing confidence in the deterrent effects of law enforcement—down from 26 percent to 16 percent between 1967 and 1981, according to the Harris survey.[22]

TABLE 2.4 The Political Salience of Crime in the United States, Selected Years 1973–1980, Forced-Choice Questions

Question: "We are faced with many problems in this country, none of which can be solved easily or inexpensively. I'm going to name some of these problems, and for each one I'd like you tell me whether you think we're spending too much money on it, too little money, or about the right amount."

| | Percentage Responding "too little" | | | | | | |
	1973	1974	1975	1976	1977	1978	1980
Halting the rising crime rate	64	67	65	65	65	64	69
Dealing with drug addiction	65	60	55	58	55	55	59
Improving and protecting the nation's health	61	64	62	60	56	55	55
Improving and protecting the environment	61	62	53	55	47	52	48
Improving the nation's education system	49	50	49	50	48	52	53
Solving the problems of the big cities	48	50	47	42	40	39	40
Improving the conditions of blacks	32	31	27	27	25	24	24
Welfare	20	22	23	13	12	13	13
The military, armaments and defense	11	17	17	24	24	27	56
Space exploration program	7	8	7	9	10	8	18
Foreign aid	4	3	5	3	3	4	5

SOURCE: *General Social Surveys, 1972–1980: Cumulative Codebook* (Storrs, Conn.: Roper Center, July 1980), 71–74.

These basic conclusions must be qualified by the distinct streak of moderation that continues to run through public attitudes even in recent years when punitive values are, generally speaking, at or near their peaks. In the first place, it is worth noting that while support for capital punishment has grown steadily during the last couple of decades, Gallup data indicate that it was no higher in 1981 than it was in 1953.[23] Moreover, while it is true (see Table 2.6) that people are significantly less supportive of economic and social approaches to crime and more inclined toward such punitive responses as longer and tougher sentences, that is not the whole story. At least as late as 1976, the punitive response was chosen by slightly fewer respondents than the

TABLE 2.5 Attitudes Toward Capital Punishment, United States

Question: "Do you favor or oppose the death penalty for persons convicted of murder?"

Year	Percent Favor	Percent Oppose	Percent Not Sure
1980	67	27	6
1978	66	28	6
1977	67	26	6
1976	66	30	5
1975	60	33	7
1974	63	32	5
1973*	60	35	5
1972*	53	39	8
1970†	47	42	11
1969†	48	38	14
1965†	38	47	15

* The question for 1972 and 1973 was: "Are you in favor of the death penalty for persons convicted of murder?"

† The question for 1965, 1969, and 1970 was: "Do you believe in capital punishment (death penalty) or are you opposed?"

SOURCE: Timothy J. Flanagan, David J. van Alstyne, and Michael R. Gottfredson, eds., *Sourcebook of Criminal Justice Statistics—1981* (Washington, D.C.: Bureau of Justice Statistics. 1982), 210–11. Nicolette Parisi, Michael R. Gottfredson, Michael J. Hindelang, and Timothy J. Flanagan, eds., *Sourcebook of Criminal Justice Statistics—1978* (Washington. D.C.: National Criminal Justice Information and Statistics Service 1979), 326.

Percent agreeing that courts do not deal harshly enough with criminals:

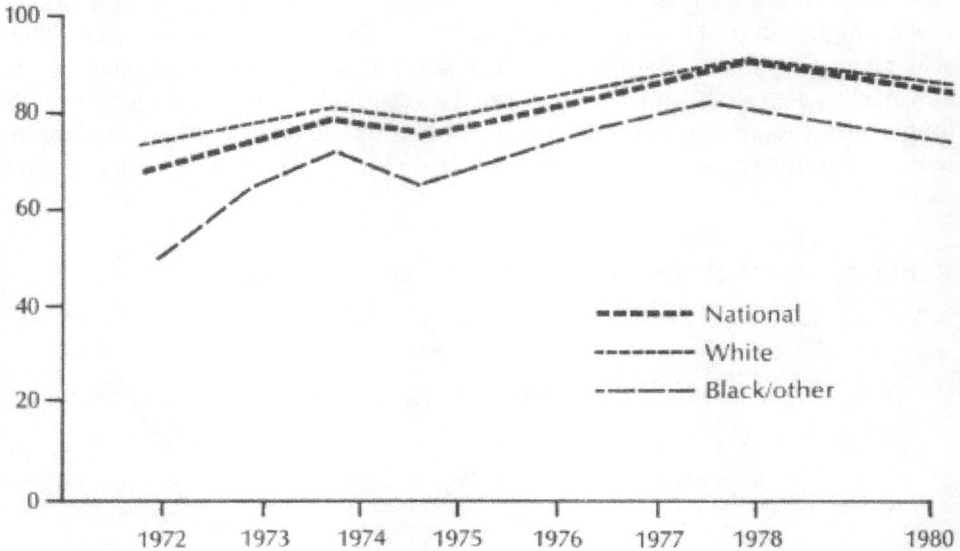

FIGURE 2.2 Public Attitudes in the United States about the Harshness of the Courts, 1972–1978 and 1980. Those surveyed were asked: "In general, do you think the courts in this area deal too harshly or not harshly enough with criminals?" (Source: Timothy J. Flanagan, David J. van Alstyne, and Michael R. Gottfredson, eds., *Sourcebook of Criminal Justice Statistics—1981*, Washington, D.C.: Bureau of Justice Statistics, 1982, 206.)

social and economic approaches. Similarly, {47} while support for rehabilitation dropped from 73 percent in 1970 to 49 percent in 1981, even in the latter year "rehabilitation" was far more popular as a response to crime than "punishment," which was supported by only 17 percent of the population, and than "protecting society," which was supported by 31 percent.[24] It remains an open question whether society in the early 1980s should be best termed as more punitive or less moderate in its approach to crime.

Efforts to find an empirical explanation for the more punitive attitudes of Americans have led outside the circle of victimization, fear, and salience. Arthur Stinchcombe and his associates began with the hypothesis that the punitive drift in public attitudes could be explained by the heightened fear and the increased salience of crime. They found that this was not really the case. With respect to salience, there were only very weak, albeit positive, relationships.

> Thinking crime is an important national problem and thinking
> crime is a problem in the streets of one's own neighborhood have

about the same impact on one's attitudes toward social control...
and in neither case can we explain the surge in punitiveness.[25]
{48}

TABLE 2.6 Preferred Ways of Dealing with Crime, United States, 1972, 1974, and 1976

Question: "Now I'd like to get your views about the best ways to deal with some of our domestic problems at home. First, which two or three of the approaches listed on this card do you think would be the best way to reduce crime?"

	*Percent**		
	1972	*1974*	*1976*
Putting more policemen on the job to prevent crimes and arrest more criminals	22	29	26
Reforming our courts so that persons charged with crimes can get fairer and speedier justice	37	45	46
Improving conditions in our jails and prisons so that more people convicted of crimes will be rehabilitated and not go back to a life of crime.	40	39	28
Really cracking down on criminals by giving them longer prison terms to be served under the toughest possible conditions	35	34	43
Getting parents to exert stricter discipline over their children	48	42	45
Cleaning up social and economic conditions in our slums and ghettos that may breed drug addicts and criminals	61	54	46
Don't know	3	3	3

* Since multiple replies were called for, these figures total more than 100 percent.

SOURCE: Nicolette Parisi, Michael R. Gottfredson, Michael J. Hindelang, and Timothy J. Flanagan, eds., *Sourcebook of Criminal Justice Statistics—1978* (Washington, D.C.: National Criminal Justice Information and Statistics Service, 1979), 326.

Correlations among fear, victimization, and punitive sentiments are still less consistent with the original hypothesis. Blacks are more victimized and more fearful, but they are not more punitive. Women are more fearful but neither more victimized nor more punitive.

> In general, black people are more afraid (and, it might be added, more victimized) than whites but not more punitive; in general, southerners are less afraid than northerners but not less punitive; and women are generally more afraid than men and somewhat less punitive.[26]

The strongest correlate of punitive preferences is what Stinchcombe and his associates refer to as the "rural hunting culture," and these are groups that, because of their distance from urban crime, are both less fearful and less victimized.[27] Stinchcombe et al. speculate that blacks are not more punitive because, having "experienced first hand a strict law-and-order regime," they are leery of its impact on their lives.[28] While no comparable speculation is offered with respect to women, the more general point seems {49} to be that punitive attitudes are best thought of in terms of a broader ideology of crime and punishment—a position that is compatible with the symbolic view of American politics I develop in the pages just ahead, as well as in the next chapter. Conversely, this view runs counter to both mainstream and Marxist approaches,[29] to which we now return.

THE POLITICIZATION OF CRIME

Crime seems to bubble to the surface of American politics in erratic patterns, rather like the measures of active salience shown in Table 2.3. Wilson, pursuing the mainstream line of argument, would have us believe that the politicization of crime reflects demands forced on political leaders by the public—democracy at work. Quinney's Marxist perspective leads him to precisely the opposite conclusion: crime is politicized by the ruling class in order to legitimate the repression of political opponents. Each explanation is inappropriately one-sided. Crime, at least over the last couple of decades, has been a target of opportunity that issue-seeking politicians have been happy to embrace. Politicization is a lesson in neither democracy nor repression but is a simple exercise of fishing in troubled waters. This explanation fits best with contrasting patterns of latent and active salience, as well as with the other data just discussed. At the conclusion of this chapter, I also argue that to the extent that we see crime as a target of opportunity, we shall also better understand the inconclusive way in which politicization has been transformed into operative policy.

Democracy at Work

According to Wilson, it is a simple matter to trace and explain the rise of crime as a political issue over the last couple of decades. The bottom line is that the crime rate, particularly the rate of violent crime, went up dramatically and that the public suffered all the unhappy consequences of increases in street crime: greater personal victimization, higher levels of fear, disruption of community activities, flight to the suburbs, and so on. The public, outraged by the way in which crime was intruding into their lives, demanded that politicians do something about it.[30]

What is remarkable to Wilson is that it took so long for political leaders, as a whole, to respond and that it was conservative Republicans, rather than liberal Democrats, who first seized the issue.

> Not only was the crime issue important to millions of voters, most of the voters who were the victims of street crime were Democrats—blacks, poor whites living in big cities, and upper-middle-class Jewish professionals living in midtown Manhattan. By contrast. Orange County suburbanites who complained {50} a lot about crime rarely experienced it and would vote Republican anyway. Furthermore, crime—unlike Vietnam and inflation—was not an issue for which the Democrats had to explain away their part in causing it.[31]

Why did the Democrats pursue this self-defeating course? According to Wilson, the blame can be placed squarely on a liberal elite that gained control of the Democratic party in the mid-1960s and proceeded to ignore the expressed needs of the party's traditional urban consistuency.[32] Only after the McGovern debacle of 1972 did the tide turn definitively, allowing crime to reach the agenda of both parties. As Wilson sees it, then, antidemocratic tendencies thwarted, at least for a time, the will of the people, who were trying to call attention to their embattled condition.

This understanding does not stand up to empirical scrutiny. Wilson's interpretation of politicization as democracy in action can be diagrammed as shown in Figure 2.3. Wilson sees simple and direct causal links, which have their source in a rising crime rate and result in the expression of punitive policy preferences to politicians. The available data, however, cast a good deal of doubt on crucial links in this chain of politicization.

While victimization and fear have risen in rough parallel, thus lending a surface credibility to Wilson's position, the levels of fear within the society are too high to be accounted for by direct victimization. Moreover, women and the elderly, as we have learned, are more fearful than they "should" be, according to simple extrapolations from victimization, while young males are, according to the same criteria, less fearful than they "should" be. It is also the case that the predicted patterns of punitive reactions do not develop. Women and blacks, who are both more fearful, are not more punitive. Conversely, rural residents are more punitive, although they live far from crime and the fears it engenders.

Nor should we emphasize too heavily the overall disruptive influences of crime on patterns of life. Skogan and Maxfield did find among their respondents in Chicago, Philadelphia, and San Francisco that the more fearful and the more vulnerable segments of the society—women, the elderly, and blacks —took more precautions than others.[33] But neither the nature nor the extent of the precautions taken indicates a drastic curtailing of activities.

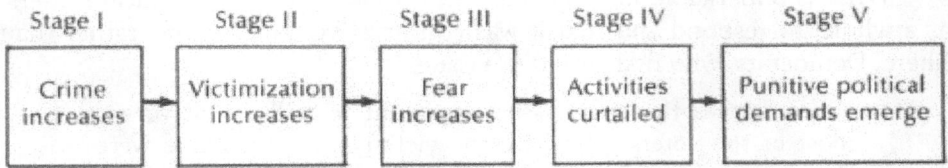

Stage I	Stage II	Stage III	Stage IV	Stage V
Crime increases	Victimization increases	Fear increases	Activities curtailed	Punitive political demands emerge

FIGURE 2.3 Mainstream Interpretation of the Politicization of Crime.

> By far the most common risk-reduction strategy adopted by residents of these cities was to go out by car rather than walk at night: Almost 50% of those {51} questioned indicated that they did this "most of the time." About one in four indicated that they frequently went out with other people and avoided certain places in their neighborhoods because of crime, and one in five usually "took something" (a euphemism we employed to grant anonymity to gun users) when they went out at night.... In all, 33% of our respondents reported doing two or more of these things most of the time, 27% one of them, and 40% none of them.[34]

These findings seem generally consistent with the conclusion drawn by DuBow and his associates after a careful review of the available research on behavioral responses to crime.

> There is considerable evidence that people's behaviors are less affected by crime perceptions than is often thought. We found that for decisions about transportation usage, home relocations, recreational patterns, and going out at night (for the elderly) crime risks are minor considerations.[35]

The inference I am inclined to draw is that people tend, for better or worse, to adapt to crime rather than let it impinge on their activities. If so, it seems unlikely that crime spontaneously generates the insistent public demands implied by Wilson's formulation.

In sum, the picture portrayed by the data suggests patterns that are much too complex to be compatible with Wilson's idea of the politicization of crime as democracy at work. Our response to crime seems to be largely independent of changes in the actual incidence of violent crime, which, as has been made clear, most of us learn about indirectly and unreliably. If we are to make sense of the weak and inconsistent relationships between victimization and fear, on the one hand, and between fear and punitive predispositions, on the other, it is less important to understand crime itself than the images of crime conveyed by the culture. And our reaction to these images depends on who we are and what we believe in. The politicization of crime must be thought of in cultural and personal terms rather than as a direct reaction to a rising crime rate.

But before going on to propose an explanation of politicization that is more complex and more in keeping with the available data, let us consider Quinney's Marxist view of these matters.

Repressive Manipulation

Quinney does not explicitly and systematically address himself to the politicization of crime. He is much more concerned with the repressive policy consequences of that process, especially with the Law Enforcement Assistance Administration, which, according to Quinney's way of thinking, has financed and coordinated those policies. Nevertheless, a Marxist understanding of the process of politicization may be readily inferred from {52} the Marxist theory of crime, which we have considered, as well as from some of Quinney's incidental comments concerning the background of President Johnson's 1965 declaration of war against crime.

For Quinney, unlike Wilson, the origins of politicization are not to be found in the rising crime rate but in the dislocations of capitalism, which account for increases in crime. And according to Quinney, the initial responses came, not from the public, but from the ruling class, which understood that the capitalist order was threatened.

> Since the mid-1960's, with the increasing crisis of capitalism, official and public attention has focused on rising crime and its control. A solution to the crisis has become simply fighting the domestic enemy—*crime*. In a presidential message to Congress in 1965, the "war on crime" was launched. The President declared that "we must arrest and reverse the trend toward lawlessness," suggesting that "crime has become a malignant enemy in America's midst."[36]

In order to legitimate its crackdown on crime, the ruling class cloaks its repression in a conception of justice that portrays the criminal, rather than the capitalist system, as the source of social disorganization.[37]

Quinney's view thus suggests a sequence in the process of politicization that is at odds with Wilson's view, according to which politicization begins with increases in the rate of violent crime and leads to public demands for punitive measures for coping with crime. The point of departure for Quinney is the crisis of American capitalism rather than increases in crime, and while the culmination is superficially the same—punitive political demands—these demands are manipulated rather than spontaneous.

Given Quinney's rather sketchy consideration of politicization, a detailed discussion of Figure 2.4 must be based in part on his more extended analysis of the Marxist theory of crime.

The criminogenic nature of capitalism was considered in Chapter 1 and need not be dealt with again at this point. Figure 2.4 makes clear, however, that the major disruption in people's lives is not caused by crime—as Wilson would have us believe—but is in the Marxist view a result of the declining fortunes of capitalism, which bring ever greater misery to more and more of the population. On the other hand, the diagram tends to obscure the complex reaction of the ruling class to its problems. Wars were declared on both crime and poverty by the Johnson administration, but {53} from a Marxist perspective, the war on poverty was an epiphenomenon that was doomed to failure for two related reasons.

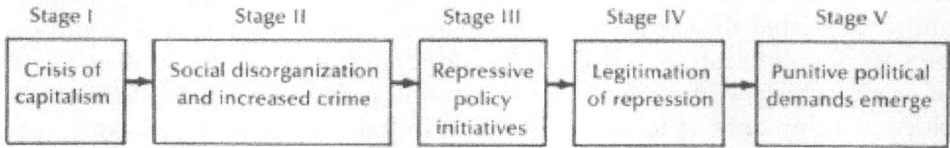

Stage I	Stage II	Stage III	Stage IV	Stage V
Crisis of capitalism	Social disorganization and increased crime	Repressive policy initiatives	Legitimation of repression	Punitive political demands emerge

FIGURE 2.4 Marxist Interpretation of the Politicization of Crime.

First, the cost of social programs quickly outstrips the resources of a declining capitalist economy. The result, according to Marxist theory, is a fiscal crisis of the state—or, one might say, a tax revolt—and a predictable decline in social welfare benefits.[38] More fundamentally, the only way to deal directly with the crisis of capitalism would be to introduce far-reaching structural changes. As Quinney points out, however, "[t]o drastically alter the society and the crime-control establishment would be to alter beyond recognition the capitalist system."[39] Of course, reforms of this magnitude would be unacceptable to the ruling classes, whose interests and values are inextricably tied to the prevailing capitalist economic order. Accordingly, repression is the only feasible alternative.

This repression must be made to appear legitimate. The public's attention is therefore redirected from the cause of society's problems—the decline of capitalism—to the symptoms—crime and criminals. In this instance, what is involved is a campaign to underscore the wickedness of criminals and the critical importance of punishing them for violating the rights of others in the society. As Quinney sees it, intellectuals such as James Q. Wilson have been enlisted in this campaign, which has resulted in a "new justice model." This model equates justice with "protecting acknowledged 'rights' within the current order and...distributing punishment according to desert."[40] More gener-

ally, legitimation entails the "expropriation" or "manipulation" of consciousness. Quinney quotes approvingly from the European Marxist André Gorz:

> As much as over the workers, the factories, and the state, [the
> dictatorship of capital] rules over the society's vision of the
> future, its ideology, its priorities and goals, over the way in which
> people experience and learn about themselves, their potentials,
> their relations with other people and with the rest of the world.
> This dictatorship is economic, political, cultural and psycho-
> logical at the same time; it is total.[41]

Ideology, as well as coercion, has always been an important instrument of
capitalist domination.

There are several persuasive aspects of this Marxist understanding of the
politicization of crime. The basic Marxist scenario offers a plausible explanation for why conservative Republicans seized the initiative in the fight
against crime—an explanation that contrasts with Wilson's notion that the
Republicans stepped in solely because the Democrats were unresponsive.
Marxists also provide some economic background for the way in which the
war on crime triumphed over the war on poverty. The Marxist view, moreover,
seems to fit somewhat better with the available data. If fear of crime outpaces
actual victimization and if the public focuses disproportionately on the most
reprehensibly violent kinds of crime, it is, {54} Marxists tell us, because ruling
elites have both the will and ways to make the public as fearful and vindictive
as possible. It is in the obvious interest of these ruling elites to divert attention
from the failure of capitalism to anxiety about crime. The considerable
strength of the Marxist view, whether or not we accept it, is that it exposes us
to the political economy, and to the ideological dimensions, of the politicization of crime.

But the Marxist model, at least as presented by Quinney, tends to overstate the conspiratorial and manipulative elements of the politicization of
crime. We come to accept, and are effectively mobilized in support of, the
official line on crime not simply because a campaign has been organized and
orchestrated by political leaders. Law-and-order values are, in addition, in
harmony with pervasive cultural themes; and they also satisfy deep personal
needs. Therefore, political leaders need not enter into overt or covert con-
spiracies with the media in order to pull the wool over our eyes. Without any
prompting whatsoever, the news and entertainment media promote law-and-
order values—strictly for market reasons. Particularly when under pressure—
whether from crime or other kinds of stress—the American public is receptive
to the hard line on crime. Whereas Wilson's mainstream view exaggerates the
voluntarism of politicization, Quinney's Marxist presentation simply ignores
the extent to which we willingly, even eagerly, participate in our own seduction.

Cultural Seduction

The politicization of crime is an interactive process combining elements of responsiveness with elements of manipulation. Politicians do not so much "expropriate our consciousness" as take advantage of punitive predispositions about crime that are rooted in American culture. The public engages and disengages from the politicization process for reasons that have at least as much to do with the place of crime in the culture as with the impact of criminal victimization on our lives. In the next chapter I develop, apply, and consider the implications of this cultural interpretation of politicization. For the time being, I simply want to describe the process, juxtapose it to the mainstream and Marxist views, and consider its compatibility with the data presented at the outset of this chapter.

To recapitulate, these data indicate that our attitudes toward crime are only tenuously linked to the crime rate. Victimization research strongly suggests that the fear of crime is more a product of rather distorted public images of crime than of crime per se. Similarly, punitive attitudes are, to a significant degree, independent of actual risk and a reflection, instead, of basic values. Finally, there is reason to believe that although crime is only occasionally an urgent or overriding concern of the American public, there does seem to be an enduring residual sensitivity to crime that makes for relatively easy politicization. In other words, if a forced-choice question in {55} a survey of public opinion can transform crime into a primary political issue, it seems reasonable to believe that our underlying anxieties and punitive predispositions can be rather easily brought to the surface by an enterprising political candidate.

The first point to be made, then, is that neither a high crime rate nor an increase in the rate of crime is, in principle, a necessary prerequisite to the politics of law and order. Of course, candidates' messages warning of a crime problem will find a more receptive audience when there is some independent confirmation or prior awareness of a crime wave. Ordinarily, increases in the actual rate of crime will probably start the ball rolling, but research suggests that media attention to crime has less to do with the crime rate, as such, than with the general news climate, competition among newspapers and television stations, or even with decisions by the police about publicizing crimes.[42]

Second, there is the process by which an increase, or a perceived increase, in the crime rate is shaped into the distorted images that, according to the research, exaggerate the most terrifying crimes and mislead people into thinking of the predatory stranger as the typical criminal. This is the stage that generates the fear of crime. Politicians may contribute to this process, and they certainly capitalize on it, but they do not create it. Nor is there any reason to believe, as Quinney suggests, that political leaders are in league with the media to generate this fear.

Law-and-order political candidates, then, simply take advantage of opportunities provided by the public's state of mind to build an effective election campaign. Nor is it necessarily the case that these politicians are cynical manipulators of the public's anxieties. As members of the public, politicians may be just as outraged about the crime problem as their constituents are, and may be just as inclined to believe that cracking down on criminals will solve or at least alleviate the problem. Some politicians are, no doubt, calculating and manipulative, but if this is truly a cultural phenomenon, we must accept the fact that its roots go deeply into the American psyche.

The cultural perspective diagramed in Figure 2.5 leads to a more complex and contingent model of politicization than do the mainstream or Marxist views just considered. The arrows in the figure convey the basic flow of politicization. Increased crime, increased media attention to crime, or both, are the starting points. While these two points of departure lead to victimization and vicarious victimization in largely independent ways, it remains true that increases in the actual amount of crime probably contribute to increased media attention. Both forms of victimization make the public more fearful, but this fear may trigger either punitive or nonpunitive reactions in the public. Politicians capitalize on, and contribute to, these public emotions by promising punitive and nonpunitive solutions to the crime problem. Thus, the arrows between stages IV and V point in both directions. It is also reasonable to believe that the hoopla {56} surrounding political campaigns sends feedback to the media and further increases media attention to crime.

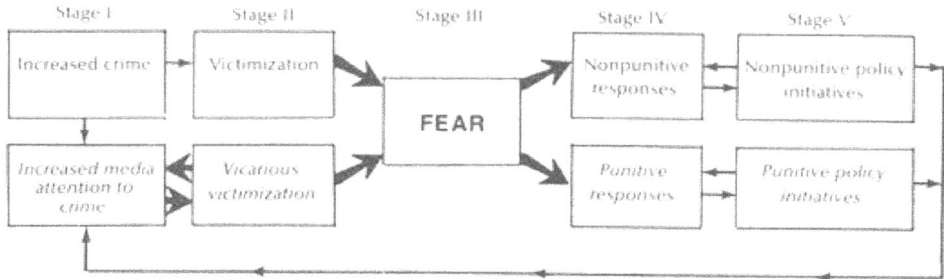

FIGURE 2.5 Cultural Interpretation of the Politicization of Crime.

The bigger arrows call attention to the mediating effects of cultural forces on the course of politicization. Vicarious victimization is attributable to the public's fascination with crime. The media are both responding to and shaping our fascination—thus the arrows go in both directions. Moreover, because we tend to dwell on the most odious forms of crime, we are to a substantial degree responsible for our own fear. As Skogan and Maxfield have demonstrated, actual crime and direct victimization are sufficient to account for only a minor portion of the heightened fears of recent years.[43] Similarly, whether we respond punitively or nonpunitively to our fears is culturally determined— attributable, that is, to the values and emotions which we bring to our thinking about crime rather than to a reliable demonstration that one approach actually works better than the other.

All three theories of politicization explain why hard-line political initiatives have become commonplace during the period beginning in the middle 1960s. Only my cultural perspective is consistent with the available data. The mainstream perspective is the most difficult to square with the data, which reveal significant discontinuities between victimization and fear, on the one hand, and between fear and punitive values, on the other. The Marxist approach fits better with the data in that it explains the discontinuities by reference to a manipulative conspiracy to make scapegoats of criminals. The Skogan and Maxfield study suggests, however, that more fundamental forces are at work and lead people to magnify, in their own thinking and in their contacts with others, the more terrifying kinds of crime. This tendency, as well as the commercial success of books, movies, and television shows that highlight crimes of violence, suggest that only an appreciation of the place of crime in American culture will provide adequate access to the politics of law and order.

Before going on to this extended consideration of crime and culture, it {57} makes sense to recall the policy implications of looking at politicization in this manner. Despite their significant differences, both mainstream and Marxist views suggest rather direct connections between politicization and policy. If democracy is really at work, we can expect political leaders to make concerted efforts to implement their policy promises. Conversely, since politicization is, for Marxists, a justification for the repression the ruling elite wishes to carry out, there is every reason to expect that repression to be forthcoming. If, however, the politics of law and order develops out of a search for salable issues, there is good reason to wonder whether the politicians, once elected, will be particularly assiduous in fulfilling their campaign promises, particularly once it becomes apparent how elusive a target crime is and how many interests are vested in the status quo.

NOTES

1. See, generally, Herbert Jacob and Robert L. Lineberry, *Governmental Responses to Crime: Executive Summary* (Washington, D.C.: National Institute of Justice, June 1982).

2. Wesley G. Skogan and Michael G. Maxfield, *Coping with Crime: Individual and Neighborhood Reactions* (Beverly Hills, Calif.: Sage, 1981), 47.

3. Ibid.

4. The best single source of this information is provided by the extensive surveys conducted by the Law Enforcement Assistance Administration (LEAA). Twenty-six American cities were surveyed between 1972 and 1974. Respondents were asked whether they had been victimized by crime *in the preceding twelve months* and, if so, about the nature of the crimes committed against them. In addition, they were asked about their attitudes toward crime—their fear of it, the extent to which they had altered their activities in response to it, their evaluation of police services, and a variety of related questions. This was a one-time-only study, although a national sample is questioned periodically on victimization alone. See James Garofalo, *Public Opinion About Crime: The Attitudes of Victims and Non-Victims in Selected Cities* (Washington, D.C.: National Criminal Justice Information and Statistics Service, 1977), 13–14. Skogan and Maxfield have also collected some important data that are analyzed together with the LEAA data in their *Coping with Crime*, and survey research organizations have posed victimization questions from time to time.

5. Wesley G. Skogan, "Public Policy and Fear of Crime in Large American Cities," in *Public Law and Public Policy*, ed. John A. Gardiner (New York: Praeger, 1977), 6–7.

6. Bureau of Justice Statistics, *Criminal Victimization in the United States, 1979* (Washington D.C.: U.S. Government Printing Office, 1981), 2 and 7.

7. Skogan and Maxfield, *Coping with Crime*, 42–43.

8. Fred DuBow, Edward McCabe, and Gail Kaplan, *Reactions to Crime: A Critical Review of the Literature* (Washington, D.C.: National Institute of Law Enforcement and Criminal Justice; 1979), 14–15. There is no better starting point for an inquiry into the voluminous and disparate research record on {58} public reactions to crime than this thoughtful synthesis of the literature.

9. Ibid., 19.

10. Skogan and Maxfield, *Coping with Crime*, 45.

11. Ibid., 60.

12. Ibid.

13. Skogan, "Public Policy and Fear of Crime," 9.

14. George Gerbner and Larry Gross, "Living with Television: The Violence Profile," *Journal of Communication* 26 (Spring 1976): 173–98.

15. *Coping with Crime*, 179.

16. Ibid., 175.

17. Ibid., 157 and 155.

18. Ibid., 161–62; and Gerbner and Gross, "Living with Television."

19. On vulnerability, see Skogan and Maxfield, *Coping with Crime*, Chap. 5.

20. Timothy J. Flanagan, David J. van Alstyne, and Michael R. Gottfredson, eds., *Sourcebook of Criminal Justice Statistics—1981* (Washington, D.C.: Bureau of Justice Statistics, 1982), Fig. 2.8, p. 188, and Table 2.12, p. 190.

21. Ibid., Fig. 2.8, p. 188.

22. Ibid., Table 2.31, p. 201.

23. Ibid., Fig. 2.12, p. 209. Support for capital punishment fell from the early 1950s to the middle 1960s when it began its climb to the earlier levels.

24. Ibid., Table 2.35, p. 208.

25. Arthur L. Stinchcombe, Rebecca Adams, Carol A. Heimer, Kim Lane Scheppele, Tom W. Smith, and D. Garth Taylor, *Crime and Punishment—Changing Attitudes in America* (San Francisco: Jossey-Bass, 1980), 72.

26. Ibid., 67.

27. Ibid., 112 and 117. Interestingly, it is also the case that the great increase in the ownership of handguns is largely among those who already owned long guns—that is, those who belong to the "rural hunting culture," ibid., 117–18.

28. Ibid., 125.

29. Ibid., 131.

30. James Q. Wilson, *Thinking About Crime*, (New York: Vintage, 1977), 72–73.

31. Ibid., 73.

32. For Wilson's intriguing analysis of the liberals' rise to power within the Democratic party, see ibid., 75–83.

33. Skogan and Maxfield, *Coping with Crime*, 205.

34. Ibid., 191. It is not clear, incidentally, that taking "something" necessarily means carrying a gun—as opposed to some other weapon or potential weapon, or even a dog.

35. DuBow, et al., *Reactions to Crime*, 66.

36. Richard Quinney, *Class, State, and Crime*, 2nd ed. New York: Longman, 1980, 9–10.

37. Ibid., 15–24.

38. Ibid., 89–91.

39. Ibid., 54.

40. Ibid., 22–23.

41. Ibid., 55.

42. Mark Fishman, "Crime Waves as Ideology," *Social Problems* 29 (June 1978): 31–43.

43. Skogan and Maxfield, *Coping with Crime*, 60.

3

Crime, Culture, and Political Conflict

At the heart of the connection between crime and culture is the myth of crime and punishment—that is, traditional beliefs about the nature, consequences, and appropriate responses to crime. This belief system has powerfully punitive overtones and deep roots in American culture. Nevertheless, the myth of crime and punishment is not without its competitors, which are also well rooted in the culture. One objective of this chapter is to understand how, why and when the myth of crime and punishment is likely to win out over more forgiving ways of thinking about crime.

Because the American public is responsive to the myth of crime and punishment, politicians are tempted to campaign on the issue. Not only is the public united in its opposition to crime, especially street crime, but it is also an issue that arouses strong feelings. Moreover, at least as portrayed by the myth of crime and punishment, crime is a rather straightforward problem whose diagnosis and treatment are embodied in widely accepted and universally understood moral truths. The politician who embraces the cause of law and order need not, for example, confront nor communicate abstruse economic ideas.

Of course, crime is no panacea to politicians. The public is not always responsive, and we must consider the rather volatile combination of forces that sustains the politics of law and order. Then, too, there is the problem of delivering on campaign promises. What happens when the mythical world of political campaigning meets the harsh realities of policy making? There is no need to worry about politicians, who have ways of obscuring their failure to deliver on campaign promises. Nonetheless, since crime is infinitely more complex and intractable than is suggested by the myth of crime and punishment, there will be a necessary discontinuity between the politics of law and order and its policy consequences. This discontinuity is {60} addressed in a preliminary way at the close of this chapter and is the principal theme of succeeding chapters on the police and the criminal courts.

THE MYTH OF CRIME AND PUNISHMENT

The core of the myth of crime and punishment is a simple morality play that dramatizes the conflict between good and evil: because of bad people, this is a dangerous and violent world. The myth helps us make sense of this precarious situation by signaling the dangers of, and revealing the solutions to, problems posed by crime. We learn how to identify criminals, who are portrayed as predatory strangers. We are led to think of criminals as persons fundamentally different in character (and appearance) from law-abiding members of society; criminals are unknown predators awaiting their opportunity to attack persons and property. This frightening image triggers off a second and more reassuring feature of the myth of crime and punishment: the idea that the appropriate response to crime is punishment. Punishment is both morally justified and practically effective. The moral case can be found, among other places, in the Old Testament with its prescription of an eye for an eye. In more practical terms, punishment is defended as a workable way of controlling crime through deterrence and incapacitation.

The available evidence suggests that the myth of crime and punishment offers, at best, a very restricted view of the world of crime. Surely the image of the predatory stranger is misleading and exaggerated. Most crimes are not committed by predatory strangers. Some of the most violent crimes—murder, rape, and assault—are most frequently committed by acquaintances. A systematic study of felony arrests in New York City confirms this and further indicates a prior relationship between defendants and victims in almost 40 percent of most other crimes.[1] Nor is it accurate to think of brutal and malicious crimes or criminals as typical. The most frightening crimes—robbery, rape, and murder—amount to only about 5 percent of the total crimes committed in any given year.[2] Similarly, criminals come with a great variety of proclivities, and for many of them violence is seen as only the last resort— something to be avoided whenever possible.[3] Basic questions may also be raised about the crime-control and moral messages of the myth of crime and punishment. Available data on deterrence and incapacitation are, at best, inconclusive.[4] Moreover, before taking too much solace in the stern morality of the Old Testament, ought we not pause to consider moral codes that stress forgiveness and look to redemption?

If the myth of crime and punishment skates on such thin ice, how can it have such a powerful grip on our imaginations? Why do we respond to it at {61} all? There are both proximate and more fundamental explanations. The proximate explanation has to do with the pervasive presence of the myth of crime and punishment in our culture. More fundamentally, the myth of crime and punishment resonates well with contemporary insecurities.

Cultural Roots

The myth of crime and punishment draws its sustenance from two re-assuring themes with roots deep in American culture. There is, in the first place, easy identification with the vigilante tradition. Even more important is the way in which the myth of crime and punishment evokes the deep-seated American belief in individual responsibility. Taken together, these two traditional themes provide the cultural foundation for the myth of crime and punishment.

Americans have often taken the law into their own hands when, as on the frontier, the state's presence was weak or nonexistent. A number of objections can be raised against vigilantism: It uses unreliable procedures for establishing guilt and innocence, it tends to foster disrespect for the law; and it can readily give way to racial and ethnic extremism. But, at least on the frontier, vigilantism seems to have been readily accepted and to have served an important purpose.

> In the short run, the vigilante movement was a positive facet of the American experience. Many a new frontier community gained order and stability as the result of vigilantism that reconstructed the community patterns of values of the old settled area while dealing effectively with crime and disorder. A host of distin-guished Americans—statesmen, politicians, capitalists, lawyers, judges, writers and others—supported vigilantism by word and deed.[5]

Vigilantism has been understood as one of the vehicles through which civility and the rule of law were imposed on the chaotic conditions of frontier life.

At the heart of vigilantism is a penchant for swift, severe, and violent punishment. After all, almost by definition, a spontaneous, informal, and per-haps underground movement does not have the wide variety of punishment modes at its disposal that are available to the state.

> A vigilante roundup of ne'er-do-wells and outlaws followed by their flogging, expulsion, or killing not only solved the problem of disorder but had an important symbolic value as well. Vigi-lante action was a clear warning to disorderly inhabitants that the newness of the settlement would provide no opportunity for the erosion of the established values of civilization. Vigilantism was violent sanctification of deeply cherished values of life and prop-erty.[6]

On the surface, the message of vigilantism is that, all else failing, effective action against crime involves taking the law into one's own hands. But the {62} more basic message is that the punitive response to crime works. In this sense the vigilante tradition lends credibility to the myth of crime and punishment.

Swift, certain, and severe punishment for those who violate society's rules is also consistent with the basic American ideal of individual responsibility. The punishment suffered by criminals is, in effect, payment for their antisocial behavior. Punishment forces individuals to accept responsibility for their criminal acts. Surely, if criminals get off scot-free, so the argument runs, they are escaping responsibility. And as the lesson sinks in, the assumption is that criminals will see the error of their ways—their efforts to take the easy path or act out their primitive impulses by aggressing against fellow human beings—and will begin to behave like responsible members of society. Punishment is also offered as an object lesson to other members of society, to divert them from the same temptations of crime. In short, crime without punishment seems to threaten what conservatives perceive as our dwindling commitment to individual responsibility.

Cultural Presence

The media focus on crime in a variety of forms and formats. Crime is presented to us in fictional forms by television and radio drama as well as in films and novels. Electronic and print media also provide nonfiction accounts of crime in their news reports. While there is some research available on all this, most of it is rather unsystematic.[7] By far the most ambitious and useful work has been a long-term study of television drama conducted by George Gerbner, Larry Gross, and their associates at the Annenberg School of Communication at the University of Pennsylvania.[8] It is on their findings that I draw, but other media research leads in roughly the same direction.

Gerbner and Gross have had trained observers monitoring and coding television drama since 1967 in an effort to understand just how American life is portrayed. One of their primary concerns has been the images of violence conveyed by television drama, and their findings have yielded a picture strikingly similar to that implicit in the myth of crime and punishment. Television drama portrays a world of violent conflict between good guys and bad guys. We learn what kinds of people are likely to be victims and by whom they are likely to be victimized. Finally, we get the reassuring message that predatory violence does not pay *if* it is dealt with directly and punitively.

The first thing to note is the grossly misleading sense of violence that pervades television drama. While there has been some variation from year to year, from network to network, and from time slot to time slot, the {63} exaggeration of violence has remained fairly constant. Consider the following summary comparison of 1979 with 1978:

> In prime time, 70 percent of all programs still contained violence.
> The rate of violent episodes was 5.7 per hour, up from 4.5 in 1978.
> Nearly 54 percent of all leading characters were involved in some
> violence, about the same as in 1978. In weekend-daytime (child-

ren's) programs, 92 percent of all programs contained some violence, down from 98 percent in 1978. The rate of violent episodes was 17 per hour, down from 25 the year before. Nearly 75 percent of all leading characters were involved in violence, down from 86 percent in 1978.[9]

Thus the audience of television drama is led to see violence as a way of life—at or near the surface of interpersonal relations.[10]

While the overall level of violence establishes an initial affinity with the myth of crime and punishment, even more revealing is the moral message conveyed by the story line and the patterns of victimization. "The victimization of the 'good' woman is often the curtain-raiser that provokes the hero to righteous 'action.'"[11] The picture emerges of heroic males regularly and successfully using lethal violence as a way of avenging wrongs and, by implication, deterring crime.

> Geared for independent action in loosely-knit and often remote social contexts half of all characters are free to engage in violence. One-fifth "specialize" in violence as law breakers or law enforcers. Violence on television, unlike real-life, rarely stems from close personal relationships. Most of it is between strangers, set up to drive home lessons of social typing. Violence is often just a speciality—a skill, a craft, an efficient means to test the norms and settle any challenge to the existing structure of power.[12]

The correspondence between Gerbner and Gross's summary of their findings and the myth of crime and punishment is really remarkable. All the elements are present: a threatening environment, disproportionately populated by predatory strangers, their victims, and their adversaries; and punitive solutions— indeed, capital punishment—ultimately providing predators with their just deserts.

Another striking feature of these findings is the way in which they match the fear of crime data discussed in the previous chapter. Women particularly old, lower-class, and nonwhite women, tend to be more victimized than men. Among the men, the picture is more ambiguous. Old and lower-class men are more likely to be killed than to kill, but old men are slightly more likely to victimize than to be victimized.[13] There is, in any case, greater correspondence between television drama and fear than between actual victimization and fear.

This leads quite naturally to the question whether our exposure to television drama is really responsible for the attitudes we have toward crime. Gerbner and Gross claim a causal relationship based on survey {64} research that indicates that, generally speaking, heavy television watchers have a view of the world that corresponds more closely to TV imagery than do those who spend less time in front of the television set.[14] Heavy viewers (1) tended to exaggerate the proportion of the population involved in law enforcement, (2) were more likely to believe that most people cannot be trusted, and (3) sensed a greater likelihood of being involved in violence.[15] These causal inferences have proven controversial, but the result of exchanges with their critics has led Gerbner and Gross to refine rather than abandon their initial conclusions. They now believe that heavy television watching cultivates a "mainstream" outlook on life. The "fundamental underlying process is that of convergence into a 'mainstream' television view of the world."[16] That is, television tends to raise levels of fear and distrust among the least anxious while having a moderating influence on the most anxious.

The causal issues are not directly germane to the argument I am developing. The point is not that people learn the myth of crime and punishment, or even a complementary set of attitudes, from television drama or from the media generally. The point is only that the values and understandings that comprise the myth of crime and punishment are indeed an important part of our cultural milieu, and they help define our common consciousness. I am less interested in whether television shapes our understanding than in its capacity to reflect that understanding.

CRIME AND CULTURE

So far, my claim has been that the myth of crime and punishment has its roots deep in American culture and continues to project a powerful presence in contemporary society. How are we to account for its staying power? Why do we continue to accept a view of the world that presents so distorted an image? The obvious answer is that the myth of crime and punishment meets our current needs in some way or other, and the purpose of this section is to explore its appeal in contemporary circumstances.

My intention is not to claim an unassailable primacy for the myth of crime and punishment. While the myth is well entrenched in traditional American values, there are alternative belief systems with equally strong traditional roots. The myth of rights, as I have argued elsewhere, offers us the rule of law, the Bill of Rights, due process, and a host of other symbols of legitimacy, which are regularly invoked in debates over policy choices to be made in the criminal process.[17] Other myths are also available. The myth of redemption is based on the idea that people can straighten out their lives if their consciences can be awakened. The myth of rehabilitation, which is of more recent vintage, banks on trained professionals to {65} provide the kind of guidance necessary to reintegrate offenders into the society.

The suasive power of the myth of crime and punishment tends to wax and wane according to social conditions. More specifically, the appeal of the myth of crime and punishment is greatest when predatory street crime is deemed to be a serious problem and, more generally, at times of perceived social crisis. Insofar as street crime is concerned, the appeal of the myth of crime and punishment is in part instrumental. *Relatively speaking*, a rather strong crime-control case can be made for the myth of crime and punishment. But there is also a strong affective side to the attractions of the myth of crime and punishment, and this affective component provides the real key to understanding the attractions of the myth of crime and punishment in times of crisis.

Crime Control

While the myth of rights may lend considerable impetus to due process policies, these policies ring hollow as a response to perceived increases in violent crime. As Herbert Packer pointed out a good many years ago, due process tends to run at cross purposes to crime control.

> Two models of the criminal process will let us perceive the normative antinomy at the heart of the criminal law. These models... represent an attempt to abstract two separate value systems that compete for priority in the operation of the criminal process... I call these two models the Due Process Model and the Crime Control Model.[18]

It is safe to say that this intellectual insight is part of the American public consciousness these days. Whether or not it is true that the due process decisions of the Warren Court handcuffed the police, "common sense" tells us that the "costs" of due process are likely to include fewer arrests and fewer convictions.

Some would argue that due process restrictions do not decrease the effectiveness of law-enforcement officials but prod them to adopt higher standards and better training. Perhaps there is some truth in this rejoinder, but there is no gainsaying that due process is, as Packer put it, an "obstacle course" deliberately designed to protect defendants and make life more difficult for police and prosecutors.[19] This point is dramatically illustrated each time offenders have their convictions reversed on "technicalities"—events that are likely to get media attention in direct proportion to the brutality of the crime.

Redemption and rehabilitation are more purposeful strategies for coping with crime, but they are not necessarily more credible. Redemption is essentially a religious or moral idea, which many Americans are {66} prepared to embrace. It is, however, more likely to be associated with divine, familial, or communal intervention than with the impersonal institutions of criminal process. The rehabilitation response is likely to carry more weight, and in the past it was readily accepted by the public. Its eclipse may be simply cyclical. Any strategy for coping with crime will ultimately be discredited because crime is part and parcel of the human condition. But insofar as the image of the predatory stranger dominates our sense of what crime is all about, neither redemption nor rehabilitation appears to be a workable strategy. How likely are we to believe that persons so bestial as the predatory stranger will reward our investment of faith and rehabilitative dollars?

In sum, both punitive and more permissive policies can invoke on their behalf cherished American values. Punitive policies have a distinct initial edge because they have a much longer tradition of association with the problems of crime in America. This edge is increased once crime becomes a public issue— once the sense of a crime wave begins to take hold. The crime wave is, after all, evidence that the legal and rehabilitative professionals who run the system are failing. Moreover, once we perceive that the society is being overrun by predatory strangers, we are no longer interested in guaranteeing them rights that might well allow them to escape punishment. Nor are we likely to think of them as fellow citizens who can be redeemed or rehabilitated. Thus, in large measure, the success of law-and-order symbols depends on frightening images of crimes and criminals.

A circular quality has crept into this argument and must now be addressed. In trying to explain the appeals of the myth of crime and punishment, I have argued that, in purely practical terms, it has a distinct edge over competing myths. But this instrumental case rests in large measure on the very exaggerated images of crime and criminals that I am trying to explain. If, in other words, we were more prepared to think about the full range of crime and the reasons for it, we would be forced to think differently about criminals; more particularly, we would begin to realize what we and they have in common, as well as those things that divide us. And if we ceased thinking about criminals as a breed apart, it would be easier to accept the possibility of redemption, rehabilitation, or, for that matter, social and economic reform as appropriate responses to crime.

In short, the attractions of punishment depend heavily on violent and frightening conceptions of crime. We are thus driven back to the basic question—our fascination with violent crime. Why is it, as Skogan and Maxfield discovered, that our discussions of crime tend to be dominated by the most horrifying and least typical kinds of criminal behavior?[20] Similarly, why is it that the reporting of crime news follows precisely the same path—"disproportionately report[ing] violent personal crimes"?[21] To respond that these unusual events are simply the most newsworthy is to beg {68} the question. Nor does it explain the prominent part played by crime and violence in our popular culture—books, films, and television drama.

Culturally speaking, it is altogether fair to say that our problem is not too much crime but too little. Even though crime exists—and exists in what the public chooses to think of as epidemic proportions—we still feel compelled to invent it, as the accompanying *Doonesbury* cartoon reminds us. I would now like to speculate on the attractions of the world of crime and punishment for B.D. and a great many other Americans.

Projecting Our Insecurities

This society's intense preoccupation with crime as a source of enter-tainment is at least in part a reaction to the amorphous stress of our daily lives. Over fifty years ago, Harold Lasswell made this kind of argument in his study of *World Politics and Personal Insecurity*.[22] Lasswell used a Freudian framework to explore the close ties between personal insecurity and a procliv-ity for orthodoxy and violence. In addition to Lasswell's ideas, I also want to look to a literary source, Bruce Jay Friedman's comic novel about the police, *The Dick*, to illustrate and convey, if not necessarily to authenticate, my argu-ment.[23]

Lasswell, writing in the 1930s, was concerned with economic insecurity and its tendency to promote public support of "rigid centralization, revolu-tionary upheavals, and international war."[24] The theory is broad enough to be applicable to a variety of personal insecurities, and when taken together with *The Dick*, to provide significant insight into the public's fascination with crime and violence.

Lasswell claimed that the internal tensions generated by personal in-securities lead people toward violence, which is best able to release these tensions. We therefore project our fantasies into matters in which violence is an accepted mode of problem solving.

> The accumulating tensions [within the personality] ... create a situation favorable to orgiastic release through the violence pat-terns which are all along recognized as potential, and which ap-pear to furnish release in maximal assertion against the un-friendly features of the environment. *The flight into action is preferable to the torments of insecurity*; the flight into danger be-comes an insecurity to end insecurity. The demand for security takes the foreground.[25]

Thus crime and punishment provide the symbols that our unconscious seeks. Lasswell's theory suggests why the tensions of modern life can generate support for the myth of crime and punishment and at the same time helps to explain why cops and robbers has become a national pastime with a powerful grip on our imaginations. {69}

Friedman's novel gives us added understanding of the phenomenon. It does not really matter whether Friedman knows much about the police—ap-parently he does not. They are only the ostensible subject of his novel. What Friedman is writing about, and what he does understand, are our fantasies about crime, cops, and criminals. A perceptive social critic, Friedman senses the symbolic importance of crime in American culture in a fashion that fits remarkably well with Lasswell's theory.

The central character of *The Dick*, Ken LePeters (née Kenneth Sussman), emerges as the incarnation of our fantasies. LePeters is a bourgeois, fortyish

Jew turned homicide detective. Clearly he is out of his element. Indeed, he is not really a homicide detective at all but the public relations man for a homicide bureau. As a kind of quasi dick, he is entitled to drive a police car, which he frequently takes onto the highway with lights flashing and siren screaming. Other perquisites of a true homicide detective are, however, denied to him. He wears a "badgette" instead of a badge and is not permitted to carry a gun. He functions, as he puts it "in a demilitarized zone between dick and PR man...enjoy[ing] the parade of slaughter before him, at the same time clicking his tongue and deploring the homicidal violence of it."[26]

LePeters is puzzled and uneasy about his fascination with crime and violence. He has been raised to respect civility and rationality, and yet he is attracted to the crude and brutal people among whom he works.

> For the most part, theirs were the simple virtues—a man put in thirty years on the job, bowled a bit, told a few fag jokes, watched the late show, had a faithful wife, and loyally practiced sex in one position, leaving the tricky stuff to foreigners. The flag gave a man goose bumps, and anyone who didn't like the country was invited to get the fuck out of it.... And what was a man's solemn hope? That when he finally got laid to rest there'd be someone around to deliver that most sought-after of all homicidal ac-colades: "By God, that fella was a good dick."[27]

After musing briefly about his own inclinations toward higher things, LePeters looks more deeply into himself.

> Who exactly was he kidding? Could he actually say that his heart was quiet when he heard "The Star Spangled Banner" or saw the Marines storm a beachhead on a late-night Iwo Jima movie? When some dick proposed that we settle our differences with the Red world by "lobbing a few into the Kremlin men's room" wasn't there one slender pocket within him in which for a frozen instant the question was asked, "Why not?" LePeters had cop in him all right, and more than he liked to admit.[28]

But why is LePeters attracted to police work? Why, despite his liberal values, is he drawn to these coarse and boorish men?

In order to answer this question, we must get a feeling for the elemental forces that are awakened in LePeters and how they do battle {70} with his liberal self-image. One example should suffice. LePeters is often the butt of homicide bureau practical jokes. Consider the day he is forced into an in-terrogation room with a tough-looking black suspect.

> He tried to get out, but then took a deep breath, switched per-sonalities, and startled himself by how quick he got into the swing of things. "Take your hat off," he told the suspect.... "I got an eyeball witness who'll swear he saw you there the day it hap-

> pened. You jerk me off, you cop-fighting jive-ass, I'll frame your
> butt so good you'll do forty years in solitary."

When the suspect immediately crumbles and begins to pour out a confession, LePeters feels "giddy, as though he had flung a basketball the full length of the court—blindfolded—and seen it go right through the hoop." He is also "horrified, his shoulders crushed with sorrow. 'I'm not a real dick. Forget what you said and take my word for it, they don't have a thing on you.'"[29]

If LePeters yields to primordial urges, it is in part because they enable him to assert control in problematic situations. Moreover, unlike LePeters, his fellow officers live without anguish and ambivalence. These themes emerge most clearly during LePeters's Caribbean vacation—a desperate effort to escape personal and professional insecurities. While on the trip he falls in with a retired dick, a cocky little fellow by the name of Boners, who arranges a deep-sea fishing trip for the two of them. When the captain hooks a huge fish, he calls out for LePeters to reel it in while warning Boners to stay out of the way. ("Not you, you'll bust your ass.") LePeters proceeds to struggle with the fish for more than an hour. Boners, in the meantime, "offended by the [captain's] mysterious rebuke...sulk[s] in the corner of the boat." Finally, he reaches the breaking point, "yank[s] out a pistol, and with perfect aim drill[s] two shots through the fish's head." The skipper, "holding a suddenly slack line" demands an explanation. Boners calmly "cool[s] his gun, then slip[s] it back in a concealed holster." He explains simply: "I don't take shit from fish." LePeters immediately identifies with Boners. "A young detectivey swagger came over him of the sort he never experienced around the bureau; indeed, he wished he had taken along a gun so that he could rip off a few rounds in support of his gutsy hell-for-leather little friend."[30]

Clearly, there is no longer any ambivalence; LePeters unequivocally accepts the liberating pleasures of direct and violent action. He had struggled with the fish, remaining within the conventions of angling. He had agonized over the captain's insult to his friend. Should he not have taken a stand in behalf of the demeaned dick? Boners, for his part, had taken things decisively in hand. He had solved all the problems in one swift and brutal act: no guilt, no equivocation, no piling of complexity onto complexity. In short, action instead of anxiety.

LePeters may not be altogether typical, but the temptation, in {71} Lasswell's terms, to displace "infantile, childish, and juvenile affects upon symbols of ambiguous reference" (or "public objects") is probably typical.[31] In other words, LePeters's attachment to liberal values may be stronger than that of the average American, but his need to displace personal insecurities is commonplace. He is worried about his marriage and his career, and these worries are compounded by his perception of social crisis, which also seems to impinge on his life. Caught up in these worries, LePeters finds the simple and direct world of cops and robbers very inviting. Despite his liberal aversion to the crudeness and violence of the police vision of the world, this vision is seductive insofar as it allows LePeters to recapture an infantile sense of omnipotence.

It stands to reason that if we turn to the world of crime for solace, we are unlikely to be receptive to messages of enlightened liberalism. We do not want to hear that we are all responsible or that there is no definitive solution to the problems of crime, nor that we should turn the other cheek. All this is unwelcome because it only adds to our sense of helplessness. Why should we reject the comfort of punitive policies? We have neither the time nor the resources to check the evidence and coolly appraise the policy options. But, more important, what if we were to find out that the liberals are correct—that there is no answer and that we are all responsible? That would mean re-assuming the burden in the world of crime that we are fleeing from in our own lives.

Lasswell and Friedman thus tell us that the politics of law and order may have less to do with traditional political cleavages, manipulation by elites, and rational policy calculations than with our insecurities. In times of insoluble problems that appear to multiply endlessly, it is not surprising that childish fantasies of cops and robbers are irresistibly diverting. If so, the politics of law and order must be seen at least partially as the projection of personal insecurities into the policy arena. Our preoccupation with self leads us to take refuge from the complexity and frustration of contemporary life in the simple, liberating truths of crime and punishment.

Reaffirming Community

It is not only in their role as diversions from the trials and tribulations of everyday life that crime and punishment are emotionally and inextricably linked. Durkheim tells us in *The Division of Labor in Society* that an equally powerful emotional mechanism is operative when we think about crime as a social problem.[32] While we may believe that we evaluate punishment in practical terms—that is, according to its capacity to deter or incapacitate—Durkheim claims that its primary appeal is "passionate and in a great part non-reflective."[33]

Indeed, the first part of Durkheim's argument is that we are not really {72} drawn to punishment as a way of "correcting the culpable or intimidating possible followers" at all.[34] As he sees it, punishment is addressed to the law-abiding rather than lawbreakers. Punishment's "true function is to maintain social cohesion intact, while maintaining all its vitality in the common conscience."[35] Those who commit crimes threaten our sense of community because crime is an act that violates our "beliefs, traditions, and collective practices."[36] Punishment is a reassuring signal that we are still authoritatively committed to long-standing community values.

But why must this official reaffirmation of community be punitive? Why not rehabilitation or restitution, for example? According to Durkheim, the community must react in terms that are *emotionally* commensurate with the injury inflicted on the "collective sentiments." The reaffirmation must be proportional to the affront.

> [Punishment] would necessarily lose its energy, if an emotional reaction of the community did not come to compensate its loss, and it would result in a breakdown of social solidarity. It is necessary, then, that it be affirmed forcibly at the very moment when it is contradicted, and the only means of affirming it is to express the unanimous aversion which the crime continues to inspire, by an authentic act *which can consist only in suffering inflicted* upon the agent.[37]

Neither rehabilitation nor restitution, Durkheim seems to be saying, provides an emotionally convincing demonstration of our continued adherence to traditional norms. "[T]he criminal must suffer in proportion to his crime."[38]

Is a society that is willing to settle for something other than punishment really a society that no longer believes in its own values—"a society where the whole common conscience would be nearly gone?"[39] Most people are inclined to disagree. Liberals tend to deny that punishment is, as Durkheim suggests, somehow necessary and proper. Conservatives, who are generally more in tune with Durkheim, defend punishment as a crime-control measure rather than a security blanket or a signal of reassurance.

While I am not sure that I am prepared to accept all the implications of Durkheim's argument, his essential insight strikes me as instructive. Surely the more powerful the affront to our fundamental social bonds, the greater the anxiety and anger that is likely to be generated. And, just as certainly, do we not need definite reassurance that this behavior is the exception and is not becoming the rule? To get a more immediate sense of the role of punishment and, more particularly, of the tensions among punishment, due process, and community, I want to look once again to popular culture. *The Magician*, a crime novel by Sol Stein, is particularly good, but there are other popular films and novels as well that evoke the same basic emotions.[40] {73}

The ostensible antagonists in *The Magician* are two high school boys—Ed Japhet, a young man of many talents, and Stanislaus Urek, who heads a gang of school hoodlums. At the heart of their conflict is Ed's refusal to pay for "protection" from Urek's gang. The dramatic incident that focuses their conflict is an unprovoked attack by the Urek gang. The attack occurs after Ed, an amateur magician, has transfixed the entire student body with a dazzling display of magic. Urek, because of his animosity toward Ed, tries to disrupt the show but ends up being embarrassed by Ed in front of everyone. After the show, Ed, his girlfriend Lila, and Ed's father, a teacher in the school, are set upon by the gang. Ed is choked so severely by Urek that a tracheotomy is required and is also beaten with a chain, which is then used to smash the windshield of the Japhets' automobile. To compound the incident, Urek, while out on bail, attempts to kill Ed in the hospital by cutting one of the tubes that Urek incorrectly assumes is keeping Ed alive.

Although the battle between Ed and Urek is the initial focus of the novel, George Thomassy, Urek's defense attorney, quickly becomes the center of attention. He is the real magician, and his magic consists of transforming a premeditated and murderous assault on Ed into a spontaneous juvenile scrap in which the distinction between the good guys and the bad guys becomes completely blurred. Thomassy's reconstruction of the fight is too long to be reproduced here, but it involves damaging admissions on the witness stand by both Lila and Mr. Japhet. Lila admits that it was not at all uncommon for the boys to pull girls' hair at school. Yet it was Urek's grabbing of Lila's hair that brought Ed to her defense and precipitated the fight that so severely injured Ed. Under Thomassy's clever and relentless questioning, Mr. Japhet acknowledges that Ed actually struck the first blow. Of course, everyone who is familiar with what has happened knows Urek's motives and realizes that the hair-pulling was incidental to Urek's clear plan to revenge himself against Ed.

For our purpose, the novel is useful because of the way in which it arouses and channels *our* anger. There is Ed's initial beating and then the additional horror of Urek's attempt to murder a helpless Ed in the hospital. As it begins to dawn upon us that Urek is going to be able to use Thomassy's legal deceptions to escape punishment, our anger is compounded by a powerful sense of impending injustice. And it becomes all too clear why the upstanding people in the novel become progressively disenchanted with the official institutions of society. Mr. Japhet cannot even convince Ed to testify.

> "All you've got to do is answer the questions you're asked truthfully."
> "I don't *have* to do anything."
> "I know you wish all this hadn't happened. So do I. But Ed, now the processes of justice are in train...."
> Ed laughed. "I'm sorry, Dad, I didn't mean to laugh...." {74}
> "What are you getting at?"
> "You were quoting the processes of justice at me."
> "Ed, all I hope is that somewhere along the line I have taught you how to make the most of your life, that's all."
> "That's a joke."[41]

It is a joke because Ed has suffered precisely as a result of his efforts "to make the most" of his life. Mr. Japhet understands this as he makes clear subsequently on the witness stand.

> "My son, *the worse for him*, resisted this extortion by refusing to pay the monthly charge for leaving his locker alone. If he were an

> adult in business and did the same thing, he would have been
> attacked, as he was attacked in school.[42]

The failure to punish compounds the initial failure to protect and somehow conveys a sense of official complicity in the antisocial behavior.

Of course, we still have not reached the issue of severity. Is an eye for an eye really an emotional necessity, and will it successfully "heal the wounds made upon collective sentiments?"[43] *The Magician* cannot, of course, answer either question definitively. It does provide some insight into the first issue. For example, it is difficult not to identify with Mr. Japhet's murderous inclinations as he struggles to get Urek to release his grip on Ed's throat.

> Mr. Japhet pulled the back of Urek's coat collar without effect,
> then drummed his fists fruitlessly on Urek's hunched back, wish-
> ing he had a gun to blow the boy's head off.[44]

Insofar as we feel this way, we finally get emotional satisfaction from the book's climactic struggle between Ed and Urek. Urek, once again the aggressor, is killed by Ed, who in desperation resorts successfully to the karate he learned in order to defend himself.[45] The book ends on a note of irony as the police steer Ed toward a patrol car and Mr. Japhet goes "inside to phone Thomassy."[46]

To the extent that commensurate punishment is an emotional (and perhaps a social) necessity, we are once again reminded of how closely the attractions of the myth of crime and punishment are tied to an exaggerated and misleading sense of the dangers of street crime. If we perceive a society haunted by an increasing army of predatory strangers, we will ask the institutions of criminal process to strike back and thus will reassure ourselves that the norms and values of the society are intact. Conversely, if we think of crime in more complex and less threatening ways, our emotional needs for retribution will be proportionately reduced. Durkheim, therefore, helps us to realize that the appeal of punishment arises from within us but that the rhetoric and imagery of law and order contribute directly to these internal needs. {75}

The Cultural Perspective

The several components, just considered, that sustain the myth of crime and punishment are analytically distinct but not so discrete in practice as my presentation may have suggested. Our anxieties are diffuse. Consider, for example, a study in Portland, Oregon, that indicated how anxiety about crime and social isolation blend together for the elderly.

> There was no relationship between the degree of social isolation
> and whether respondents had or had not been victims of crime,
> but greater isolation was related to the higher anxiety about
> crime.[47]

Similarly, the data reveal that various forms of incivility or unusual behavior "may be interpreted as a sign of the social disorder and moral decay of which crime is a part and, hence, be as threatening as more victim-oriented crime."[48] Crime can become a convenient symbol for condensing a variety of stresses in our lives. Our frustrations are simply redirected into the issue of street crime for which punishment, we have learned, is a swift and effective remedy. According to this way of thinking, support for cracking down on criminals may be generated by a convergence of cultural forces rather tenuously linked to a concern with the kinds of predatory street crime that threaten life, limb, or property.

Taken together, the cultural forces sustaining the myth of crime and punishment might seem overwhelming. How is it, then, that we are not in a perpetual state of siege? The answer is to be found in the volatility of these forces. One theme emphasized in this section has been that the myth of crime and punishment is particularly compelling when we are most frightened by crime and extremely anxious about other threats to our way of life or our peace of mind. At such times, the sustaining forces feed upon one another, producing a kind of multiplier effect. In less stressful periods, we are presumably less receptive to messages that exaggerate our sense of criminal jeopardy, and the whole process reverses itself. Because we are less receptive, we will probably be subjected to fewer such messages, since they are less likely to sell soap or swing votes. For these reasons, the politics of law and order, to which we now turn, seem to come and go in a rather mysterious fashion.

THE POLITICS OF LAW AND ORDER

The temptations to politicize crime are very strong. Insofar as politicians share the fears of their fellow citizens, it is only natural that they think about dealing with crime as an important political responsibility. But crime is a political opportunity as well as a responsibility. For the politician casting about for a campaign issue, crime has some compelling attractions. {76} Most fundamentally, the public cares deeply about the issue, and the politician can expect considerable support from the media in capturing the public's attention. Crime is also an issue for which the myth of crime and punishment provides a simple and credible answer that the public is only too happy to embrace. Indeed, once public anxieties are aroused, it would be difficult, if the analysis I have presented in this chapter is correct, to sell any answer other than punishment. Finally, punitive solutions tend to bring politicians to office in distinctly favorable circumstances. Given a threat to its security, the public is likely to be permissive with its grants of money and authority.

It could be argued that in the long run, the crime issue is bound to backfire. Crime is, after all, an intractable problem, and there is good reason to doubt whether cracking down will be particularly effective. Will the voters not turn on the erstwhile law-and-order candidates once it becomes clear that they, as elected officials, are unable to deliver on their campaign promises? Although this could happen, it is really not all that likely because of the sharp discontinuity between politics and policy.

This discontinuity stems from the distance that separates policy makers from the public. To borrow a distinction originally drawn by Murray Edelman, political campaigns are conducted at the "symbolic" level; actual policy making involves a much more "concrete" form of politics.

> For most men most of the time politics is a series of pictures in the mind, placed there by television news, newspapers, magazines, and discussions. The pictures create a moving panorama taking place in a world the mass public never quite touches, yet one its members come to fear or cheer, often with passion and sometimes with action.[49]

The public ordinarily responds to symbols rather than direct experience and is not really aware of the "concrete" effects of public policy. In contrast, political elites who participate regularly in the decisions that actually allocate resources are in a position to appreciate and calculate the costs and benefits of policy choices.

The policy promises made in political campaigns are part of a cycle of symbolic politics and have no necessary connection to concrete problem solving. This cycle is comprised of reassurance from the politicians in return for support from the public. In evoking such widely shared truths as the myth of crime and punishment, politicians tell the public what it wishes to hear, namely, that a complex and troubling problem can be solved in a simple and time-honored fashion. The public thus contributes to its own seduction. Indeed, as Lance Bennett argues, the politician who offers proposals that "fall outside the range of acceptable alternatives dictated by social myth" is asking for trouble.[50]

> Policies become means of affirming the larger images of the world on which they are based. In most policy areas it is more acceptable to suffer failure {77} based on correct theories than it would be to achieve success at the price of sacrificing social values.[51]

Campaign promises, shaped by political myths, provide political leaders with the authority to govern and become "a set of lessons about how people should act and how they should apply values to social dilemmas."[52]

Once in office, there is no reason to assume that political leaders will actually pursue the punitive paths inherent in the myth of crime and punishment. In all likelihood, punitive programs will be developed and presented with the great fanfare appropriate to the symbolic level of politics. Nor should we necessarily think of these policy initiatives as disingenuous. They may or they may not be honest efforts to fulfill campaign promises.

Either way, it is at this point that politicians are drawn into interactions with one another and with public officials, and for all these elites the stakes of the policy game are concrete and well understood. It is clear, in the first place, that crime, like other policy problems, is not amenable to simple solutions. In addition, since all reforms tend to alter the status quo and jeopardize vested interests, resistance to punitive policy programs can be taken for granted. Under these circumstances, it is reasonable to expect that even sincere politicians will look for ways to rationalize symbolically what they are unwilling or unable to accomplish concretely.

With these introductory principles in mind, it is time to look more carefully and explicitly at the politics of law and order.

Campaigning on Crime

There is ample evidence that crime has been a political issue at the national level since Barry Goldwater got the ball rolling during his unsuccessful bid for the Presidency in 1964.

> Tonight there is violence in our streets, corruption in our highest offices, aimlessness among our youth, anxiety among our elderly…. The growing menace in our country tonight, to personal safety, to life, to limb and to property, in homes, in churches, in the playgrounds and places of business, particularly, in our great cities, is the mounting concern of every thoughtful citizen in the United States.[53]

Crime seems to have been an issue in most of the subsequent presidential elections including 1980 when the Reagan-Bush Committee pointed out that "Ronald Reagan demonstrated his commitment to neighborhood safety and fair and effective criminal justice during his eight years as Governor of California. During this period, he signed more than forty anti-crime bills, and took other steps to strengthen the criminal justice system."[54] {78}

These law-and-order campaigns tended to follow a path easily predictable on the basis of the myth of crime and punishment. First, anxieties are aroused by manichean portrayals of crime. Consider, for example, President Eisenhower's contribution to the Goldwater nominating convention of 1964.

> [L]et us not be guilty of maudlin sympathy for the criminal who, roaming the streets with switchblade knife and illegal firearms seeking a helpless prey, suddenly becomes upon apprehension a poor, underprivileged person who counts upon the compassion of our society and the laxness or weakness of too many courts to forgive his offense.[55]

We are also instructed about the contribution of permissive judges to this problem. Candidate Richard Nixon's 1968 campaign speeches are typical:

> Our judges have gone too far in weakening the peace forces as against the criminal forces. Our opinion-makers have gone too far in promoting the doctrine that when a law is broken, society —not the criminal—is to blame.
>
> Our judges and courts must take a large measure of responsibility for the current lawlessness.[56]

If the courts are the villains of the criminal process, the police are the would-be heroes. "If I am elected," claimed candidate George Wallace in 1968, "that in itself is going to give some moral support to the police and firemen and other law-enforcement officials in the country."[57] Thus the burden of fear is magically lifted by assurance that punitive measures, like stiffer sentences or more aggressive policing, will protect us from predatory strangers.

At the local level, it is more difficult to generalize. The best available source of information is a comparative study of five cities during the thirty years between 1948 and 1978.[58] In two of those cities, Philadelphia and Minneapolis, police officers rode the law-and-order issue into the mayor's office.[59] In Newark, Hugh Addonizio, who served as mayor from 1962 to 1970, identified himself with the law-and-order position, although less centrally, it appears, than was the case with Frank Rizzo in Philadelphia or Charles Stenvig in Minneapolis.[60] In San Jose, it was not until the 1978 mayoral election that crime became a truly central campaign issue, and even then the law-and-order candidate was badly defeated.[61] Finally, we come to Phoenix, where crime apparently has not become a central campaign issue, but only because incumbents have managed to stay ahead of potential competitors by taking a strong law-and-order stand.[62] Broadly speaking, then, in local as well as national politics, there has been a tendency for political leaders to call our attention to the dangers of crime and to promise us a crackdown.

From time to time and place to place, the scenario has varied a good deal. There are instances when all candidates seem to get carried away with punitive policies. In the 1968 presidential campaign, for example, even {79} Hubert Humphrey, despite a liberal constituency and a more balanced tone, clearly joined in celebrating the police as the key to crime control. "You get law and order by getting enough police on the job who are capable, trained, qualified, well-paid, and backed by their superiors."[63] At other times, liberals have risen in defense of restraint and the rule of law, as in the 1965 New York mayoralty election when John Lindsay supported a civilian review board for purposes of imposing "traditional notions of due process" on police practices.[64] Increasingly in recent years the punitive message has been softened by appeals to make criminal process more efficient and equitable, although, as in Reagan's 1980 program, calls for "strong penalties" and procedures to ensure judicial compliance have also been prominent.[65] Another pattern observed at the local level has been the politicization of street crime in combination with civil disorder.[66] And of course there have been frequent occasions when crime was not an issue at all or was a marginal issue.

Crime and Politics

How can these variations be explained? The available data are sketchy, so any explanation must be considered speculative. Nevertheless, there are good reasons for rejecting both the mainstream view of politicization as democracy at work and the Marxist notion of overt manipulation. The crime issue is neither imposed on us by a coalition of media executives and political elites nor does it emerge democratically from an increasingly victimized grass-roots constituency. Instead, what is operative is a complex and unpredictable process in which politicians seeking to obtain or retain office capitalize on public anxieties, which are only tenuously linked to the actual incidence of crime. In sum, the politics of law and order is best understood in terms of political conflict, which is shaped, to a significant degree, by the powerful symbols of American culture that determine how we understand the world around us.

The first problem with the mainstream explanation is that most of us experience crime abstractly and indirectly. We are therefore subjected to confusing and misleading messages by the agents of our vicarious victimization. Do we really know whether the crime rate is increasing or decreasing—much less anything about the rate of change? Consider the following leads to stories about crime appearing in the *New York Times*, clearly one of the more sober and responsible newspapers.

February 9, 1982: "Homicides Involving Robbery in New York Rising, Study Shows."

February 27, 1982: "New York City Felonies Rose Far Slower Last Year Than in '80." {80}

March 25, 1982: "30 of 73 New York Precincts Show Decreases in Felonies."

The issue is not whether these headlines or the stories can be reconciled with one another but whether the casual reader will add up all this information and come to a conclusion or will simply shape that ambiguous information to fit preconceived ideas. Even when the picture is clearer, our response may well be clouded by "extraneous" considerations. It is no doubt true, for example, that the sharp increases in street crime beginning in the middle 1960s contributed to our anxieties and, consequently, to the emergence of crime as a political issue. It is just as certain to me that fear of street crime was inextricably linked to anxieties about the expropriation of the streets by a variety of dissident and disaffected Americans, thus lending impetus to the process of politicization.

The agents of vicarious victimization also give us an exaggerated sense of jeopardy. This is true of neighbors and the news media as well as politicians.[67] It is hardly surprising, then, that the average American is more frightened by crime in general than by the impact of crime on his or her own life.[*] Respondents in several studies—even respondents from high-crime areas—perceived other neighborhoods as more dangerous than their own.[68] There is a parallel inclination to think of the increase in crime nationally as more severe than local increases and to believe that the national increase involves more serious kinds of crime.

> There was a strong tendency to believe that major personal crimes (murder, rape, robbery, assault) were the main factors in the perceived increase in national crime. On the neighborhood level, however, respondents thought that major property crimes (burglary, larceny, and other forms of theft) were equally responsible for an increase in crime.[69]

These same respondents "overwhelmingly agreed that crime affects the behavior of people in general, but were less likely to see crime as an influence on the behavior of people in their own neighborhoods."[70]

Nor is there any reason to expect politicians to spread oil on these troubled waters. Quite the contrary. Looking, for example, at the flurry of pronouncements about crime as the 1982 election campaigns heated up, it would be hard to believe that the overall rate of violent crime had leveled off in 1973. "Crime is the hidden social issue of the 80s—not abortion or busing," according to Democratic Representative Charles E. Schumer of Brooklyn. "Ten years ago crime was a Brooklyn issue. Five years ago it was a metropolitan New York issue. Now it's a national issue."[71] If this is true, and Representative Schumer was just one of a host of political figures offering this view in the spring of 1982, it is perhaps because politicians {81} contribute to our exaggerated sense of jeopardy. In September of 1981, President Reagan opened his speech to the International Association of Chiefs of Police by declaring: "Crime is an American epidemic—it takes the lives of 25,000 Americans, it touches nearly one-third of American households, and it results in at least $8.8 billion per year in financial losses."[72] In August 1982, Attorney General William French Smith told the House of Delegates of the American Bar Association that violent crime had increased by 85 percent over the last decade and asked them to support Reagan administration proposals "that would restore the balance between the forces of law and the forces of lawlessness."[73]

At first glance, all of this might seem to lead inevitably to the conclusion that the Marxists have the right idea. Surely the media and the politicians seem to be working hand in glove to build our fears and trigger our punitive

---

[*] I exclude from this generalization the small fraction of the public personally victimized by violent crime who may be expected to have a heightened level of fear.

impulses. The result is, moreover, clearly manipulative. Crime ends up being portrayed as a cause rather than an effect of social disorganizations; our deep-seated social, economic, and political problems are reduced to the dimensions of cops and robbers.

Manipulative opportunities are, however, much more contingent than the Marxist analysis presented by Quinney would have us believe. The forces generating the politics of law and order are so unstable and uncoordinated that it seems misguided to think of them as a political coalition, much less a conspiracy among ruling elites. Instead, the politics of law and order rests on the attraction of a common target of opportunity—the punitive predispositions of the American public—to a variety of largely independent actors: news and entertainment media, politicians, and the crime-control establishment. Each seeks to market a similar but not identical message to an inconstant public. The generative forces behind the politics of law and order are thus unstable because the purposes of the elites converge and diverge for reasons only tangentially related to crime as such. This underlying instability is increased because law-and-order symbols seem to resonate with varying degrees of intensity, depending on time and circumstance.

Fishman's analysis of the development of a "crime wave" in New York clearly indicates that the connections between the media and public officials are more serendipitous than conspiratorial. News people searching for stories on a slow shift ran across some reports of crime with elderly victims. Crime against the elderly became a theme for linking these discrete events. This theme was picked up by others in the media, thus amplifying the coverage and laying the foundation for a crime wave: "[E]very crime incident that can be seen as an instance of the theme, will be seen and reported as such."[74] The journalists could not provide the "continuous supply of crime incidents" necessary to transform the theme into a wave, but law-enforcement agencies are willing and able to play that role.[75] {82}

> [W]hen the police perceive that the media are interested in a certain type of crime (for example, crimes against the elderly), they include instances of it in the police wire whenever they can. Thus, the police bolster emerging crime waves as long as those waves pertain to crimes the police routinely detect (that is, street crime).
>
> The police-supplied incidents that make up the media's crime wave pool all support prevailing notions of "serious crime." The crime wave pool leads the media to reproduce a common image that "real crime" is crime on the streets, crime occurring between strangers, crime which brutalizes the weak and defenseless, and crime perpetrated by vicious youths.[76]

Finally, the mayor was only too happy "to assume from the outset that the crime wave represented something real" and to come forward with a program for defending the innocent elderly of New York City.[77] A crime wave is, in short, constructed on the convergence of a variety of distinct objectives.

Perhaps the most uncertain participants in the process of politicization are the media. Media executives are concerned with market shares and ratings, and therefore with entertainment value. Not surprisingly, then, television drama seems to have a cyclical quality to it—corresponding, presumably, to changing public tastes. Medical dramas, crime shows, sporting events, and situation comedies follow one another in a desperate effort to set, or keep up with, fashions. News is also show business. Of course, a good crime story will draw "front page" treatment, but as Fishman's study indicates, the incurporation of that story into a theme that is suitable for subsequent development into a wave is largely fortuitous—an editor in need, stumbling across some reports that seem to hang together. They are, moreover, hung together for purposes of "presentational order"—in other words, according to professional criteria.[78] Thus the media do not sell crime and punishment for its political message but for its payoff in advertising revenue.

It is difficult to estimate how much instability this lends to the generative forces of law and order. No doubt, there is some constancy. The message of crime and punishment is regularly invoked in a variety of adventure programs, not just in crime series. Yet, in times of relative tranquility, those messages may not be particularly seductive. And insofar as the focus is shifted from crime shows per se, the media contribution to fomenting a war against crime is likely to be reduced.

Political leaders operate in a comparably cyclical setting. The law-and-order issue is likely to vary in its appeal, and most political leaders will continue to pursue the issue only as long as it is electorally salable. The initial precondition for the politics of law and order is a public perception that crime threatens the social order, although other threats to society and other personal insecurities are also germane. In any case, our receptivity to the symbols of law and order are only partially under the control of {83} political leaders. Moreover, after the law-and-order pitch has been successfully used for a while, the marginal utility of each successive call for law and order is likely to be reduced. In part, this may simply be a question of fashion: the political public, like the entertainment public, becomes harder and harder to rouse if the message is not varied. In addition, if the crime rate actually drops after the election of law-and-order candidates, it will become increasingly difficult to capitalize on the issue because it will have lost some of its sense of urgency. If, as is more likely, there is no significant decrease in crime, the message of law and order is, in some measure, discredited. Finally, with respect to the period we have considered, law and order no doubt lost some of its appeal as the images of its most ardent advocates were tarnished by Watergate.

The only really constant force in the battle on behalf of law and order is the crime-control establishment. Law-enforcement officials have a long-term interest in the myth of crime and punishment. The symbols of law and order reinforce the importance of their skills and enhance their status and rewards. Unlike political leaders and media executives, they have nowhere else to turn, and so they can be expected to continue to plug away at a variety of threats to law and order in a continuing effort to convince the public that with the necessary resources they can successfully thwart these threats. They do have some capability for influencing our sense of threat because they compile the statistics and are the principal source of information for the media. When one combines the incentive of law-enforcement officials to promote the politics of law and order with their opportunities to do so and adds the public's latent receptivity, it is clear that we should not underestimate the law-and-order capabilities of the crime-control establishment. But, ultimately, the politics of law and order depends on a broader configuration of generative forces.

Politics and Policy

The connection between politics and policy is much less direct than either the mainstream or the Marxist view suggests. Quinney claims that political leaders are willing and able to seize upon the pretext provided by the politicization of crime to initiate repressive policies. He draws this conclusion from an analysis of the Law Enforcement Assistance Administration, which, according to his way of thinking, served as the hub of a wheel of repression— providing a clearinghouse for ideas, a conduit for money, and a coordinating agency for programs.

> The major part of LEAA's budget goes to states and localities to improve criminal justice activities and develop new techniques of control. Funds are also provided for training law-enforcement agents and for research to improve criminal justice. The result is a coordinated system of legal control for the {84} advanced capitalist society. All levels of the state and the agencies of the law are linked in a nationwide system of criminal justice.[79]

Wilson is less forthcoming on policy, but he seems to believe that responsible political leaders do, in the long run, take advantage of politicization to implement sensible programs for controlling crime. His own preferences run to proactive policing, deterrent-oriented sentencing, and methadone programs for dealing with heroin-related crimes.[80]

Neither of these two positions takes sufficient account of the discontinuity between political campaigning and policy making. Campaigning is largely a symbolic exercise in which the politicians do their best to conceal what is really at stake. Policy making, in contrast, pitches politicians headlong into the arena of concrete politics where they must interact with public officials who are keenly aware of the stakes of the game. These officials understand, as do most politicians, that crime is not amenable to simple solutions. Moreover, since all reforms alter the status quo and threaten vested interests, resistance to law-and-order policies can be taken for granted. It therefore seems equally naive to assume that policy consequences of the politics of law and order will be either as repressive as Quinney argues or as purposefully directed toward crime control as Wilson implies.

The rise and demise of the LEAA is instructive. The best available study leads to conclusions altogether different from those developed by Quinney and at the same time casts substantial doubt on Wilson's view.[81] The LEAA was established under the Crime Control and Safe Streets Act of 1968, which remains to this day the principal piece of federal legislation traceable to the politics of law and order. A superficial case can be made for either Wilson's or Quinney's position, but neither case stands up to careful scrutiny.

The repressive bias of congressional legislation generally, and the expenditure of funds by LEAA in particular, is abundantly clear. The Antiriot Act of 1968 was obviously aimed at political dissidents rather than street criminals and figured in some of the celebrated "political trials" of the early 1970s.[82] The Crime Control and Safe Streets Act extended the use of wiretapping and sought to invalidate the Supreme Court's *Miranda* decision, which broadened the rights of defendants in state criminal proceedings.[83] As to the LEAA itself, a major portion of the funds it expended, particularly in the early days, went to the police and was used, among other things, for a variety of threatening hardware that increased police firepower and surveillance capabilities.

Wilson's position is born out principally by LEAA support of research and experimentation in law enforcement. LEAA took the lead in funding extensive studies of victimization that provided a much more reliable picture of patterns of crime and the public's reaction to them. There were also demonstration grants to fund a variety of experiments involving the {85} diversion of juveniles from the criminal justice system, neighborhood justice to resolve minor criminal disputes by informal mediation, and reforms aimed at more effective policing.[84] While it is true that only a small portion of LEAA funds were so expended, LEAA was continually associated with this kind of work.

Nonetheless, the essential reality of LEAA before its rather protracted demise was neither repression nor experimentation, according to Malcolm Feeley and Austin Sarat, because the agency was never sufficiently purposeful to carry out either mission.

> [C]ritics argued that the bulk of the money made available to the states through the Law Enforcement Assistance Administration was spent for police equipment, much of which was outlandishly expensive to say nothing of lethal. With benefit of hindsight, however, these "hardware" purchases appear more ridiculous than repressive (e.g., antiriot tanks for small towns), and, at any rate, such extravagant equipment purchasing did not last long.[85]

The shortcomings of LEAA support to develop effective programs of crime control were rooted not so much in the paucity of funds as in the erratic course of policy.

> With each new administrator came new priorities for dis-
> cretionary funds, priorities which did not cumulate. Although
> discretionary funds have been used to support some valuable
> programs, no truly national approach to crime has been de-
> veloped.[86]

The politics of law and order was sufficiently powerful to generate campaign promises and follow-up legislation, but relatively little in the way of consistent public policy.

Feeley and Sarat explain the shortcomings of the LEAA in terms consistent with the distinction between concrete and symbolic politics. There were, in particular, two points along the way when concrete interests triumphed over symbolic promises. Those who wrote the act were influenced by a variety of interest groups that blocked a clear legislative mandate. "The result was a failure to specify substantive objectives, specific goals, and a strategy for achieving them. The goals of the Safe Streets Act are almost purely procedural."[87] Implementation was equally problematic as state planning agencies without well-defined legislative objectives attempted to influence well-entrenched law-enforcement officials at the local level.

> As organs of state government, [state planning agencies] must
> function within an established criminal justice system that is
> overwhelmingly local in structure, funding, and orientation. As
> dispensers of funds, they control less than 5 percent of the total
> criminal justice budget in any state and thus have no real clout
> especially with respect to larger agencies or in large cities, where
> the problems of crime are most apparent.[88] {86}

The policy consequences of the political forces that led to the creation of the LEAA were, therefore, a good deal less imposing than Wilson hoped or Quinney feared.

Something like this same pattern can be expected when we look more generally in subsequent chapters at the influence of the politics of law and order on operative policy in the principal agencies of urban law enforcement, the police, and the criminal courts. External pressures are likely to be substantially neutralized by vested interests and established patterns of the police and the court bureaucracies. This is not to say there will be no repression or no purposeful policy change. Nevertheless, it would be unrealistic to expect the daily workings of criminal process to be substantially transformed by the politics of law and order. Instead, what we shall discover as the most likely consequences of the politicization of crime are modest changes in a punitive direction—changes, moreover, that seem to be of dubious value, at best, in the nation's effort to control crime.

The politics of law and order grew, in part, out of the increase in street crime that developed in the mid-1960s, but that is only part of the story. The increase in crime must be seen against the many crises of American society during that period. The latter half of the 1960s and the early 1970s were years of rapid and unsettling social change. Traditional norms and values were under pressure in a great many areas of American life, and "law and order" became a symbol of resistance to unwelcome changes of all sorts—in race relations, education, and family life as well as in crime.

Crime tended to become the focal point of much of this discontent because it is such a simple and straightforward issue. There is, in the first place, very little ambiguity about the good guys and the bad guys. Virtually everyone can readily agree that an increase in the crime rate is deplorable. Judgments about changes in race relations, education, and the family are much more elusive and contentious. It is also relatively easy to agree on the right way to solve the crime problem. The myth of crime and punishment informs us that we can control crime by cracking down on criminals firmly and expeditiously. The culture provides no comparable magic wand to wave over the other unsettling features of American life.

But the attractions of punitive solutions go beyond the consensus they engender and their traditional place in American culture. Punishment, as Durkheim has pointed out, provides unequivocal reassurance that the society's norms and values are still intact—fully supported by the powers that be. Punishment also, Lasswell has suggested, has a cathartic effect—assuring us that complicated problems are amenable to simple solutions. At times of stress, we are therefore tempted to seek refuge in the simple world of crime and punishment. Small wonder, then, that crime has {87} become something of a national pastime. It reaffirms our sense of community, and its simple truths are a refreshing change from the frustrating uncertainties of contemporary society.

The upshot is that the generative forces of the politics of law and order are complex and contingent. While the punitive predispositions that fuel the politics of law and order are cultural constants, they surface politically in unpredictable combination with unsettling kinds of social change. Crime per se—or at least a public perception of increasing criminal jeopardy—may be a necessary, but it is hardly a sufficient, condition of the politics of law and order. The politics of law and order thrive only together with a more extended sense of social malaise, which drives the public toward the consolations provided by the myth of crime and punishment. At such times, our problem is not too much crime but, culturally speaking, too little—a need the media are only too happy to meet. Given this climate of opinion, crime becomes a very attractive campaign issue.

An awareness of the complexity and the contingent character of the politics of law and order is the first step toward appreciating the distance that separates campaign promises from changes in operative policy. In the chapters ahead, the emphasis shifts from crime as an issue for enlisting electoral support to policy making in criminal process. More specifically, the objective is to assess the impact of the politics of law and order on operative policy in police departments and criminal courts.

The net effect of the politics of law and order will be neither the repression that Marxists fear nor the pragmatic reforms that the mainstream counts on. Instead, we shall see little overall change. Moreover, while such change as does take place will tend to have a punitive bias, this cracking down seems unlikely to make either the police or the criminal courts more effective agents of crime control. There is, in particular, no reason to believe that the punitive drift in criminal process occasioned by the politics of law and order will be effective against the predatory strangers who are the public's primary concern.

The policy limitations of the politics of law and order are, in part, a product of the symbolic character of politicization. Politicians ordinarily gain electoral success by telling the public what it wants to hear. When fear of street crime runs high, politicians have every reason to believe that the public is looking for promises to crack down on criminals firmly and expeditiously. Certainly the politician who, in a climate of fear, champions due process, redemption, or rehabilitation faces an uphill struggle. Thus politicians are more or less forced to promise simple punitive solutions to complicated and intractable problems. Whether they realize it or not during the campaign, political candidates end up making promises that they cannot possibly keep.

The other obstacle to effective reform is the powerfully entrenched values and interests of lawyers and police officers who control the agencies {88} of criminal process. These officials have a stake in the status quo and are resistant to change. This is not to suggest a cynical disregard for public safety and an exclusively self-interested approach to policy choices. There are legitimate differences of opinion about how best to control crime, and, generally speaking, the officials of criminal process are inclined to believe that they are doing the best they can under the circumstances. Certainly they believe that they have a better understanding of how to cope with crime than the politicians, who are poorly informed and who, they feel, yield too readily to political pressures. Moreover, there is probably some recognition by all concerned that whatever is done will have only a marginal impact on crime. With the crime-control stakes relatively low and with no way to demonstrate conclusively that one approach is better than the other, it is understandable that even conscientious public officials tend to be influenced by their own responsibilities.

The essential objective of the following inquiry into criminal process is, then, to analyze the policy consequences of the politics of law and order. The guiding premise of this inquiry is that the only way to accurately assess the extent and direction of policy change is to understand the patterns of values and interests of the essential actors in police departments and criminal courts. We must understand the world as they understand it if we are to gauge successfully their response to the policy initiatives associated with the politics of law and order. Similarly, we must understand the balance of power within the agencies of criminal process in order to figure out just how much resistance can be mounted against policy reform. In the final analysis, operative policy does not reflect some objective truth or general consensus about the nature and causes of crime but the several bureaucratic realities of the agencies of criminal process. It is to those realities that we now turn.

NOTES

1. Vera Institute of Justice, *Felony Arrests: Their Prosecution and Disposition in New York City's Courts*, rev. ed. (New York, Longman, 1981), 19. It is, of course, true that any study that focuses on arrests tends to overstate the proportion of prior relationship crimes since these crimes are the most easily solved because identification of the assailant is relatively easy.

2. Michael J. Hindelang, Michael R. Gottfredson, and Timothy J. Flanagan, eds., *Sourcebook of Criminal Justice Statistics—1980* (Washington, D.C.: Bureau of Justice Statistics, 1981), 290.

3. Charles E. Silberman, *Criminal Violence, Criminal Justice.* (New York: Random House, 1978), 59.

4. Ibid., 183–97.

5. Richard Maxwell Brown, "The American Vigilante Tradition," in *Violence in America: Historical and Comparative Perspectives*, rev. ed., ed. Hugh Davis {89} Graham and Ted Robert Gurr (Beverly Hills: Sage, 1979), 173–74.

6. Ibid., 154.

7. Fred DuBow, Edward McCabe, and Gail Kaplan, *Reactions to Crime: A Review of the Literature* (Washington, D.C.: National Institute of Law Enforcement and Criminal Justice 1979).

8. For a systematic description of this research, see George Gerbner and Larry Gross, "Living with Television: The Violence Profile," *Journal of Communications* 26 (Spring 1976): 173–97.

9. George Gerbner, Larry Gross, Michael Morgan, and Nancy Signorielli, "The 'Mainstreaming' of America: Violence Profile No. 11," *Journal of Communications* 30 (Summer 1980): 13.

10. Violence, for purposes of the study, is defined "as the overt expression of physical force (with or without a weapon, against self or others) compelling action against one's will on pain of being hurt and/or killed or threatened to be so victimized as part of the plot.... ['A]ccidental and 'natural' violence (always purposeful dramatic actions that do victimize certain characters) are, of course, included." Ibid., 11–12.

11. Gerbner and Gross, "Living with Television," 190.

12. Ibid., 184.

13. Ibid., Table 5, p. 199.

14. Heavy viewers were those who watched television for an average of four or more hours per day, while those averaging two hours per day or less were classified as light viewers. Ibid., 191–92.

15. Ibid., 192–93.

16. Gerbner et al., "The 'Mainstreaming' of America," 25. Among the principal critics to whom this response is addressed are Anthony N. Doob and Glenn E. Macdonald, "Television Viewing and Fear of Victimization: Is the Relationship Causal?" *Journal of Personality and Social Psychology* 37 (February 1979): 170–79. For further research indicating that television, in this case television news, shapes the viewers concerns and fears, see Shanto Iyengar, Mark D. Peters, and Donald R. Kinder, "Experimental Demonstrations of the 'Not-So-Minimal' Consequences of Television News Programs," *American Political Science Review* 76 (December 1982): 848–58; and Walter B. Jaehnig, David H. Weaver, and Frederick Fico, "Measuring Media Influence: Reporting Crime and Fearing Crime in Three Communities," *Journal of Communication* 31 (Winter 1981): 88–96.

17. Stuart A. Scheingold, *The Politics of Rights: Lawyers, Public Policy, and Political Change* (New Haven: Yale University Press, 1974), 13–22.

18. Herbert L. Packer, *The Limits of the Criminal Sanction* (Stanford, Calif.: Stanford University Press, 1968), 153.

19. Ibid., 163.

20. Wesley G. Skogan and Michael G. Maxfield, *Coping with Crime: Individuals and Neighborhood Reactions* (Beverly Hills, Calif.: Sage, 1981), 155.

21. Ibid., 131. The same process has been discovered in a study of British newspapers by Roshier. See ibid.

22. New York: McGraw-Hill, 1935.

23. New York: Bantam, 1971.

24. Lasswell, *World Politics and Personal Insecurity*, 231. {90}

25. Ibid., 75; italics added.

26. Friedman, *The Dick*, 256.

27. Ibid., 255.

28. Ibid., 256.

29. Ibid., 35–36.

30. Ibid., 141–42.

31. *World Politics and Personal Insecurity*, 39.

32. New York: Free Press, 1964.

33. Ibid., 108.

34. Ibid.

35. Ibid.

36. Ibid., 84.

37. Ibid., 108; italics added.

38. Ibid.

39. Ibid.

40. Sol Stein, *The Magician* (New York: Dell, 1973). Among the films I have in mind are *Walking Tall* and *First Blood*.

41. Ibid., 244–45.

42. Ibid., 252; italics added.

43. Durkheim, *The Division of Labor in Society*, 108–9.

44. Stein, *The Magician*, 55.

45. Ibid., 296.

46. Ibid., 300–301.

47. Marlene A. Young Rifai, "The Response of the Older Adult to Criminal Victimization," *Police Chief*, February 1977, 48–50, as reported in DuBow et al., *Reactions to Crime*, 25.

48. DuBow et al., *Reactions to Crime*, 8.

49. Murray Edelman, *The Symbolic Uses of Politics* (Champagne-Urbana: University of Illinois Press, 1967), 5.

50. W. Lance Bennett, *Public Opinion in American Politics* (New York: Harcourt Brace Jovanovich, 1980), 397.

51. Ibid.

52. Ibid.

53. Quoted in Malcolm M. Feeley and Austin D. Sarat, *The Policy Dilemma: Federal Crime Policy and the Law Enforcement Assistance Administration, 1968–1978* (Minneapolis: University of Minnesota Press, 1980), 35.

54. Reagan Bush Committee, "Reagan & Bush" (Arlington, Va., undated, unpublished campaign material), 69.

55. Quoted in Adelaide H. Villmoare, "Law and Order and the American State: Ideological Bases of Legitimacy" (unpub. n.d.).

56. *U.S. News and World Report*, 15 July 1968.

57. *Ibid.*, 21 October 1968.

58. Anne Heinz, Herbert Jacob, and Robert Lineberry, eds., *Crime in City Politics* (New York: Longman, 1983).

59. Peter C. Buffum and Rita Sagi, "Philadelphia: Politics of Reform and Retreat," and Marlys McPherson, "Minneapolis: Crime in a Politically Fragmented Arena," both in Heinz et al., *Crime in City Politics*.

60. Dorothy H. Guyot, "Newark: Crime and Politics in a Declining City," in {91} Heinz et al., *Crime in City Politics*.

61. Kenneth A. Betsalel, "San Jose: Crime and the Politics of Growth," in Heinz et al., *Crime in City Politics*.

62. John S. Hall and David L. Altheide, "Phoenix: Crime and Politics in a New Federal City," in Heinz et al., *Crime in City Politics*.

63. *U.S. News and World Report*, 21 October 1968.

64. Villmoare, "Law and Order."

65. "Reagan & Bush," 70.

66. See McPherson, "Minneapolis," 175; and Guyot, "Newark," 70–71.

67. Skogan and Maxfield, *Coping with Crime*, 127–62.

68. DuBow et al., *Reactions to Crime*, 4.

69. James Garofalo, *Public Opinion About Crime: The Attitudes of Victims and Non-Victims in Selected Cities* (Washington, D.C.: National Criminal Justice Information and Statistics Service, 1977), 15.

70. Ibid., 32.

71. Steven V. Roberts, "Emerging Issues: Crime, Energy, and Polish Debts," *New York Times*, 16 March 1982.

72. *New York Times*, 29 September 1981.

73. *Seattle Times*, 11 August 1982.

74. Mark Fishman, "Crime Waves as Ideology," *Social Problems* 29 (June 1978): 537.

75. Ibid., 538.

76. Ibid., 540.

77. Ibid., 540–41.

78. Ibid., 534–35.

79. Richard Quinney, *Class, State, and Crime*, 2nd. ed. (New York: Longman, 1980), 129.

80. James Q. Wilson, *Thinking About Crime* (New York: Vintage, 1977), Chaps. 5, 7, and 8.

81. Feeley and Sarat, *The Policy Dilemma*.

82. John T. Eliff, *Crime, Dissent, and the Attorney General: The Justice Department in the 1960's* (Beverly Hills, Calif.: Sage, 1971), 108–11 and 201–11.

83. Richard Harris, *The Fear of Crime* (New York: Praeger, 1968), 58–63.

84. See, for example, *Exemplary Projects* (Washington, D.C.: National Institute of Law Enforcement and Criminal Justice, 1978). 31 pp.

85. Feeley and Sarat, *The Policy Dilemma*, 137.

86. Ibid., 53.

87. Ibid., 135.

88. Ibid., 146.

90

Part III

Criminal Process

{Page 95}

4

Traditional Policing

The law-and-order political climate of the last couple of decades has generated a great deal of interest in police policies for coping with street crime. Political leaders, police officials, and social scientists have all turned their attention to schemes that promise to make the police more effective agents of crime control. It is, however, unlikely that the politics of law and order have actually led to much reform of traditional police practices. On the contrary, the climate of concern that has resulted in so much attention to policy innovation has also generated political pressures that reinforce traditional ways of doing things. That irony is the underlying theme of Chapters 4 and 5.

It must be acknowledged at the outset that there are problematic features to the case that can be made for reform. The simple truth is that despite a good deal of research and experimentation, we do not really know how to control crime, and reformers are sharply divided on how best to proceed. In the final analysis, then, the case for reform is essentially negative in that it rests on the manifest inadequacies of traditional ways of doing things. In Chapter 5, we look directly at the struggle for reform and at the perverse impact of the politics of law and order on that struggle. The focus of the present chapter is on the inertial forces that resist changes in the status quo.

There are essentially three reasons why the police are unwilling, perhaps even unable, to recognize the problems with established police practices. Resistance to reform is, in the first place, a kind of reflex action against outside interference.

> [T]he police view most issues—whether they arise from a city manager's efforts to "reform" a department, an alderman's effort to name a new deputy chief, or {96} a Negro organization's efforts to establish a civilian review board—as a struggle for control of the department by "outside" forces.[1]

It is also true that any reform will upset the delicate institutional equilibrium that balances the interests of managers of police organizations with those of rank-and-file police officers. Finally, the police have their own way of thinking about crime and criminals, their own subculture, which accounts for the practices they have developed and makes them resistant to change. While the reflexive reaction against outside interference speaks for itself, the organizational and subcultural barriers to reform provide the main focus of this chapter and therefore warrant a few additional introductory comments.

Organizational barriers to reform do not really have a great deal to do with crime control, although they may be presented as if they do. Rank-and-file officers are concerned with salary, working conditions, and status, as well as with catching criminals. Managers have as big a stake in the effective administration of the police organization as in curbing crime. These organizational tensions are ordinarily resolved by way of compromises that reflect the long-term balance of power within each police department. Substantial resistance to policy changes that would undermine these hard-won compromises is only to be expected. In any case, reform signals are certain to be filtered through particularized calculations of costs and benefits that have very little to do with crime control as such.

A more focused and in a sense more principled source of resistance to reform is the police subculture. To understand this subculture is to understand the common ground that unites managers and rank-and-file officers against important currents of reform. It is also to understand the punitive drift of police policy preferences, as well as the tenacity with which the police cling to these preferences. Although managers may, because of their organizational and political responsibilities, sometimes take a more moderate stance, beneath the surface there is a basic acceptance of rank-and-file values. Accordingly, this agreement on a punitive approach to policing is ingrained in subcultural values and poses a substantial obstacle to reform, as becomes clear in the next section. In Chapter 5 we consider the drawbacks of punitive policing, as well as the way in which the politics of law and order tends to reinforce these objectionable practices.

SUBCULTURAL VALUES

To posit a police subculture is not to suggest that all police officers are alike or that they respond in lockstep to the problems of policing. Police officers, like the rest of us, come in a wide variety of shapes, sizes, abilities, and sensibilities. They can be good or bad, cagey or naive, brave or cowardly, {97} harsh or sympathetic. William K. Muir captures this variety and then boils it down into four modes of police response to problematic situations ranging from evasion to confrontation.[2] Similarly, James Q. Wilson has shown that police departments tend to adopt distinctive styles of policing that vary according to the political and social setting.[3]

There do, however, seem to be certain modal tendencies, at least in the medium to large urban areas where most research has been conducted. According to the substantial body of literature on police values, the police have developed their own distinctly punitive view of the world. In this section, I begin by making a case for the existence of a police subculture and then go on to look at the content of that subculture.

Before analyzing the police subculture, I want to look briefly at two preliminary questions. First, is it inevitable that the police develop a punitive subculture? Apparently not. For example, David Bayley has discovered a Japanese police subculture with a community service orientation.[4] Even in the United States, Samuel Walker tells us, a social reform conception of police professionalism was briefly entertained within police circles.[5] Muir argues that effective training can instill more humane values.[6] Still, it is the punitive image of the crime fighter that predominates among American police officers. Accordingly, I am inclined to argue that the explanation for the punitive character of the American police subculture is to be explained by our cultural milieu.[*]

But if the police subculture is ultimately shaped by American cultural values, does it really make sense to talk about a separate subculture among American police officers? My answer is that the police subculture is not so much separate as an *in extremis* version of the underlying American culture. When Americans in general become preoccupied with crime, we also move in punitive directions, but our preoccupation with crime tends to be abstract and episodic, as was pointed out in the previous chapter. The real difference between police officers and the rest of us is that coping with crime is their full-time job. There is, in short, reason to believe that they and we share the same values but that the police are distanced from us primarily by the nature of their work. At least that is the argument I make in the pages that follow.

---

[*] I do not mean to argue that the punitive police subculture is a uniquely American phenomenon. Perhaps Japan is the exception that proves the rule. I am inclined to believe that the way in which punitive values have been incorporated into the overall police subculture is best understood in terms of the peculiarities of the American cultural milieu.

The Case for a Police Subculture

Three features of police work lend credence to the claim that the police look at the world in their own special way. The police tend, first, to be a homogeneous social group—they come from similar social backgrounds. {98} Second, the police share an especially stressful working situation. Finally, the police live and work within a largely closed social system that tends to cut them off from outsiders and their ideas. Taken together, these three characteristics suggest why the police might develop their own distinctive patterns of values and interests that generate internal cohesion as well as tensions with outsiders.

Police officers are disproportionately recruited from the working class or the lower middle class.[7] Minority groups are significantly underrepresented. In the past it was not unusual for a particular segment of society to dominate a given police department—with the New York or Boston Irish cop being prototypical. As late as the early 1960s in New York City, a class of police recruits was 80 percent Catholic and 95 percent white.[8] Nearer the end of the 1960s in Denver, the religious mix was more evenly distributed between Catholics and Protestants, but black and Hispanic minorities were underrepresented.[9] Even if allowances are made for a broadening of representational patterns in recent years and different areas of the country, it appears accurate to think of the police as reflective of middle America—that is, without many officers drawn from either the upper or the lowest strata of society. This general picture is further sharpened by the educational level of police officers, who tend to come to the force with little more than a high school education.[10] Given these roots in middle America, it is hardly surprising that the police are politically conservative and embrace traditional American values.[11]

If the backgrounds of police officers underscore what they share with the American mainstream, the setting within which the police work begins to reveal the distance separating them from the rest of us. The police work under circumstances that make their relationships with others extremely problematic. Typically, the police officer must work in a setting that is crisis-laden and indeterminate. Violence, danger, or both are close to the surface. Interactions in a world of latent violence may frequently take on the trappings of what Muir refers to as "extortionate transactions."

> In a world in which relationships are based on threat, everyone is
> either a victim or a victimizer, one party perceiving that the other
> is trying to get something for nothing.[12]

The police must somehow assert authority in such situations, but because things are frequently so fluid, officers are necessarily given a lot of leeway to deal with problems as they see fit. As Michael Lipsky puts it, the police "often work in situations too complicated to reduce to programmatic formats.

Policemen cannot carry around instructions on how to intervene with citizens, particularly in potentially hostile encounters."[13]

The police, in brief, have the responsibility for coping with sordid and dangerous situations from which the rest of us are ordinarily protected—largely because the police intervene on our behalf. Under these circumstances, {99} it stands to reason that the police develop quite different understandings of what life is *really* like. Consider the reaction of criminology professor George Kirkham to his temporary tour of duty as police patrol officer.

> I found that there was a world of difference between encountering individuals, as I had, in mental-health or correctional settings and facing them as the patrolman must: when they are violent, hysterical, desperate. When I put the uniform of a police officer on, I lost the luxury of sitting in an air-conditioned office with my pipe and books, calmly discussing with a rapist or armed robber the past problems which led him into trouble with the law....
>
> Now, as a police officer, I began to encounter the offender for the first time as a very real menace to my personal safety and the security of our society....
>
> Like crime itself, fear quickly ceased to be an impersonal and abstract thing. It became something which I regularly experienced. It was a tightness in my stomach.... I could taste it as a dryness in my mouth.... For the first time in my life, I came to know—as every policeman knows—the true meaning of fear.[14]

Such experiences distance the police from others in the society, whom the police regard as naive and idealistic.

Finally, the police tend to be isolated; they seldom escape from the closed social system of their own department. The lack of social interaction with outsiders is in part a function of the formal institutional structure within which the police work and in part a function of the personal distance that has just been discussed. Social interaction with outsiders is inhibited by irregular hours that put the police out of phase with those working nine-to-five jobs. There also seems to be a kind of mutual discomfort when the police mix socially with those outside the force. As Abraham Blumberg puts it:

> Since an officer's total life is colored by his occupation, police find that in most instances their circle of friends are other police and their families. This is not a consequence of lack of personal affability or congeniality, but instead is due to the perception of others who make the possibility of social interaction more difficult than it might otherwise be.[15]

Officers have told me that they are often embarrassed in social situations by special treatment that may range from an uncomfortable kind of deference to even more unwelcome entreaties to fix tickets or explain the sins of the police department.[16]

There is an understandable reluctance to confide in those who cannot possibly share the intense and jaundiced police view of people. As a veteran police officer puts it to a rookie cop in *The New Centurions*:

> You can't exaggerate the closeness of our dealings with people....
> We see them when nobody else sees them, when they're being
> born and dying and {100} fornicating and drunk.... We see
> people when they're taking anything of value from other people
> and when they're without shame or very much ashamed and we
> learn secrets that their husbands and wives don't even know, se-
> crets that they even try to keep from themselves, and what the
> hell, when you learn these things about people who aren't insti-
> tutionalized, people who're out here where you can see them
> function every day, well then, you really *know*. Of course, you get
> clannish and associate with others who know. It's only natural.[17]

Even the more prosaic problem of relaxing and blowing off steam among people who are expected to respect police authority causes difficulties.* Clear-ly, the upshot of this social isolation is to cut the police off from unfamiliar views. Even the modest stimulation that might come from other departments is denied by policies that discourage lateral transfers—meaning that officers must start at the bottom if they move from one department to another.

Thus, shared ideas are constantly reinforced by informal social networks. These informal networks are increasingly supplemented by police unions and similar organizations that transform police values into policy positions both to rally the rank and file and to proclaim and press police preferences on the public and administrators as well.

Police Values

There have been a great many studies of police attitudes, and these studies reveal substantial agreement among police about their own work, the public, criminal process, and how to deal with criminals and crime. Peter Manning has neatly summarized this research by extracting ten assumptions that police officers seem to share.

1. People can not be trusted; they are dangerous.

---

* Another Wambaugh novel, *The Choirboys* (New York: Dell, 1975), chronicles the extrav-agant diversions to which police can be driven by the stress of their work. Even allowing for some considerable hyperbole, it can easily be understood why the police would want to keep this conduct under wraps. But if Wambaugh is correct, a release of tension and an understanding peer group are necessary if the police are to maintain some kind of personal equilibrium.

2. Experience is better than abstract rules.

3. You must make people respect you.

4. Everyone hates a cop.

5. The legal system is untrustworthy; the policemen make the best decisions about guilt or innocence.

6. People who are not controlled will break laws.

7. Policemen must appear respectable and be efficient.

8. Police can most accurately identify crime and criminals. {101}

9. The major jobs of the policeman are to prevent crime and to enforce the laws.

10. Stronger punishment will deter criminals from repeating errors.[18]

One need not consider this list complete nor accept each assumption at face value to acknowledge that it captures the general spirit of the literature on police attitudes.[19] A careful look at these assumptions reveals two aspects of the police officer's view of the world and suggests a third that is of equal importance to an understanding of the relationship between the police subculture and their policy preferences.

Clearly, *the police are cynical*. People are "dangerous" and "can not be trusted." There are a couple of ways of interpreting this mistrust. One can conclude that the police believe that people are just no damn good—that any people "who are not controlled will break laws." This is surely part of the story, but there is another part as well: what Muir refers to as a "dualistic" view of human nature.[20] The police tend to divide the world into good guys and bad guys. If is, of course, the bad guys, the criminals, who preoccupy the police. It is not so much that *all* people are dangerous but that police officers must deal disproportionately with bad guys. It is, therefore, "in the nature of the policeman's situation that his conception of order [is]...shaped by a persistent *suspicion*."[21] At least until they have had a chance to sort out the good guys from the bad guys, it is prudent for police officers to assume danger.

The police rely heavily on their sorting capabilities. They believe that they "can most accurately identify" criminals. The police take pride in what Charles Silberman refers to as their "personal radars," which they rely on "to tell them who is and who is not worth stopping."

> [A] good officer closely studies the way people react to his presence—whether they show concern as he approaches, or change their behavior after they think he is out of sight. Body language can provide any number of clues.... "Gandy was standing a little too casually there in the parking lot," the hero of Joseph

> Wambaugh's novel, *The New Centurions*, explains to the rookies riding with him. "He was to cool and he gave me too much of an 'I got nothing to hide' look when I was driving by and eyeballing everybody that could possibly be the guy."[22]

Body language may reveal who has done something wrong—or is about to do so. Equally revealing are people's past records and the company they keep. In this way, criminality tends to become associated for the police officer with personal or social identity rather than specific criminal acts. Accordingly, the police officer tends to look with favor on preemptive actions like street stops and decoys.

A second theme manifest in Manning's ten assumptions is the *primacy of force* in coping with crime and criminals. Force emerges explicitly only in the belief that stronger punishment deters crime. But force is implicit in {102} the perception that people must be brought under control. At least, the primacy of force is implicit when taken together with the literature from which Manning's list is drawn.

There is a strictly business aspect to police attitudes toward force. The nightstick, the blackjack, and the gun are simply "tools of the trade," according to Jonathan Rubenstein, who goes on to explain: "The use of force is not a philosophical issue for a policeman. It is not a question of should or whether, but when and how much."[23] Muir tells how the most exemplary of his respondents learned to understand the importance of force.

> Throughout the interview Justice returned frequently to the efficacy of "fear." Of certain youths he would say, "You can't do much when they don't fear the law, ... when they are not afraid of anything." Coercion was essential to gaining control of individuals who were otherwise ungovernable.... To Justice, a policeman could not be "afraid" to fulfill his threats.[24]

In these strictly instrumental terms, police officers think of force as an integral part of their repertoire. This professionalization of force was graphically portrayed by a film made at a convention of the International Association of Chiefs of Police where displays of weaponry were as commonplace as the books promoted by publishers at academic meetings.

Even in this relatively benign form, it is important to realize how a preoccupation with force tends to distance police from the rest of us. Consider, for example, the purely instrumental character of the following instructions for the use of the nightstick as spelled out in a police training manual:

> If a word association test were given the average citizen, and the words "police club" were mentioned, the corresponding word that would likely come to their minds would be "head." It seems natural for the club to be used on the opponent's head, yet if there were a cardinal rule for the use of the police club, it would

be "not to hit a person on the top of the head with the police club.".…

1. It can kill them. If you want to kill the person, use the gun, that's what it is for.…

2. You seldom knock them out.… Many times the club will break.

3. If the club breaks, it is psychologically defeating…to put every-thing you have into a club, and then end with just a stump in your hand. (It makes things worse because…it just makes him more angry and violent.)

4. The victim usually bleeds profusely.…

5. It brings "police brutality" charges.…

6. The person can be left insane.…

7. The officer opens himself for attack.…[25]

Clearly, force is part of the daily life of the police officer in a way that is very difficult for an outsider to grasp. Realizing this, the police learn to use {103} their sticks in ways that will be least shocking to the public. In so doing, the police are once again insulating us from the harsh realities of the real world as they see it.

But there is another, more expressive aspect to force among police officers. I recall the story of a friend of mine who directed a county police force that had responsibility for policing the rural areas beyond the boundaries of a medium-size western city. He believed that he lost the confidence of the rank and file when, upon taking command, he directed his officers to turn in privately owned submachine guns that they had been taking on patrol. He replaced them with high-powered rifles that were clearly more effective weapons for dealing with the occasional wild animal they were called upon to kill. The chief's perception was that those submachine guns were an important symbol, which had nothing whatsoever to do with efficient police work. That story takes on added credence when considered together with a statement made some years ago by the national president of the Fraternal Order of Police in testimony before the Violence Commission:

> When I was a young officer I received instructions: if someone spits in your face wipe it off and turn your back; if someone curses with the vilest language pretend you don't hear. This is idiotic. The first person who spits in my face will lose his teeth; they have it coming to them.[26]

Once again we see that force has an expressive as well as an instrumental aspect. There is reason to believe that the police take pride in their ability to use force and that the use of force provides them with satisfaction quite independent of its instrumental effects.

There is no way of estimating the relative importance of this expressive aspect of force nor, indeed, should it be thought of as unconnected to purposeful policing. Muir, for example, identified a small group of officers among his respondents who look at force in expressive terms. He characterized this group as "enforcers" and described one of them in the following terms:

> Russo's moral philosophy, his stringent standard of success and failure, was so one-dimensional, so uncomplicated by contradictory purpose, that it made imperative the use of the policeman's fullest capacity. The law may have forbidden maximum force, but Russo perceived it to be an act of betrayal and cowardice to knuckle under to the law. His need for moral worth, his "pride," would eventually overcome his timidity; defiance of the laws and the regulations would be the hallmark of good police conduct.[27]

What Muir thinks of as a minority position, others see as deeply ingrained in the police subculture. Stark notes that police regularly use force in the face of citizen disrespect, when, as the Los Angeles police put it, citizens fail the "attitude test." Stark's conclusion is that the police simply believe that "the way to instill...respect in those who lack it is with a night-stick, {104} a blackjack, or a squirt of MACE in the face."[28] According to Albert Reiss:

> There are strong subcultural beliefs that the officer who ignores challenges from citizens loses the respect of the citizenry and makes it difficult for other officers to work in the precinct. No challenge to authority, therefore, can go unmet until there is acquiescence to it. The police code prohibits "backing down."... Therefore, threats to use coercive authority quickly yield to use of force.[29]

From this expressive perspective, coercion serves a deterrent function.

The expressive resort to violence is thus different from the instrumental use of violence, and this distinction has important policy implications. When the police indulge in expressive violence, their concern is less with the most satisfactory resolution of a particular incident than with teaching the public a lesson. Consider the reflections of a Berkeley, California, police officer on the coercive police response to a mid-1960s' street demonstration.

> If the parents of these cocksuckers had beat 'em when they were young, we wouldn't have to do it now.... There's a whole bunch of these assholes who've learned respect for law and order tonight. You better believe that, buddy.[30]

Insofar as the police feel entitled, or even obligated, to use violence to teach citizens a lesson, they are relying on force in circumstances when it is not, strictly speaking, necessary. It is this expressive dimension to the use of force that leads to "police brutality" and to tensions with the public, who are likely to be alienated by "gratuitous" violence. The violence is gratuitous because its focus is at least as much on moral regeneration as on law enforcement or peacekeeping.

There is a third theme, *the police officer as victim*, that emerges only marginally in Manning's ten assumptions but that is very prominent throughout the police literature. There are a number of aspects to this sense of victimization, but the essential message is that the police are physically and psychologically damaged by their jobs, and adding insult to injury, they are not respected by the public they serve. There may be reason to question whether the police are, relative to other occupational groups, in such serious jeopardy, but little doubt that the police feel victimized in a number of ways.[31]

At the core of the idea of police officers as victims is the familiar belief that police work is dangerous, that an officer may be killed or severely injured at any time. But it is not just officers who suffer physically who are perceived as victims. This perception has more to do with psychic than with physical injuries. The threat of injury hangs over the heads of all officers. "Every policeman lives with fear," as Rubenstein puts it.[32] Not only are police officers in constant jeopardy, according to this way of thinking, they are also stuck with some of society's dirtiest jobs. "I'm just sick.... I just {105} saw the asshole of the world get a blue enema," says one of Wambaugh's officers about his vice work.[33]

The essential victimization is understood to set in as the police develop defenses to protect themselves from the degradations and suffering they must constantly confront. As the police harden themselves against their daily experiences, they feel themselves losing their capacity for intimacy and, more generally, tend to cut themselves off from their friends and even from their families. One of the costs of a police career thus becomes a denial to police officers of the normal personal and social relationships open to others. Again, I turn to Joseph Wambaugh, whose stories are filled with lonely and embittered "blue knights" with unsuccessful marriages and without intimate friends. For these officers, their only real life is on the streets. Consider Kilvinsky in *The New Centurions* as seen through the eyes of one of his admiring trainees, who is already beginning to sense the isolation of police work.

> The intimate friends were few in number, and at this moment... he could think of no one he really wanted to be with. Except Kilvinsky. But Kilvinsky was so much older and he had no family now that his ex-wife was remarried. Every time Kilvinsky came to his house for dinner he played with Gus's children and then became morose.... Once [Kilvinsky] had taken little John...and tossed him in the air with his big sure hands until John and even Gus who watched were laughing so hard they could hardly breathe. And inevitably Kilvinsky became gloomy after the children went to bed. Once when Gus asked him about his family he

said they were now living in New Jersey and Gus realized he must not question him further.[34]

Capping off the course of victimization is the feeling, to return to Manning, that "everyone hates a cop." Blumberg reports a "recurring theme among police officers to the effect that they do not get the support, understanding, and fair treatment they expect from the people they serve."[35] The public, for whom the police are sacrificing their physical, psychological, and social well-being, fail to appreciate or even acknowledge this sacrifice. Understandably, this is a particularly bitter pill to swallow and cannot help but further estrange the police from the public.*

Two important points emerge from this consideration of the police subculture. First, the subculture nurtures a strong image of police officers as effective crime fighters whose primary approach is direct action against criminals—even to the point of taking the law into their own hands. After all, to refer one last time to Manning's list: "The legal system is untrustworthy; the policemen make the best decisions about guilt or {106} innocence." Second, the police seem to have little respect for, and are largely isolated from, the public. The police feel that they know best how to cope with crime and that they should not be subjected to second guessing by a public divided between those who are part of the world of crime and those who are naively oblivious to its causes and consequences.

ORGANIZATIONAL TENSIONS

The message of the police subculture seems clear enough. The job of crime control should be left to the experts; they should be free from outside interference to act when, where, and how they deem necessary. But who are the experts? The managers, who have responsibility for making policy, and the rank-and-file officers, who work the streets, do not see eye to eye on how best to proceed. As a result, traditional practices are something of a compromise, although with a distinct edge to rank-and-file preferences.

Both political and organizational forces determine how the balance will be struck between managers and the rank and file. Historically, the police have been very closely linked to partisan politics, and the result has been what

---

* On this point, at least, there is some reason to believe that the police may be parties to their own victimization, since opinion surveys tend to show strong support and approval of the police among the general public. See James Garofalo, *Public Opinion about Crime: The Attitudes of Victims and Nonvictims in Selected Cities*. (Washington, D.C.: National Criminal Justice Information and Statistics Service, 1977), 10–11. Of course, a sense of martyrdom has its own rewards.

Wilson aptly characterizes as a "watchman style" of policing that invests the rank and file with a great deal of discretion.[36] Political reform movements, going back at least to the early part of this century, have managed to insulate the police to some extent from politics, leading to a "legalistic style" of policing, with which managers sought to restrict rank-and-file discretion.[37] Even under the most favorable circumstances, however, managers are working under substantial handicaps in their battle against rank-and-file discretion, as we see at the conclusion of this section.

Policy Preferences

The rank and file, according to the available literature, like to acquit their responsibilities by establishing a presence on the street, by building up a reliable network of informants, or both. Generally speaking, patrol officers think in terms of the former, and detectives think in terms of the latter.[38] Above and beyond the effectiveness of each of these practices, they are attractive to the rank and file because they are part of established patterns, and more important, because control remains at the street level. Of course, this increase in discretionary authority makes police managers uneasy.

At the heart of establishing a presence on the street is routine passive patrolling: walking the beat or cruising in a radio car. The basic assumption is that criminals will be hesitant to engage in crime simply because they know that the police are present. {107}

> By their continuous, moving presence, so the theory goes, crime will be prevented because would-be criminals will be aware of and deterred by the police presence. Furthermore, this patrolling may enable the officer to witness a crime in progress or to discover and stop fugitives, suspicious persons, and stolen cars.[39]

If one accepts the basic premise of passive patrolling, the more police that are on the streets, the greater will be the crime-fighting capabilities of the patrols. Yet there is research indicating that short of vast numbers of police, which would be unacceptable in both fiscal and civil liberties terms, routine patrols do not deter crime.

Although it is unlikely that the rank and file would be persuaded by this research, officers on the street have not traditionally relied on passive patrolling alone. When street cops decide to "crack down on crime" they are likely to become more aggressive in their patrol practices. For example, patrol officers will increase the number of street stops in a manner consistent with their understanding of neighborhood people and patterns.

Patrol officers, as Rubenstein demonstrates, develop a territorial view of their responsibilities. Officers connect both their safety and their effectiveness with knowing as much as possible about their territory and the people who work and reside there.

> The police are organized to control the streets and the successful patrolman is an informal specialist in street use. He combines his knowledge of local behavior with his conception of how the public streets are used to analyze and perform many of his routine obligations. He informally rationalizes his search for activity and minimizes, in his own terms, the need for conflict with the people by constantly evaluating the character of the ground he patrols and uses.[40]

Accordingly, patrol officers decide who to stop and when to stop them, as well as the mode of intervention, on the basis of their experience with, and understanding of, local patterns.

Informants are the second traditional response of the police to crime. The police enter into exchange relationships with informants, who provide information about criminal activity. The currency of exchange is sometimes money and sometimes small favors, but seems most often to be immunity from prosecution. Informants are particularly important in vice work because there is ordinarily no victim and therefore no complainant to notify the police that a crime has been committed or help identify the criminal. But in all crimes in which the assailant is unknown to the victim, informants are important. "To exaggerate just a bit," Charles Silberman tells us, "the police can solve a crime if someone tells them who committed it; if no one tells them, they do not know what to do."[41] The individual {108} officer's professional success is thus directly dependent on establishing a reliable network of informants.[42]

The managers have a distinctly different view of all this. Having come up through the ranks and being part of the police subculture, the managers understand street-level priorities and share rank-and-file values. But managerial links to the rank and file are attenuated by responsibilities to the politicians and the public. Discretionary practices, moreover, run at cross purposes to managerial efforts to establish control of the police organization.

Both the informer system and the patrol officers' territorial attachments thus pose threats to police managers. While managers recognize the need for informants, the proprietary attitudes of rank-and-file officers toward their informants is another matter.

> A policeman's information is his private stock which nobody else may presume to make claims on, unless invited to share. What each man learns and does is not a subject for discussion unless he chooses to initiate the talk or is asked by his superiors.[43]

In treating the information provided by informants as their "private stock" and in routinely protecting informants from arrest, prosecution, or both, the rank and file are, in effect, asserting their independence from managerial coordination. There is also the possibility of a scandal should things get out of hand—a more than remote possibility, as we see in the next chapter. Insofar as officers come to think of their beats as their own fiefdoms, they will not be amenable to central direction and may well get involved in selective enforcement for personal gain. Certainly, close ties between police officers and particular neighborhoods have in the past been associated with corruption and political favoritism.[44] Because their authority and, indeed, their jobs are on the line, managers have a stake in curbing rank-and-file discretion, but they have not been particularly successful in doing so.

The persistence of discretionary authority, despite its obvious drawbacks for the police manager, provides some important insights into the nature of policing. First, the political setting determines whether police executives are really in a position to think of themselves in managerial terms. Second, because policing is inherently discretionary, there are some built-in limits to even the most dedicated manager's capabilities for control of street-level behavior.

Political Accommodation

Political culture, Wilson argues persuasively, is the primary link between politics and police policy. {109}

> By political culture is meant those widely shared expectations as to how issues will be raised, governmental objectives determined, and powers for their attainment assembled; it is an understanding of what makes a government legitimate.[45]

Cities develop their own kind of politics, and police departments are more or less compelled to adopt styles of policing suited to local conditions. Consistency between police style and political culture is maintained primarily through the hiring and firing of police chiefs.

> The most important way in which political culture affects police behavior is through the choice of police administrator and the molding of the expectations that govern his role.[46]

The chief understands that retention of his position depends on working out policies that do not run against the local political grain.

"Caretaker" politics is particularly conducive to discretionary policing. As Wilson explains it, caretaker politics has less to do with providing public service than with securing and consolidating electoral power. Whether electoral power is centralized within a united political party or divided according to "personal followings and ad hoc alliances," the results are roughly the same. Patrol officers are encouraged to deal informally with situations within a pattern of selective enforcement that protects those associated with the machine and grants favors in return for political support.[47]

The resultant "watchman style" of policing is characterized by the informality of interaction between the police and the public.

> The police are watchman-like not simply in emphasizing order over law enforcement but also in judging the seriousness of infractions less by what the law says about them than by their immediate and personal consequences, which will differ in importance depending on the standards of the relevant group—teenagers, Negroes, prostitutes, motorists, families, and so forth. In all cases, circumstances of person and condition are taken seriously into account—community notables are excused because they have influence and, perhaps, because their conduct is self-regulating; Negroes are either ignored or arrested, depending on the seriousness of the matter, because they have no influence and their conduct, except within broad limits, is not thought to be self-regulating.[48]

Clearly, the watchman style invests street-level officers with a great deal of discretion to go about the business of crime control pretty much as they see fit. Only when police activities threaten some vested political interest is rank-and-file discretion restricted.

In this setting, then, it is not the managers but the politicians who interfere with the rank and file. Chiefs in caretaker cities need not be concerned about corruption and favoritism so long as these deviant behaviors are consistent with the interests of the established politicians. {110} The fate of police managers and political machines are inextricably intertwined. A scandal may bring the whole regime crashing down, but absent such a scandal, the chief will stay in power so long as he is willing to play ball.[49]

In reform, or what Wilson calls "good government," cities, managers are in a much better position to impose limits on the discretionary authority of patrol officers. Traditionally, this has been accomplished through adoption of a "legalistic" style of policing.[*] Police officers in legalistic departments are called on "to handle commonplace situations as if they were matters of law enforcement."[50] What this means, in essence, is a formalization of relationships between police and citizens. A high proportion of contacts initiated by the police with citizens is supposed to lead to a citation or an arrest. To the extent that this formalization prevails, there is obviously less discretion, as well as fewer opportunities for corrupt practices to develop. More generally, formalization produces a paper record, which allows administrators to keep track of rank-and-file work habits. "A legalistic department will typically...put

---

[*] These so-called police styles are as, Wilson points out, "abstraction[s] from reality" (see note 1, p. 149) and are meant to convey basic tendencies rather than describe the detailed operations of any particular police department. Two additional police styles are discussed in Chapter 5, and it should be kept in mind that elements of each style tend to coexist in all departments. The mix of styles varies from time to time and place to place in relation to the prevailing political culture.

all patrolmen...under some pressure to 'produce.'"[51] Moreover, in order to maintain the impersonality deemed necessary for enforcing the law in a detached and uniform fashion, administrators also try to disrupt the territorial attachments of patrol officers. Officers are rotated through the city on a regular basis, thus substituting "stranger policing" for the close neighborhood ties associated with the beat cop.[52]

Both the public and rank-and-file police officers tend to find legalistic policing objectionable, but patrol officers pose the more serious problems. The public gets uniform but more intrusive policing. Citizens are less likely to "get a break," but in "good government" cities, this is presented to the public as the price that must be paid to avoid corruption. The good government spirit is very nicely conveyed by the reaction of a resident of Highland Park, Illinois, to the introduction of legalistic policing.

> The old [police] department was very friendly; every officer seemed to know you. If you were going too fast they would give you a warning instead of a ticket. But I suppose the way the department operates today is the only right way to go about it. The laws should be enforced to the letter.[53]

Patrol officers are not so easily convinced. "When the new chief [in Highland Park] installed a legalistic police style, the citizenry did not rebel but the police officers did."[54] Patrol officers object to legalistic policing because it is intrusive for them also. The paper record is, in essence, a way {111} of forcing them to account for their time, and their discretion is sharply restricted. Patrol officers understandably resent these restrictions on their independence and prefer the watchman style with its conception of street-level autonomy.

Organizational Accommodation

Despite the formal hierarchies and military appearance in police organizations, effective control over operative policy tends to flow from the bottom up rather than from the top down. Police officers are, as Lipsky demonstrates, street-level bureaucrats who are in a position to thwart policy directives from headquarters.[55] Moreover, as Muir makes clear, the chiefs have very limited capabilities for inducing the rank and file to accept new ways of doing things.[56] Chiefs can battle against traditional practices, Muir seems to tell us, if they have sufficient political support, but even then only at great cost and with limited success.

The leeway accorded the rank-and-file is inherent in the variety and particularity of their work. In part, there is a problem of not being able to formulate general rules to deal with the kaleidoscopic world that the police must confront. Like other street-level bureaucrats—social workers and legal services attorneys, to cite just two of Lipsky's examples—police officers "have discretion because the nature of service provision calls for human judgment that cannot be programmed and for which machines cannot substitute. Street-level bureaucrats have responsibility for making unique and fully appropriate responses to individual clients and their situations."[57] Effective service, in other words, requires that the police adapt to the special circumstances of each encounter. The ill-defined police mission further complicates matters. Police are charged with crime control, but there is no agreed upon means to that end. They are also expected to maintain order, which may or may not involve making arrests. Providing emergency services to the community is another responsibility thrust upon them. To further complicate matters, it is the officer's definition of a situation rather than some prior legal category that determines the appropriate response. Consider, for example, a family dispute. There are often grounds for making an arrest, but for a variety of reasons most officers are inclined to settle for spreading oil on the troubled waters. Much the same thing is likely to be true of neighborhood disputes or even tavern brawls. Officers must exercise judgment because we expect them to be Dick Tracy, Officer Friendly, and Florence Nightingale, each at the appropriate time.[58]

Police work is also dangerous and calls for very quick decisions. "Time to develop even a minimum degree of certainty appears to be unavailable to officers who shoot innocent people because they feared the consequences {112} of what they say was the civilian's intention to reach for a weapon."[59] Decisions to use deadly force "do not," as Justice Jackson remarked of a comparable dilemma, "pretend to rest on evidence, but are made on information that often would not be admissible and on assumptions that could not be proved."[60] While rules for the use of deadly force are regularly formulated, they cannot alter the contingent nature of such decisions. "Police reformers are unable to deal adequately with the heartfelt claims of policemen that they require discretion in order to protect themselves."[61]

The inherent difficulties of limiting discretion tend to be compounded by an organizational backlash when the managers do step in. Muir has chronicled the determined and apparently successful efforts of the "Laconia" chief directed at "tempering *the most offensive practices* of those policemen who had been inclined to brutality, rudeness, or venality."[62] Even this effort to curb *abuses* of discretion appears to have been very costly to the chief.

> Retaliation, demoralization, curtailed experimentation, secrecy, and disillusionment were some of the most severe costs of the wholesale use of the purely punitive process. Reliance on cruel discipline ultimately produced sharply diminishing returns and would have been disastrous except for the fact that the chief supplemented his terrifying actions with acts of moral leadership, which reinstilled principle, morale, willingness to take risks, candor and faith.[63]

Part of the chief's problem, according to Muir, was that he had to act punitively, and it appears from Muir's account that chiefs in general must rely on the stick because they have so few carrots available to them. Moreover, this was a chief with more personal resources than most—a man who could aid his own cause by intervening personally and effectively in training programs designed to reduce rank-and-file misbehavior.[64]

While Muir concludes that the chief was successful in curbing inappropriate behavior, there is good reason to believe that the chief's reward was a vote of no-confidence from the rank and file. Muir does not discuss the chief's downfall and makes an effort to conceal the locale of this study. It is, however, relatively easy to put two and two together and figure out that the chief in question did not survive his reform. Regardless of the final outcome, Muir's presentation makes it clear that the chief's effort to impose a reasonable level of civility led to turmoil, which undermined both the morale and the effectiveness of the Laconia police force. In other words, reform programs tend to threaten the viability of police organization.

Traditional practices, I have been arguing, are shaped in part by the values and in part by the interests of the police. Insofar as police values are {113} concerned, there is a good deal of consensus. The police like to think of themselves primarily as crime fighters, and there is substantial agreement that the most effective way to deal with criminals is directly and punitively. With respect to police interests, the perceptions of managers and of the rank and file diverge rather sharply. The rank and file identify their interests with a large measure of discretionary authority that enables them to maintain exclusive control of their assigned territory and their sources of information. But such extensive leeway for the rank and file jeopardizes managerial authority, which is already attenuated by the chief's dependence on elected officials, especially the mayor, at whose pleasure chiefs ordinarily serve. Accordingly, managers attempt to impose legalistic constraints of various kinds on rank-and-file discretion.

This tension between managers and the rank and file is part and parcel of traditional policing and tends to be handled in different ways depending on the political style of the city, the personality of the chief and the extent of political support he enjoys, and the cohesion and militance of the rank and file. Where, for example, the chief is in a relatively strong position and a reform style of politics tends to prevail, policing can be expected to turn in a legalistic direction, and the more punitive and unruly impulses of the police subculture may be significantly curbed. Conversely, when the rank and file has the upper hand, where political machines are operative, or both, the discretionary modes of the watchman style are likely to prevail. In this setting, patrol officers and detectives will be able to play their crime-fighting roles pretty much as they see fit—as long, at least, as their activities do not work at cross purposes to the preferences of important politicians and their influential constituents.

However the balance may be struck between legalistic and watchman style policing in *normal* times, the politics of law and order are likely to push policy in punitive and discretionary directions. Rank-and-file priorities for fighting crime are, unfortunately, extremely problematic, as we see in Chapter 5. The essential message of the rather complex arguments that follow is that law-and-order pressures have stifled the forces of reform and breathed new life into some of the most suspect features of traditional policing.

NOTES

1. James Q. Wilson, *Varieties of Police Behavior: The Management of Law and Order in Eight Communities* (New York: Atheneum, 1970), 231.

2. William K. Muir, Jr., *Police: Streetcorner Politicians* (Chicago: University of Chicago Press, 1977), 57.

3. Wilson, *Varieties of Police Behavior*, Chaps. 5–7.

4. David H. Bayley, *Forces of Order: Police Behavior in Japan and the United States* (Berkeley: University of California Press, 1976), esp. Chaps. 3 and 5. {114}

5. Samuel Walker, *A Critical History of Police Reform: The Emergence of Professionalism* (Lexington, Mass.: Heath, 1977), Chap. 4.

6. Muir, *Police*, Chap. 12.

7. John H. McNamara, "Uncertainties in Police Work: The Relevance of Police Recruits' Backgrounds and Training," in *The Police: Six Sociological Essays*, ed. David J. Bordua (New York: Wiley, 1967), 193.

8. Ibid., 199. Dorothy Uhnak's novel *Law and Order* (New York: Simon and Schuster, 1973) provides insight into the interpenetration of police and Irish-Catholic working class values in New York City and the evolution of that interpenetration between the 1930s and the 1960s. See also Arthur Niederhoffer, *Behind the Shield: The Police in Urban Society* (Garden City, N.Y.: Doubleday, 1967), 142–44.

9. David H. Bayley and Harold Mendelsohn, *Minorities and the Police: Confrontation in America* (New York: Free Press, 1968), 3–4.

10. Ibid. 4; McNamara, "Uncertainties in Police Work," 194; and Muir, *Police*, 233.

11. Unfortunately, with respect to many matters like education and ethnic or religious background, the available evidence is dated and in no sense comprehensive. There is, however, no reason to believe that changes in police recruitment practices have been sufficiently thoroughgoing to root out established norms. See Hubert G. Locke and Samuel E. Walker, eds., "Institutional Racism and American Policing: A Special Report," *Social Development Issues* 4, no. 1 (Winter 1980).

12. Muir, *Police*, 38.

13. Michael Lipsky, *Street-Level Bureaucracy: Dilemmas of the Individual in Public Service* (New York: Russell Sage, 1980), 15. Of course, there are a variety of constitutional, legislative, and departmental restrictions, but these are more proscriptive than prescriptive.

They set limits rather than define courses of action. Even these "negative" rules are extremely difficult to enforce.

14. George L. Kirkham, "What a Professor Learned When He Became a Cop," *U.S. News and World Report*, 22 April 1974, 70–72.

15. Abraham S. Blumberg, *Criminal Justice: Issues and Ironies*, 2nd ed. (New York: New Viewpoints, 1979), 85. Blumberg, however, believes that police isolation may be decreasing. "Regardless of what a number of now dated studies may show, it is my experience in contact with a variety of police departments that the 'new breed' of police recruit is more prepared to reach beyond the narrow police circle in establishing a friendship network... and that the 'social isolation' of police is somewhat exaggerated" (ibid).

16. Skolnick perceptively discusses this same phenomenon. Jerome Skolnick, *Justice Without Trial: Law Enforcement in Democratic Society* (New York: Wiley, 1966), 49–51.

17. Joseph Wambaugh, *The New Centurions* (New York: Dell, 1970), 161; italics in the original.

18. Peter K. Manning, "The Police: Mandate, Strategies, and Appearances," in *Criminal Justice in America: A Critical Understanding*, ed. Richard Quinney (Boston: Little, Brown, 1974), 175.

19. See, for example, Niederhoffer, *Behind the Shield*; Skolnick, *Justice Without Trial*; {115} William A. Westley, *Violence and the Police: A Sociological Study of Law, Custom, and Morality* (Cambridge, Mass.: MIT Press, 1970); Muir, *Police*, and Blumberg, *Criminal Justice*, Chap. 3.

20. Muir, *Police*, 22–25.

21. Skolnick, *Justice Without Trial*, 47–48.

22. Charles E. Silberman, *Criminal Violence, Criminal Justice*, (New York: Random House, 1978), 211–12.

23. Jonathan Rubenstein, *City Police* (New York: Ballantine, 1973), 323.

24. Muir, *Police*, 20–21.

25. Rodney Stark, *Police Riots: Collective Violence and Law Enforcement* (Belmont, Calif.: Wadsworth, 1972), 68–69.

26. Ibid., 62.

27. Muir, *Police*, 26.

28. Stark, *Police Riots*, 61.

29. Albert J. Reiss, *The Police and the Public* (New Haven: Yale University Press, 1971), 150. See also McNamara, "Uncertainties in Police Work," 207–15.

30. Stark, *Police Riots*, 61.

31. For a systematic presentation by a social scientist of the case that the police are victimized by their work, see William H. Kroes, *Society's Victim—The Policeman: An Analysis of Job Stress in Policing* (Springfield, Ill.: Charles C. Thomas, 1976).

32. Rubenstein, *City Police*, 298.

33. Wambaugh, *The New Centurions*, 201.

34. Ibid., 127–28.

35. Blumberg, *Criminal Justice*, 83.

36. Wilson, *Varieties of Police Behavior*, Chap. 5.

37. Ibid., Chap. 6.

38. On street presence, see Rubenstein, *City Police*, 129–73. On the detectives and informants, see Skolnick, *Justice Without Trial*, 112–38.

39. James Q. Wilson, *Thinking About Crime* (New York: Vintage, 1977), 98.

40. Rubenstein, *City Police*, 152.

41. Silberman, *Criminal Violence, Criminal Justice*, 204.

42. Westley, *Violence and the Police*, 40–42.

43. Rubenstein, *City Police*, 439.

44. Walker, *A Critical History of Police Reform*, 3.

45. Wilson, *Varieties of Police Behavior*, 233.

46. Ibid.

47. Ibid., 236–37.

48. Ibid., 141.

49. On the cycles of corruption and reform, see John A. Gardiner, *The Politics of Corruption: Organized Crime in an American City* (New York: Russell Sage, 1970).

50. Ibid., 172.

51. Ibid., 174. See also 183–88.

52. Silberman, *Criminal Violence, Criminal Justice*, 208.

53. Wilson, *Varieties of Police Behavior*, 260.

54. Ibid.

55. Lipsky, *Street-Level Bureaucracy*. {116}

56. Muir, *Police*.

57. Lipsky, *Street-Level Bureaucracy*, 161.

58. Cf. Manning, "The Police," 175–84.

59. Lipsky, *Street-Level Bureaucracy*, 30.

60. *Korematsu v. United States*, 323 U.S. 245 (1944).

61. Lipsky, *Street-Level Bureaucracy*, 30.

62. Muir, *Police*, 250; italics added.

63. Ibid., 252.

64. Ibid., 253–57.

5

The Politics of Police Reform

Beginning in the 1960s, largely as a result of the tensions arising out of policing the black ghettos of urban America, law-enforcement practices were subjected to a great deal of critical attention by journalists and scholars. James Baldwin captured the essential concerns of the era when he proclaimed that the police officer "moves through Harlem…like an occupying soldier in a bitterly hostile country; which is precisely what, and where he is, and is the reason he walks in twos and threes." As Baldwin saw it, the police would inevitably tyrannize the ghetto under these circumstances.

> The only way to police a ghetto is to be oppressive. None of the Police Commissioner's men, even with the best will in the world, have any way of understanding the lives led by the people they swagger about in twos and threes controlling. Their very presence is an insult….

> It is hard, on the other hand, to blame the policeman, blank, good natured, thoughtless, and insuperably innocent, for being such a perfect representation of the people he serves. He, too, believes in good intentions and is astounded and offended when they are not taken for the deed. He has never, himself, done anything for which to be hated…and yet he is facing daily and nightly, people who would gladly see him dead, and he knows it.[1]

The course of American life during the 1960s and early 1970s added further fuel to the critical fires. Tensions between the police and blacks increased—most spectacularly during the ghetto riots that placed unprecedented demands on the police and spotlighted various kinds of abusive police behavior. Similar tensions erupted between the police and other elements of society—students, opponents of the Vietnam war, and restive minorities generally. Finally, the rising crime rate raised questions about {118} the ability of the police to deter or catch criminals. The critical literature that emerged directed attention to virtually all aspects of traditional policing, from the recruitment and training of officers to the administrative procedures and policy decisions of police managers.

Ultimately criticism gave way, at least in part, to reform, which became the principal preoccupation of students of American policing. Research and experimentation into ways of increasing the effectiveness of law enforcement and improving police-community relations began in earnest. Insofar as all this ferment has led to proposals for improved training, better equipment, more personnel, and higher pay, the police have been enthusiastically receptive. Proposals calling on the police to depart from established practices have proven much more controversial, and it is these controversial reforms that are the focus of this chapter.

Proposals for serious reform can be divided roughly between the "crime attack" strategy and the "community service" strategy—a distinction I borrow from Wilson.[2] The idea behind crime-attack approaches is that the police should seize the initiative against crime. Instead of passive patrolling throughout the city, the police are supposed to target high-crime areas and high-crime periods, as well as particularly troubling kinds of crime, for special attention—using, for example, decoys or stakeouts in an effort to catch criminals off guard. The community service approach is less direct. It operates on the assumption that what the police need most in order to cope with crime is information and that the most fruitful sources of information about crimes, whether before or after the fact, are the people of the community.[3] Accordingly, the objective of the community service approach is to maximize trust between the police and the citizenry. The primary means to that end is to assign officers on a long-term basis to particular beats and encourage officers to become as much a part of the community as possible. Neither reform strategy is entirely new, but each involves departures from established practice.

A commitment to community service calls on both police administrators and the rank and file to reconsider strongly held beliefs about police work. "[T]he police recognize," according to Wilson, "that since the vast majority of citizens commit no serious crimes and know no serious criminals, they have little information to offer."[4] Moreover, while rank-and-file officers have always appreciated the importance of an intimate familiarity with the territory and the people for whom they are responsible, their objective has been to assert their authority rather than establish relationships of mutual trust and dependence. Thus community service is an idea that is not really compatible with the values of the police subculture. The managers, for their part, can be expected to resist community service reforms on organizational as well as ideological grounds because the territorial and personal loyalties that are part and parcel of community service reforms tend to attenuate managerial control.

The crime-attack strategy requires comparatively little adjustment of {119} basic police values and is in harmony with the punitive political climate. It is, however, a strategy that divides police managers from the rank and file. Managers, at least those with progressive orientations, are likely to welcome crime-attack ideas because they rely on the techniques of modern management to mobilize and deploy departmental resources. Of course, this administrative control directly limits the discretion of rank-and-file officers, who are therefore inclined to think of crime-attack strategies as a threat to their professional autonomy.

There are, in sum, both ideological and organizational obstacles to the acceptance of progressive policing. The overall picture can be portrayed as shown in Figure 5.1. The forces of progressive policing are both divided and weak. The division is a result of the organizational implications, just discussed, of the crime-attack strategy. Moreover, progressive policing has established reasonably secure beachheads in only a relatively small number of departments. It is also true that the law-and-order political climate with its punitive bias lends a certain legitimacy to the get-tough ideas of traditional policing.

While all these matters must be discussed in greater detail, the upshot is to make the implementation of progressive reforms highly problematic. Although a reasonably good case can, and will, be made for the crime-control potential of a community service approach to policing, movement in that direction tends to be precluded by the political climate, by traditional police values, and by managerial reluctance to grant the decentralization required for a community service strategy to work properly. As for the crime-attack strategy, it is likely under the pressure of the politics of law and order to retrogress to a simple and unfortunate unleashing of the rank and file—a reversion to the watchman style. {120}

		VALUES Attitudes toward reform	
		Traditional	Progressive
INTERESTS Locus of organizational Power	Managerial	Legalistic	Crime attack
	Street level	Watchman	Community service (neighborhood team policing)

FIGURE 5.1   Styles of Policing.

THE CASE AGAINST WATCHMAN-STYLE POLICING

Rank-and-file priorities tend to be self-defeating in two important ways. First, the rank and file cannot be counted on to make policy choices that will target the kinds of street crime about which the public is most concerned. Second, get-tough policies favored by the rank and file pose a threat to police-community relations and may well undermine successful crime fighting. Before going on to examine each of these charges against watchman-style policing, let us look briefly at the way in which the rank and file approach their crime-fighting responsibilities.

There is a curious ambivalence among the rank and file concerning their crime-control capabilities. On the one hand, they realize that they are in no position to solve the crime problem, and this leads to an understandable frustration, which some officers handle better than others. According to Muir, those who make their peace with a "sense of limited purpose" can become a credit to the force.[5] Those who cannot become cynical and may vent their frustrations in a punitive style of policing.[6] Either way, police officers eventually come to understand that there are severe limitations on how much they can hope to accomplish.

On the other hand, there is a strong current of opinion among police officers that, for all their limitations, they are society's experts at fighting crime. Most generally, they "know," as we have seen, that harsh and certain penalties deter criminals. More specifically, they have great faith in their competence to distinguish the good guys from the bad guys, to ferret out threats to public order, and to control explosive situations. Consider Rubenstein's account of a veteran officer's uncanny ability to see trouble in an ostensibly tranquil setting.

"What do you see?" the lieutenant asked.

"Just the usual bunch of dirtyneckers in the playground, nothin' else."

"Look again, boy," he said, getting out of the car. They walked toward the corner, carefully scanning the people in the area. There had been fighting between white youths who lived in the neighborhood and the black students who passed through each day on their way home from school. The men had come looking for signs of trouble; *one saw them and the other did not.*

"Clever little bastards," the lieutenant muttered. He told his companion to examine the building line across the street. What was previously invisible became immediately apparent—a double row of soda bottles neatly lined up along the length of the buildings. "We'll find twice as many in the playground. You better call a sector car to block the trolleys at Fulton Street until we get this cleared up. They got an ambush all set up. The Indians are jump-in' the Indians. Look at the wires." His partner glanced overhead and saw large, wet rags twisted around the trolley wires. These would dislodge the power pole of any passing trolley and make it a sitting duck for a bottle barrage.... He [the lieutenant] walked into the playground, his stick tucked in his armpit, toward a group of children. "If you want to stay here—play—otherwise get the hell out."[7] {121}

Experienced officers, in other words, believe that they can tell the difference between a normal situation and one where trouble is brewing. They have faith in their ability to be suspicious when it is appropriate, as well as in their ability to intervene effectively.[8]

Rank-and-File Priorities

How do the rank and file traditionally reconcile their capabilities and their limitations? According to Rubenstein, they establish realistic priorities. They think of their crime-control responsibilities as extending primarily to "outside crime"—crime that occurs in places that are visible to officers while on routine patrol. Conversely, they do not worry very much about "inside crimes"—those that are hidden from the patrol officer's view. The distinction is not so much between what is actually outside and what is actually inside as between that which an officer can be expected to see or to detect while on routine patrol. A mugging in an alley, Rubenstein tells us, is an "inside crime"; but if a burglar goes in through a front door, it is an "outside crime."[9]

From the perspective of the patrol officers, this makes good sense. "Any outside crime is an affront to the patrolman's notion of himself as a guardian of his territory."[10] The rank and file simply face up to their limitations by establishing standards of performance that provide them with a maximum of self-respect. In Muir's terms, this can be considered part of the process of coming to terms with a "sense of limited purpose."

From the public's point of view, there are two obvious problems with police priorities. Research suggests, first, that routine patrolling is not an effective tool of crime control. More important, police priorities are only loosely related to the public's priorities. Let us look at each of these matters.

The most convincing case against routine patrols emerges from the Kansas City Preventive Patrol Experiment, which was a research project involving three sectors of the city. In one sector, police patrols were doubled. In a second sector, preventive patrol was abolished, with the police appearing only in response to citizen calls. Patrol practices remained unchanged in the third sector. At the end of twelve months the results indicated that the mode of patrolling had no effect on the rate of crime. Even more surprisingly, increased patrolling did not reduce citizen fear of crime or increase citizen satisfaction with the police.[11] Perhaps a really massive police presence might be able to deter crime, but only at a cost that would jeopardize the fiscal re-sources of most municipalities.[12] Such a massive police presence would also jeopardize constitutional liberties—subjecting people to a virtual garrison state. In short, only if the rank and file were given a budgetary blank check would there be any reason to {122} believe that the street-level approach would be effective, and even then the remedy might prove worse than the disease.

Absent this massive police presence, the public is stuck with dubious rank-and-file priorities. When the public demands a crackdown on crime, the ostensible objective is decisive action against predatory strangers in direct proportion to the seriousness of their crimes. The public does not expect the police to ignore criminals who are clever enough to conduct their activities "inside," where the officer's dignity will not be affronted.

> The majority of all murders and aggravated assaults occur inside and therefore are not "on" the patrolman. Once he accustoms himself to being in the presence of the battered and gory remains of the victims, he does not display much concern about these crimes (unless the victim is a child), although he knows they arouse considerable public agitation.[13]

Thus the rank and file are making their choices in their own interests. While these choices may, in a superficial sense, be in the service of safe streets, they are not really responsive to the public's fear of crime, and if we can trust Rubenstein's account, the police are well aware of what they are doing.

The rank and file also substitute personal for public priorities in their work with informants. The grant of immunity by detectives to their infor-mants amounts, in effect, to official permission to commit crime. The detec-tive's essential concern is that the informant does not commit crimes that fall within the detective's jurisdiction. As Skolnick puts it:

> Most informants—both burglars and narcotics offenders—are addicts. In general, *burglary detectives permit informants to commit narcotics offenses, while narcotics detectives allow infor-mants to steal.* Now, this summary is not entirely correct or always true, but it does accurately state a strong tendency.[14]

The depths to which this relationship can descend were illustrated by the trial of Daniel Carranza, age twenty-two, who had been a police informer for six years. New York Police Department Detective Brendan Tumulty, with whom Carranza worked, described their relationship as follows:

> He gave me a couple of things of value and we acted on some of them. But 90 per cent of the things he gave me were garbage.
>
> When he worked for me, I tried to protect him. But how long can I look the other way? I told him, "You get in trouble, don't count

on me." But what he has been looking for was a license from the
police to go out and steal.

Finally, the detective said: "I told everybody: 'Bury him.' I had a
very annoying period with this bum."[15]

The problem is that by the time Detective Tumulty decided to bury
Carranza, the informant had already committed, by his own count, two
hundred crimes, and he had confessed over one hundred of them to the {123}
police. It is not surprising that business persons victimized by Carranza were
not particularly pleased when they learned the police had failed to prosecute
him. As a former assistant district attorney told *New York Times* reporter
Leslie Maitland: "At the police level a good informant is given a license to
continue his criminal activities."[16] Since Carranza's crimes included, in addition to burglary, arson, complicity in rape, assault with intent to kill, forgery,
and armed robbery, it is difficult to square Carranza's career as an informant
with any reasonable interpretation of the public's demand for law and order.
Even if we conclude that Carranza is an exception, and there is no particular
reason to do so, Skolnick's more measured analysis indicates why we can have
little faith that police and public priorities will coincide.[17]

In sum, it would seem very difficult to make a crime-control case at all
for yielding to the rank-and-file's preference for street-level strategy. There is
no evidence that the traditional police practice of establishing control of the
streets with routine patrolling reduces crime. Indeed, Rubenstein's experience
gives us reason to believe that the rank and file bring to their patrol tactics, as
well as their use of informers, priorities that may be quite different from those
of the general public. Rank-and-file practices also pose a threat to police-
community relations, which have additional crime-control implications.

Police Misbehavior and Community Relations

Tension with the community can be generated by practices that seem to
be part and parcel of traditional police work. The abusive treatment of citizens can antagonize those who observe the police in action as well as those
who are victimized. A more subtle problem is posed by neglect of duty and by
corruption, which tend to undermine respect for the police. There is ample
evidence indicating that the rank and file, if left to their own devices, are
likely to jeopardize police-community relations in both ways. The most systematic source of evidence on such police misbehavior is a study done for the
National Crime Commission by Albert Reiss in 1966, and much of what
follows is drawn directly from that research. There are other indications of
police misbehavior, and these are also considered. In evaluating these research findings, the patterns of police misbehavior are much more revealing

than are the absolute levels. Generally speaking, the less influential elements in the society are disproportionately subjected to police abuse.

The Reiss research was carried out by 36 observers who rode around in patrol cars in Boston, Chicago, and Washington, D.C. These observers spent a total of 7 weeks of 8-hour days in each city and observed more than 5000 police encounters involving more than 11,000 citizens.[18] Reiss and his {124} associates identified three distinct kinds of police misbehavior, which I list here in the order of their frequency: (1) violations of department regulations, (2) violations of the law, and (3) unnecessarily harsh treatment of citizens. The first two kinds of misbehavior are likely to evoke disrespect for the police, while the third can be expected to engender hostility. Needless to say, citizens who either fear the police or have no respect for them are unlikely to co-operate in matters of law enforcement.

Based on this research, the police seem to provide citizens with ample grounds for disrespect. Roughly 25 percent of the officers in the three cities violated the law in ways that included accepting money to alter testimony, carrying weapons to plant on suspects, accepting merchandise from merchants, extorting money from deviants, taking items from burglarized stores, or accepting money in return for stolen goods. The most frequent violations were accepting money or merchandise illegally.[19] The police were even more likely to violate department regulations than to commit felonies or misdemeanors. Roughly 4 out of 10 officers were observed *each* 8-hour day doing such things as drinking or sleeping on duty, falsifying reports, or simply neglecting their responsibilities.[20]

The data on abusive treatment of citizens are much less alarming—at least at first glance. In only 3 of every 1000 interactions did the police use excessive force. Demeaning treatment was more frequent, occurring in about 9 percent of the cases.[21] These figures do *not* suggest a generally authoritarian and brutal mode of policing even if considerable allowance is made for police restraint during the period when they knew they were being observed. Reiss, however, warns us against taking these figures at face value. When the focus is on police encounters with suspects rather than witnesses or victims, the rate for excessive force jumps to a little more than 3 percent.[22] What these figures suggest is that while verbal and physical abuse of citizens should hardly be thought of as the rule in police encounters, such behavior is not unusual—particularly in problematic situations.

Reiss's research has not been replicated, and so there is no way of knowing the extent to which his findings are representative of other police departments or, for that matter, whether they still accurately portray the incidence of police misbehavior in Boston, Chicago, or Washington, D.C. Nevertheless, the extensive body of literature on the police does indicate that all the forms of misbehavior uncovered by Reiss are woven into the fabric of American policing, albeit with substantial variations from time to time and place to place. We have already discussed the liberties that police officers regularly take with the law when dealing with informers. Violations of the law are, of course, also an integral part of police corruption, which surfaces over and over again and was spectacularly documented more than a decade ago in New York City.[23] I think most observers would agree with Herman Goldstein's conclusion that "[c]orruption is endemic to {125} policing."[24] Similarly, there is wide agreement that the police predilection for expressive use of force can and does lead to brutality and unwarranted police homicide.[25] In sum, the literature provides less precise confirmation of Reiss's findings that police misbehavior is commonplace and not to be explained by the bad-apple theory.

To the police, much of this behavior is justified either by legitimate law-enforcement objectives or by the trying circumstances they confront day after day. How else are we to explain why so much apparently unwarranted behavior occurred while the officers were being observed? As discussed earlier, the police subculture tends to legitimate, indeed to extol, the use of physical force. Similarly, the police officers' sense of their own victimization allows them to justify the liberties they take with the law. It was on this latter ground, for example, that the police sought to justify the corrupt practices uncovered by the Knapp Commission.[26] It is not so much that the police are proud of all of these activities but that they are inclined to believe that such behavior is normal for those who work under such stressful circumstances and, moreover, that anyone who really understands what it is like to be a police officer will not find the officers' response objectionable.

More revealing than this overview of police misbehavior are the patterns that lie beneath the surface. The overview indicates only that misbehavior is hardly an aberration. The underlying patterns indicate that certain segments of the community are much more likely to be victimized by police misbehavior than others. These patterns also suggest that the higher incidence of victimization is not really attributable to legitimate law-enforcement objectives. More aggressive patrol tactics, therefore, may have the unintended consequences of accentuating divisions within the society.

It is well established that police relations with young males are especially problematic. Young males are responsible for a disproportionate amount of violent crime, and it is therefore understandable that they are a particular target of aggressive patrolling. But there is another dimension to the tension between the police and young males. Both the police and the juveniles consider the streets to be their turf. We have already considered the territorial imperatives that the rank and file bring to patrolling. The streets are also vitally important to juveniles, especially "lower-class" juveniles for whom the streets serve as "hangouts,"—as their "private space."[27] In their encounters with these juveniles, the police are looking for deference, and according to Reiss, "many believe that citizens, particularly those from the lower classes, only understand and respect coercive authority."[28] For their part, the juveniles are trying to maintain their dignity. It is no mean feat to maintain one's self-respect and at the same time try to acknowledge authority. To tread this fine line requires verbal facility and perhaps some familiarity with one's rights. Deference {126} with dignity would therefore seem to come hardest to those lower-class youth from whom the police most insistently demand it.

The basic tensions present to some extent in all police encounters are likely to be further compounded by racial cleavage. As sympathetic an observer as Wilson tells us how frequently the race factor can intrude inappropriately into decisions about whom to stop. "[A] dark skin is to the police a statistically significant cue to social status, and thus to potential criminality.... [A] black skin is taken as grounds for police suspicion and therefore for questioning and frisking."[29] Inevitably, tensions are exacerbated as the police step up aggressive tactics. The result is, to quote Wilson once again,

> to multiply the occasions on which citizens are likely to be stopped, questioned, or observed. Inevitably, the great majority of the persons stopped will be innocent of any wrongdoing; inevitably, many of these innocent persons believe the police are "harassing" them; inevitably, innocent blacks will believe that they are being "harassed" because of their race.[30]

To Wilson, these unhappy consequences are the understandable and necessary consequences of the police responding to the law of averages. Wilson fails to consider the racism that seems so serious a problem among American police organizations. This racism is not easy to document, but black officers perceive sufficient racial animosity among rank-and-file officers to lead them to organize separately.[31] It is, in any case, reasonable to hypothesize that police racism increases the likelihood of misperceptions, misunderstandings, and mistreatment, resulting in a further deterioration of relationships between police and minority communities.

Assignment practices contribute another element to the problems posed for police-community relations by aggressive patrolling. Reiss discovered in the three cities where he conducted his research that "officers with the least training and experience are assigned to the highest crime-rate precincts. Officers with the poorest records of performance like-wise are transferred to these areas."[32] Thus street-level attacks on crime may well be in the hands of less competent officers. White officers assigned to nonwhite areas are, according to Reiss's data, more likely to neglect their duty.[33] While there are no comparable data on excessive force, it is reasonable to infer that those in high-crime areas are going to get the full range of poor service from the worst police officers that are available in the city. As a result, tensions between the police and the community will develop in these areas, particularly as aggressive patrolling is increased. Conversely, those in higher-status areas, who see the best officers at their most polite, will tend to discount charges of brutality, corruption, and dereliction of duty. In other words, police misbehavior not only inflames its victims but is also politically divisive, creating as it does such different images of police in the various segments of the society.[34] {127}

PROGRESSIVE POLICING

Progressive policing is less a program than a state of mind—a willingness to acknowledge and confront the kinds of problems that have just been discussed. The roots of progressive policing can be traced to the movement to professionalize the police. Progressive policing begins with professionalization but goes well beyond this starting point to a comprehensive rethinking of the police mission and to policies appropriate to new conceptions of policing. At the outset of this chapter I identified these alternatives to traditional styles of policing as the crime-attack and community service strategies.

Professionalization, the jumping-off point for progressive policing, means, at a minimum, better-trained police officers and a police organization insulated from partisan politics. Professionalization is therefore closely associated with the kind of "good government" ideas that gave rise to the legalistic reforms considered in Chapter 4. Police managers understand professionalization in terms of the techniques of modern administration, which facilitate effective control of unwieldy police organizations. The three elements of this managerial conception of professionalism are, according to Samuel Walker, first "to centralize authority within the department, second to rationalize the procedures of command and control, and third to raise the quality of police personnel."[35] The rank-and-file have nurtured a distinctly different conception of professionalization. Police guilds or unions, whose principal mission has been to improve the wages, working conditions, and career prospects of police officers, have been the spear carriers for this rank-and-file conception of police professionalism. According to their way of looking at things, professionalization means the development of specialized knowledge that will make police officers bona fide experts at crime control and thus entitle them to enhanced status and rewards.[36] The widespread acceptance of professionalization obviously conceals sharp disagreements anchored in a very restricted sense of reform.

Progressive policing significantly broadens the field of reform. The clearest and most consistent voice of progressive policing has been the Police Foundation, established by the Ford Foundation in 1970. The Police Foundation, under the long-time leadership of Patrick V. Murphy, a former police chief in Detroit, Syracuse, Washington, and New York, has provided an agenda for progressive policing, which has refocused reformers from organizational and career issues to broader social implications of policing. In so doing, the foundation has expanded the conception of professionalization to include moral and public interest concerns.[37] The progressive agenda of the Police Foundation is conveyed very nicely by the chapter titles of a book recently published under the auspices of the foundation. {128}

Chapter 1: The Role of the Police: Should It Be Limited to Fighting Crime?

Chapter 2: Personnel Upgrading

Chapter 3: Police Organization and Management

Chapter 4: The Police and the Community

Chapter 5: Police Consolidation and Coordination

Chapter 6: Police Research and Experimentation[38]

While there is no party line on these matters, widespread agreement prevails among progressives on some basic objectives, if not on how best to achieve them. Consensus would probably extend to the upgrading of educational and training standards at all levels of policing; the establishment of closer rapport with the communities served; a larger proportion of minority police officers as a necessary, although hardly a sufficient, condition of improved relations with minority groups; and a conception of policing that goes beyond the idea of police as crime fighters.

As for the long-standing division between managers and the rank and file, the picture is not altogether clear. As Figure 5.1 indicates, there are both street-level and managerial theories of progressive policing. In practice, things are quite different.

Only the managerial version of progressive policing has had any appreciable impact on policy because, among progressives, only the managers are organized. Progressive policing is institutionalized at the managerial level in two ways. First, the Police Foundation is essentially a managers' organization and necessarily brings a manager's understanding to the problems of the police. Thus, for all its efforts to take the long view, the only coherent voice of progressive policing has a distinctly managerial bias. Second, some urban police chiefs are associated with the Police Foundation and are willing and able to put into practice some of the principles worked out within the foundation.

As for the rank and file, things are a good deal more amorphous. Given the superior training and education of many of the rank-and-file these days, substantial numbers of police officers probably would be responsive to new ideas, but they are dispersed and unorganized. Police associations that represent the rank and file generally cling to a narrow conception of professionalism. They are committed to improving wages and working conditions but are otherwise conservative and unreceptive to broader understandings of the police role.[39]

To sum up, then, the Police Foundation provides managers with a progressive alternative to the traditional views of the much larger International Association of Chiefs of Police.* No comparable counterbalance is available to

---

* The distance separating the progressive ideals of the Police Foundation from the International Association of Chiefs of Police is amply demonstrated by the recent censure of Patrick V. Murphy, the president of the foundation, by the IACP. The IACP objected to

the rank and file, whose organizations are concerned with reform only insofar as it improves the working circumstances of police officers. {129}

The Crime-Attack Strategy

The crime-attack strategy entails a concerted effort by police admin-istrators to mobilize their resources and deploy them as efficiently as possible in the service of crime control. In place of preventive patrol and ad hoc, dis-cretionary interactions with the public, the crime-attack strategy emphasizes specific targeting, aggressive patrolling, faster response time, and depart-mental programs designed to improve police-community relations.[40] Even Wilson and Boland, who are relatively optimistic about the crime-control capabilities of the crime-attack strategy, are not optimistic about the will-ingness of the rank and file to accept this managerial approach.[41] A closer look at its four elements will clarify rank-and-file objections to the crime-attack strategy.

The core idea of the crime-attack strategy is the *specific targeting of crime-control objectives*. High-crime areas are given special attention, as are time periods when the risk of crime is greater. Particular crimes are also chosen for special attention, either because the incidence of these crimes is increasing or because they are deemed particularly threatening to the social order. Given fixed resources, special attention to some matters necessarily results in reduced attention to others. For the rank-and-file, this can mean a disruption of routines—more officers on duty at peak crime times or one-person patrol cars in low-crime areas. Targeting also strengthens the hand of the administrators who rely on data—increasingly computerized data—to deploy resources in a manner consistent with the overall patterns of crime throughout the city.

Another aspect of the managerial version is *aggressive patrolling*. Officers are expected to seize the initiative in a variety of ways: decoying muggers, staking out particularly attractive robbery targets, conducting more field in-terrogations stopping more motorists for moving violations and in order to check for stolen vehicles. While at first glance aggressive patrolling may seem more appropriately classified as a street-level response, Wilson and Boland make clear its essentially managerial orientation:

> To achieve an aggressive patrol strategy a police executive will recruit certain kinds of officers, train them in certain ways, and devise requirements and reward systems (traffic ticket quotas, field interrogation obligations, promotional opportunities) to en-courage them to follow the intended strategy.[42]

Murphy's willingness to acknowledge publicly the problems of racism, corruption, and brutality within the nation's police forces. *New York Times,* 8 July 1982.

In other words, aggressive patrolling should be thought of as a managerial technique insofar as it is institutionalized within a reward system and {130} accompanied by recordkeeping designed to ensure implementation by the rank-and-file.

Reduction of response time is the third element in the crime-attack strategy. In addition to the obvious community relations benefits of reducing response time, there is also some reason to believe that faster response time leads to more arrests.[43] The key to speeding up responses is the upgrading of departmental communication so as to maximize the amount of time that dispatchers are in touch with the rank-and-file. It stands to reason that knowing where all units are and being able to contact them immediately enables dispatchers to move officers around with the least waste of time and motion. Radio cars were an obvious step in this direction, but the communication system is further improved if officers have portable radio units that maintain contact with the dispatcher even when the officers are out of the car.

From the point of view of the rank and file, while efficient communication has some advantages, it also has severe drawbacks. Continuous contact impinges on the autonomy of the officers and subjects them to more effective administrative control. When this control is used to move officers away from their established beats, the system becomes even more objectionable because it interferes with territorial commitments that are so integral to traditional conceptions of professional responsibility.

Improving police-community relations is the final objective of the managerial version of progressive policing. Such programs as neighborhood blockwatch teams or property identification schemes organized by community service officers working out of headquarters serve the dual purpose of crime control and community outreach. More generally, advocates of progressive policing expect relations with the community to improve as minority representation on the police force increases and as abusive behavior toward the public decreases.[44]

Rank-and-file reactions to all of this are likely to be lukewarm. The rank-and-file are unlikely to take outreach programs very seriously. Insofar as the programs are taken seriously, they will be seen as impinging on traditional territorial prerogatives. Efforts to curb abusive behavior are a direct threat to traditional values and discretionary authority. Finally, affirmative action programs designed to develop a minority presence at all echelons of police departments have proven a rallying point for rank-and-file organizations. The ostensible concern is the threat posed by affirmative action hiring to merit systems and service quality. As with objections to affirmative action elsewhere in the society, however, beneath the surface are the self-interest of current officers and, in all likelihood, a measure of racial bias. In any case, managerial approaches to police-community relations are resisted by police associations.

All elements of the crime-attack strategy will therefore have to be implemented over substantial opposition from organizations representing {131} the rank-and-file. The obvious issue, to which we now turn, is whether the payoff of the crime-attack strategy, in terms of crime control and police-community relations, is sufficient, given the organizational backlash that can be expected.

There are at least two different ways to pose this question. On the one hand, is it reasonable to expect police managers to follow the path of progressive reform despite opposition from the rank-and-file? On the other hand, does the crime-attack strategy substantially improve the quality of policing?

The Consequences of Pursuing a Crime-Attack Strategy

Relatively little is known about the effects of crime-attack programs on street crime. Wilson points out that figures gathered in the early 1970s by the New York Police Department were encouraging.[45] More recently, a number of programs targeting robbery in high-crime areas have produced positive results, according to figures compiled by the police in New York City.[46] More systematically, Wilson and Boland, working with 1975 data from 35 of the 46 largest American central cities, found that robbery arrest rates can be increased without higher police expenditures if administrators employ an aggressive patrol strategy.[47] By aggressive patrol strategy, they mean one that "maximizes the number of interventions and observations of the community."[48] If these findings are taken at face value, the effectiveness of the crime-attack strategy has been established. But there are reasons to be cautious about Wilson and Boland's findings, which they readily concede are only the first step toward establishing the efficacy of the proactive methods of a crime-attack strategy.[49]

Does the Wilson and Boland research really test the efficacy of the crime-attack strategy? My doubts center on the way Wilson and Boland have determined which departments are employing aggressive patrolling practices. Instead of actually investigating police practices in the various cities included in the study, they have chosen the rate at which patrol officers issue traffic citations to motorists as the indicator of aggressive patrolling. Their premise is that a police force that is aggressive in issuing traffic citations will be more likely to engage in aggressive patrolling generally—"frequent 'field stops' of suspicious persons, frequent 'car checks' of suspicious vehicles, and the use of 'decoy' or other anticrime procedures."[50] Perhaps so, but I am inclined to look upon this premise with considerable suspicion. The issuance of large numbers of traffic tickets is, according to Wilson and Boland, indicative of a legalistic style of policing, which they characterize as more aggressive than the passive orientation of watchman-style departments.[51] But the formal interactions with citizens implied by the legalistic style is hardly consistent with the {132} stop-and-frisk harassment of the crime-attack strategy. Data from an extensive study by Jacob and Rich also indicate that "robbery rates are not sensitive to changes in policing."[52] The two projects differ significantly from one another, but each seems equally reliable, thus leaving a very cloudy picture concerning the impact that the police can have on robbery—let alone on other kinds of crime.[53] Given the suspect premise on which the Wilson and Boland study is based and the contrary findings of Jacob and Rich, the crime-control case for the crime-attack strategy is at best inconclusive and will remain so until someone undertakes the "sort of fine grained analysis" that Wilson and Boland acknowledge is required to adequately test their hypothesis.[54]

Leaving aside the question of crime control, there is still reason to question the wisdom of the crime-attack strategy, which poses a serious threat to police-community relations. Even Wilson admits that there is, in practice if not necessarily in principle, an underlying tension between more aggressive patrolling and maintaining rapport with the public.

> Stakeout squads and decoys may produce dead criminals rather than arrests. Decoys sometimes have difficulty convincing either criminals or innocent bystanders that they are police officers; indeed, there have even been instances in which a decoy has been unable to convince a fellow officer that he was a cop. As a result, police decoys have sometimes been attacked by citizens and shot at by skeptical officers. In racially tense areas aggressive law enforcement, unless well managed, can give rise to community criticism.[55]

If police officers are not always able to distinguish their fellow officers from criminals, it seems reasonable to infer that they may also have trouble distinguishing between criminals and innocent bystanders. Aggressive patrolling may not only "produce dead criminals" but dead bystanders as well. Wilson clearly discounts these problems. He believes that mistakes will be minimal if aggressive patrolling is "well managed." I disagree, in part because I have less faith in the managers and in part because I see the mistakes that concern Wilson as only one aspect of a much more fundamental problem.

It is true that administrators tend to exercise a moderating influence on the rank-and-file, but that influence is not likely to make a significant impact on tensions generated by aggressive patrolling. Aggressive patrolling is inherently intrusive and demeaning. Charles Silberman puts his finger on the essential difficulty: "When an officer stops someone for questioning, he is conveying suspicion—suspicion of who the person is, what he may have done, and what image he projects to others."[56] Insofar as aggressive patrolling requires an increase in interventions, relationships with the community are likely to become ever more abrasive as the police convey their suspicions with greater frequency to larger proportions of the community.[57] {133}

While police administrators may try to cushion the shock by imposing standards of civility on patrol officers, even the relatively moderate views of appropriate street behavior held by the administrators have a distinctly coercive ring to them. Consider Muir's subtle formulation of the moderate position. He looks with considerable distaste at what I refer to as the expressive use of force—what he calls the "enforcer" approach to policing. Nonetheless, Muir thinks about police encounters as essentially coercive transactions. As he sees it, officers and those they police are adversaries locked into an "extortionate" or "antagonistic" relationship "based on threat" with "everyone... either a victim or a victimizer."[58]

> The policeman's authority consists of a legal license to coerce others to refrain from using illegitimate coercion. Society licenses him to kill, hurt, confine and otherwise victimize nonpolicemen who would illegally kill, hurt, confine or victimize others whom the policeman is charged to protect.
>
> But the reality, and the subtle irony, of being a policeman is that, while he may appear to be the supreme practitioner of coercion, in fact he is first and foremost its most frequent victim. The policeman is society's "fall guy," the object of coercion more frequently than its practitioner. Recurrently he is involved in extortionate behavior as victim, and only rarely does he initiate coercive actions as victimizer.[59]

Given this orientation, to which most police administrators would, I suspect, subscribe, it is not surprising that Muir would see coercion as an integral, though by no means sufficient, aspect of the police repertoire. In other words, administrators may seek to draw the line between instrumental and expressive uses of force, but coercion still looms quite large. Moreover, as we have seen, administrators do not seem either willing or able to consistently impose even these minimal standards on the rank-and-file.

Community Service Policing

The community service approach has been most concretely realized in neighborhood team policing programs tried out in a number of cities during the 1970s. These pilot projects were mildly encouraging in a number of ways, but the prospects for the adoption of neighborhood team policing are not particularly promising, due principally to the self-interested opposition of police managers, who perceive team policing as a threat to their authority. Interestingly, the rank-and-file, who might be expected to object to the nonpunitive orientation of team policing, seem much more accepting than their bosses.

At the heart of the concept of neighborhood team policing are the long-term assignment of officers to a particular area and the delegation of broad responsibilities to individual officers and the teams on which they {134} serve.[60] The teams are, by and large, self-contained police units, generally operating under the command of a lieutenant, who is, in effect, the police chief for the neighborhood. The duties of rank-and-file officers are expanded. They are "assigned more skilled responsibilities like investigations and community relations" and are expected "to participate in the planning and decision-making processes of the team."[61] The assumption lying behind this devolution of authority from headquarters through the team commander to patrol officers is that "law enforcement priorities" will vary from community to community and that "those officers having the greatest degree of contact with residents" have important contributions to make.[62] The whole spirit of team policing is therefore one of coordination and cooperation rather than hierarchy and command.

These organizational changes are merely the means to the essential objective of team policing—the development of a broader conception of police service among the officers and a corresponding increase in the willingness of citizens to participate in law enforcement. Officers are expected to spend less time in their patrol cars and more time on the street. Moreover, they are supposed to use that time on the street to get to know the residents. This in turn means adopting less aggressive patrol tactics and increasing the "provision of non-crime services."

> Examples of such services include referrals to other social agencies, family crisis intervention, establishment of youth athletic groups, etc. Team policing programs undertaking these activities have attempted thereby to increase police visibility and develop citizen support, trust and identity with the police.[63]

The citizens, for their part, are supposed to be drawn into such support activities as advisory councils, auxiliary patrol programs, and more conscientious reporting of crime.

One variant or another of team policing seems to have been tried out in roughly twenty-five cities all over the United States. Included have been such large departments as New York, Detroit, Cincinnati, and Los Angeles and smaller departments such as those in Richmond, Palo Alto, North Charleston, and Holyoke. Given such extensive experimentation, it might seem relatively easy to draw conclusions about how well team policing works, but unfortunately this is not the case. Both the programs and the methods used to evaluate them have varied so widely that reliable generalizations on the success of neighborhood team policing and, therefore, of the community service approach are very hard to come by. What seems to emerge most clearly is resistance to giving team policing an honest try.[64]

One of the more impressive experiments was carried out in Cincinnati partly under the auspices of the Police Foundation. Silberman provides a cogent analysis of the mixed results of this four-year experiment, which {135} ended in 1975. In formal terms, the program was set up with careful attention to the means and ends of team policing as I have summarized them above: multiservice teams, working under a lieutenant with responsibility to assign officers when, where, and how they were needed; and encouragement given to officers to get out of their cars and get to know the neighborhood and its residents. The problem is that these formal trappings were accompanied by a continued utilization of "administrative routines" that "conveyed a different message," as well as by a failure to provide training consistent with the new responsibilities:

> [E]ach Cincinnati patrol officer fills out a daily work sheet...reporting his activity.... "[A]ctivity" is defined in traditional police terms: "parkers" and "movers," arrests and suspicion stops. Time spent conversing with storekeepers and residents was not considered an important enough activity to be recorded....
>
> Several officers told me that there is an informal quota system for tickets and arrests: although there is no fixed numerical goal an officer has to meet, questions will be asked if his "output" drops significantly below what it was the month before, or if it is consistently lower than that recorded by other officers.[65]

Obviously, the officers were getting a mixed message about team policing. On the one hand, they were being told to establish rapport with the community, while on the other hand, they were being rewarded for the kind of aggressive patrol tactics that, as Silberman aptly puts it, were "most likely to anger local residents."[66]

Even this watered-down version of team policing seems to have been too much for the police managers, who perceived the whole plan as a threat to their prerogatives and prestige. Their response was to reassert control over some aspects of personnel deployment and, under some circumstances, to directly undercut the basic authority of the team leaders.

> [M]embers of middle and top management in the Cincinnati department feared that delegating authority to a patrol officer, sergeant or lieutenant meant taking an equivalent amount of authority away from them.[67]

Since the chief did nothing to assuage these concerns, it would appear that the acceptance of team policing was grudging at best and that the continued emphasis on aggressive patrol tactics was not inadvertent.

As the Cincinnati experience suggests, the fact that team policing has not entirely lived up to expectations may be less a commentary on the promise of the program than on the reluctance of police managers to give it a fair try. The rank and file, while often skeptical at the outset, seem to adjust well to properly implemented team policing programs, and these programs produce positive results. In San Diego, for example, where the role of rank-and-file responsibilities was changed to conform to community service principles, team policing officers actually developed more positive {136} attitudes toward the community, and vice versa.[68] No such successes grew out of the rather slapdash New York program.[69] With respect to the six cities evaluated in terms of crime control, the findings are particularly sketchy and inconclusive.

> [C]rime in Rochester, Holyoke and Los Angeles improved relative to the rate in control areas while Cincinnati, New York and St. Petersburg reported very little difference between team and control areas.[70]

The available data do not reveal whether the positive results were recorded by programs that more faithfully followed team policing principles. At least there seems no cause for concern that the less authoritarian approach of team policing will actually encourage crime, as hard-liners seem to believe. More generally, the evaluation research suggests that team policing, even in the half-hearted forms in which it has usually been implemented, was able to make significantly positive changes while causing little, if any, harm.

If the prospects for further experimentation with, or the widespread adoption of, team policing are dim, it is not on principled grounds. The principled objections of police managers are rooted in past experiences that are of dubious relevance to team policing. Close ties between police officers and particular neighborhoods have been associated historically with political favoritism and corruption.[71] But these legitimate problems have not figured in the administrative subversion of team policing experiments, nor have these experiments given any cause for concern. On the contrary, during the Cincinnati project corruption turned up in the central administration while the team districts remained clean.

> Chief Goodin was indicted on thirty-two counts of bribery, extortion, perjury, "soliciting for compensation," tampering with evidence, and obstructing justice. Six members of the centralized vice squad were indicted along with Goodin, who was accused of using vice squad members to shake down prostitutes and other unsavory characters. The chief was convicted on two counts and sentenced to four months in jail, with a fine of $5,000.[72]

Beyond the irony of this single example, team policing bears little resemblance to the conditions that bred corruption and political favoritism at the end of the nineteenth and the beginning of the twentieth centuries in urban America.

After all is said and done, then, managerial resistance to team policing seems to be inertial and self-serving rather than principled. Community service ideas, as implemented in team policing programs, offer the only option that shows promise of combining crime control with improved relationships between the police and the community. The decentralization, which is integral to team policing, impinges directly on managerial prerogatives, however. Understandably, if regrettably, most managers will not surrender such power voluntarily. Clearly, from the managerial point {137} of view, the crime-attack strategy, which strengthens their hand, is far and away the better way to go. It is, moreover, true that a law-and-order political climate tends to be supportive of managerial preferences, as we now see.

THE POLITICS OF LAW AND ORDER

One of the spin offs of the politics of law and order has been a serious rethinking of the problems of traditional policing and the development of progressive alternatives to traditional practices. Nevertheless, I have suggested that the prospects for progressive policing are not particularly good because the politics of law and order has also generated counterforces that tend to reinforce the already well entrenched traditional ways of doing things. It is now time to look more systematically at my rather gloomy predictions concerning police reform.

There are essentially three parts to the argument. Traditional practices rest on political and organizational accommodations that reflect long-term structural relationships and are therefore resistant to changes of any sort. Second, the politics of law and order tends to increase the influence of the rank and file and in this way to reinforce the punitive and discretionary bias of traditional policing. Finally, given this change in the balance of organizational power, police managers are likely to become even less reliable agents of moderation. Only with respect to the continuity of established practice is there any substantial supporting evidence. Insofar as the punitive tilt of organizational forces is concerned, my position is primarily speculative.

If I am right, it would be wrong to think about the politics of law and order as an effective agent of reform, as Wilson seems to suggest. He sees the crime-attack and community service strategies as good examples of serious and responsible policy making engendered by the public's increased fear of crime. As I look at things, the politics of law and order has re-created a climate of opinion and a balance of organizational forces that is inimical to community service ideas and is likely to drive crime-attack policies back toward the suspect priorities and abusive practices associated with the watchman style.

Policy Continuity

The concerns that have given rise to the politics of law and order do not feed into a policy vacuum. A variety of vested interest, which have already been considered, stand in the path of progressive policing. Accommodations between the police and the local political culture are rooted in {138} structures and values that change only incrementally and by their nature tend to be resistant to short-term fluctuations in public attitudes. Accommodations within the police organization are even more resistant to change. Politicians,

administrators, and the rank-and-file all have a stake in existing arrange-
ments, and crime control is just one of a number of issues that influence their
policy preferences.

If we really knew how to reduce crime, the other obstacles to effective
reform might not loom quite so large. The simple truth is, however, that
nobody can make a conclusive case for any mode of crime control. What we
have instead are theories, pilot projects, research findings, and street knowledge all pointing in different directions. Under the circumstances, all parties
stick to their preferred solutions, and established political and organizational
accommodations take precedence over reform.

This interpretation is consistent with the findings of Rich, Lineberry, and
Jacob, who gathered a substantial body of data on police department policies
in ten American cities over the years between 1948 and 1978.[73] They focus
primarily on the resources available to the police and on the patterns of police
arrest activity. The essential message of these data is that established practices
have considerable staying power, although there is some reason to believe
that the politics of law and order have had some impact.

It should be noted, preliminarily, that there is a substantial problem involved in adapting these findings to concerns with the politics of law and
order. The period covered by the research goes back to well before the development of the politics of law and order in the mid-1960s. Moreover, the
data are not presented in a way that permits "before and after" analysis.
Nevertheless, inferences may be reasonably drawn from contrasts between
cities where the police are insulated from local politics and cities in which the
police are politicized. To the extent that things are different in those latter
cities, it seems reasonable to attribute those differences, at least in part, to the
law-and-order political climate.

Most of the indicators show remarkable continuity through the years.
While police departments may differ from one another, they tend to develop
and stick to their own ways of doing things. The ratio of arrests to offenses
remained stable in virtually all the cities.[74] It is also true that the attention
devoted to violent crime in comparison to property crime did not change very
much either.[75] The ratio of police officers to population was a good deal more
volatile, but this was due, to some extent, to federal government programs
that funded temporary increases in personnel.[76] More generally, the data
indicate that cities with a high ratio of officers to population maintained this
"labor intensive" pattern throughout the period, while other departments
continued to make do with fewer police officers per capita.[77]

Against this general background of continuity, politicization does {139}
seem to have led to some changes. To appreciate the effects of politicization,
note, first, the across-the-board increases in resources made available to the
police during the thirty years.

> [E]ach of the ten cities increased their level of police expen-
> ditures when adjusted for population and inflation, and...nine out

of the ten cities...reported a mean annual increase in the ratio of police officers to population.[78]

While, generally speaking, this increase in available resources was not sufficient to keep pace with rising crime, in some cities it was. Similarly, arrest rates tended to fall behind crime rates in most but not all cities.[79] Although there are a number of ways of explaining these intercity variations, the answer is partially attributable to politics.

> [T]hose cities in which policing is highly politicized (that is, cities in which the police department is very active in local politics), generally tended to be those cities that increased manpower the most and also those cities in which increases in police activities either exceeded or closely followed rises in the crime rate.[80]

Politicization would seem conducive to more aggressive policing from better-financed police forces.

What are the implications of such changes? If the increased arrests were part of a systematic revision of departmental practices, some optimism might be in order—at least if one accepted Wilson's views about the effectiveness of crime-attack strategies. But the other data just discussed indicate that no such departmental transformations have been occurring. High arrest rates alone do not seem to constitute an effective crime-control program, particularly when it turns out that even the most active departments make so few serious crime arrests.

> Oakland's police officers, the most "productive" in our ten cities according to this measure, made only slightly more than one part I [serious crime] arrest per police officer per month.[81]

It does seem, however, that an aggressive arrest policy, in the context of politicization of police activities, can be indicative of greater leeway for the rank and file to engage in abusive behavior toward the public.

Rank-and-File Influence

An increasingly well organized and vocal rank-and-file has learned that it can use political action to undermine moderate politicians and police managers. Cases in point are the generally successful police campaigns against civilian review boards. The vote in a New York City referendum {140} organized by the Patrolmen's Benevolent Association was almost 2 to 1 against the board.[82] In Philadelphia and elsewhere, police associations have used a variety of tactics to undermine efforts to establish effective outside review of police practices.[83] "In Boston, Cleveland, and Detroit," according to Samuel Walker, "the rank-and-file also organized in opposition to liberal mayors seeking to improve police-community relations."[84] In at least two major American cities,

Philadelphia and Minneapolis, former police chiefs campaigning on law-and-order platforms won mayoralty elections.[85]

Without much systematic study of the political power of police associations, it would be wrong to jump to any final conclusions about their strength, staying power, or even their objectives. Not too long after the police successfully defeated Mayor Lindsay's proposal for a review board in New York City, rank-and-file efforts to defeat another Lindsay proposal, this time in the state legislature, were thwarted. This latter proposal dealt with more efficient deployment of police resources along lines consistent with the crime-attack strategy. In this instance, the police chief and the mayor were successful against the rank-and-file, although it is worth underscoring the fact that the battle was conducted in the legislature rather than by referendum.[86] More generally, in an era of tight budgets, managerial arguments in behalf of efficient deployment of resources are likely to take precedence over rank-and-file claims for increased numbers of personnel to establish a more extensive presence on the streets.

With all that said, it still seems likely, as long as the politics of law-and-order continue to predominate, that the political arena will be receptive to rank-and-file demands for a more punitive policy posture. Wilson notes that a legalistic department in Oakland shifted from moderation to a get-tough policy under the pressure of a rising crime rate.[87] One could even speculate that if the politics of law and order were to prevail for a sufficient time, the basic character of the political culture would be altered, thus undermining the forces of moderation even in those settings that have been traditionally receptive to reform, good government, and less harsh forms of law enforcement.

Punitive Policing

Under these circumstances, only a determined and resourceful police manager with solid support from the mayor can be expected to crack down firmly on rank-and-file abuses. Less able, courageous, or secure chiefs can be expected to follow the line of lesser resistance, making concessions on issues of vital importance to the rank-and-file while holding the line on matters directly related to managerial control. The most likely tradeoff would entail backing off on abusive treatment of the less influential {141} elements of the public. This was the issue that caused so many problems in "Laconia" and is likely to be equally explosive elsewhere. Conversely, chiefs could be expected to hold the line on violations of department rules and on corrupt practices.

Violations of department regulations and corruption are both serious threats to administrative authority. In the case of department regulations the threat is clear and direct. If officers are neglecting their duty, they are not available as needed; they are not under control, and this is a direct affront to the bureaucratic conception of professionalism that is so important to police managers. Moreover, violations of department regulations are *relatively* easy to deal with. Typically, officers are required to keep close track of their activity and maintain continuing contact via radio, whether in cars or portable, with the dispatcher.[88] Corruption is a less obvious threat and is more difficult to control, but it is important to police chiefs because pervasive corruption is a serious obstacle to discipline. So long as patrol officers know that their superiors are involved in corrupt practices, the opportunities to reject discipline with impunity are increased.[89] Corruption tends to generate a web of complicity.[90] More generally, police managers must live with the knowledge that they are vulnerable to charges of corruption, favoritism, and the like:

> Because police chiefs are broken by scandal, not crime, a new chief hired to put an end to scandal, will seek to put an end to the officers' discretion concerning what laws will and will not be enforced.[91]

To put this in slightly different fashion, corruption and violation of department rules run at cross purposes to any viable definition of the police mission. They are inconsistent with all notions of police professionalism. And they tend to stand in the way of mounting any sort of crime-attack strategy because they limit the effectiveness with which managers can mobilize and deploy police resources.

Conversely, police violence and incivility are much less objectionable to managers, and there are a number of reasons why managers will be reluctant to second-guess patrol officers on such matters. After all, managers have come up through the ranks, which means that they are basically sympathetic to "[t]he problem of having to make a quick decision in life-threatening circumstances."[92] Similarly, administrators share those values that lead officers to see force and intimidation as vital to asserting authority. Moreover, even if they do not accept the rank-and-file vision, administrators are aware of how central that vision is to the police officer's self-image and, accordingly, how much opposition will be occasioned by any efforts to second-guess officers who adopt a punitive orientation in carrying out their duty. As long, therefore, as force, incivility, or both are employed in the line of duty, administrators will be genuinely reluctant to intervene. While the professional administrator may be inclined in principle {142} to draw the line (as do Muir and his "Laconia" chief) between instrumental and expressive uses of force, that may well be a difficult and troublesome line to draw. Of course, when officers are simply on some frolic of their own, the chief will be more willing to act. Under those circumstances, the action contributes nothing to any crime-control objectives and is normally contrary to department regulations and, as such, an affront to administrative authority.[93]

After all is said and done, it seems unlikely that the politics of law and order is leading to a significant transformation of police practices. Those changes that have occurred have, moreover, probably done more harm than good to the cause of progressive policing. No doubt, many police managers have responded to the politics of law and order with a variety of crime prevention programs—some of which have undoubtedly paid lip service to the problems of police-community relations. But behind the facade of neighborhood crimewatch committees, a property identification program, and a corps of community service officers, the more basic trend has probably been a shift of police policy in perceptibly more punitive directions. This may not be uniformly the case. Much will depend on local conditions—the prevailing political culture, the effectiveness of the chief, the unity of the rank-and-file. But in all likelihood, the net effect of the politics of law and order has been increased rank-and-file discretion leading to heightened tensions, particularly in high-crime areas.

In some instances, the arrest rate has climbed as well. There is, however, no reason to believe that the rank-and-file, if left to their own devices, will have an appreciable impact on the street crime that worries most Americans. As we have seen, rank-and-file priorities differ significantly from those of the public. Moreover, when the police alienate the public, they cut themselves off from one of their most valuable sources of information about crime. Crime control and good police-community relations go hand in hand. The unhappy irony of the politics of law and order is that it promises to unleash forces that will make the battle against street crime gratuitously more difficult.

A similar picture emerges in the analysis that follows in Chapters 6 and 7 of the criminal courts, but there are interesting twists. The courts, too, tend to be resistant to reform as a result of well-entrenched patterns of practice. Still, because so many of the key personnel of criminal courts are elected, I would say that the courts are somewhat more permeable to law-and-order pressure than are the police. There is another significant difference. The pressures of the politics of law and order drive the police back toward an established tradition of punitive policing—toward the watchman style of "kicking ass."[94] The criminal courts do not have a {143} punitive tradition, and contrary to popular opinion, they actually work pretty well. The impact of the politics of law and order on the criminal courts is therefore especially unfortunate.

NOTES

1. James Baldwin, *Nobody Knows My Name* (New York: Dial, 1961), 65–66.

2. James Q. Wilson, *Thinking About Crime* (New York: Vintage, 1977), 100–102.

3. Charles E. Silberman, *Criminal Violence, Criminal Justice* (New York: Random House, 1978), 204–5.

4. Wilson, *Thinking About Crime*, 101.

5. William K. Muir, Jr., *Police: Streetcorner Politicians* (Chicago: University of Chicago Press, 1977), 18.

6. Ibid., 25–26.

7. Jonathan Rubenstein, *City Police* (New York: Ballantine, 1973), 218; italics added.

8. Listen to one of Joseph Wambaugh's veteran officers explaining to a rookie how he correctly spotted a suspect despite a misleading description over the police radio. "I don't honestly know how I knew. But I knew. At least I was pretty sure. The shirt wasn't red, but it wasn't green either. It was a color that could be called red by a fuzzy-eyed drunk. It was rusty brown. And Gandy [the suspect] was standing a little too casually there in the parking lot. He was too cool and he gave me too much of a 'I got nothing to hide' look when I was driving by and eyeballing everybody that could possibly be the guy. And when I came back around he had moved to the other side of the lot. He was still moving when I turned the corner but when he sees us he stops to show us he's not walking away. He's got nothing to hide. I know this means nothing by itself, but these are some of the little things. I just knew, I tell you." Joseph Wambaugh, *The New Centurions* (New York: Dell, 1970), 76; italics in the original.

9. Rubenstein, *City Police*, 341–42.

10. Ibid., 342.

11. Silberman, *Criminal Violence, Criminal Justice*, 215–16.

12. Wilson, *Thinking About Crime*, 107.

13. Rubenstein, *City Police*, 343.

14. Jerome H. Skolnick, *Justice Without Trial: Law Enforcement in a Democratic Society* (New York: Wiley, 1967), 129; italics in the original.

15. *New York Times*, 9 December 1974.

16. Ibid.

17. See also Clifford Karchmer, "Corruption Towards Performance: Goals and Operations in Proactive Law Enforcement" (Seattle, Wash.: Batelle Law and Justice Study Center, unpublished/undated).

18. Albert J. Reiss Jr., *The Police and the Public* (New Haven: Yale University Press, 1971), xiii.

19. Ibid., 155–63. These figures on violations of the law were based on reporting {144} by police officers as well as on observations. Not included were free meals and other minor favors.

20. Ibid., 164–69.

21. Ibid., 141–44.

22. As reported in Rodney Stark, *Police Riots: Collective Violence and Law Enforcement* (Belmont, Calif.: Wadsworth, 1972), 82.

23. Knapp Commission, *Report on Police Corruption* (New York: George Braziller, 1972). See, more recently, *New York Times*, 27 January 1983.

24. Herman Goldstein, *Police Corruption: A Perspective on Its Nature and Control* (Washington, D.C.: Police Foundation, 1975), 52. See also Antony E. Simpson, *The Literature on Police Corruption*, Vol. 1, *A Guide to Bibliography and Theory* (New York: John Jay Press, 1977).

25. U.S. Commission on Civil Rights, *Police Practices and the Preservation of Civil Rights* (Washington, D.C.: U.S. Government Printing Office, 1980). See also Arthur L. Kobler, "Police Homicide in a Democracy," *Journal of Social Issues* 31, no. 1 (1975): 163–84; and idem,

"Figures (and Perhaps Some Facts) on Police Killing of Civilians in the United States, 1965–1969," *Journal of Social Issues* 31, no. 1 (1975): 185–91.

26. Knapp Commission, *Report*, 5–7 and 170.

27. Carl Wertham and Irving Piliavin, "Gang Members and the Police," in *The Police: Six Sociological Essays*, ed. David J. Bordua (New York: Wiley, 1967), 57–62.

28. Reiss, *The Police and the Public*, 150. See also Michael Lipsky, *Street-Level Bureaucracy: Dilemmas of the Individual in Public Service* (New York: Russell Sage, 1980), 123.

29. Wilson, *Thinking About Crime*, 119–20. As Skolnick sees it, "a stereotyping perceptual shorthand is formed through which the police come to see certain signs as symbols of potential violence." See Skolnick, *Justice Without Trial*, 54.

30. Wilson, *Thinking About Crime*, 121.

31. See, generally, Hubert G. Locke and Jamual E. Walker, eds., "Institutional Racism and American Policing: A Special Report," *Social Development Issues* 4, no. 1 (Winter 1980). Raymond G. Hunt, "Combatting Institutional Racism in Police Departments: Application of a Problem-Remedy Strategy" (unpublished paper, 1981), presented to the U.S. Civil Rights Commission as part of a consultation on "Affirmative Action in the 1980's: Dismantling the Process of Discrimination"); and Nicholas Alex, *Black in Blue: A Study of the Negro Policeman* (New York: Appleton-Century-Crofts, 1969).

32. Reiss, *The Police and the Public*, 167.

33. This is, Reiss tells us, more a matter of class than race. Ibid., 155. Both black and white officers are, for example, more likely to use excessive force against their own race. Ibid., 147. However, given the overlap between high-crime and nonwhite areas, there are surely racial dimensions to these assignment practices.

34. James Garofalo, *Public Opinion About Crime: The Attitudes of Victims and Nonvictims in Selected Cities* (Washington, D.C.: National Criminal Justice Information and Statistics Service, 1977), 27–31.

35. Samuel Walker, *A Critical History of Police Reform: The Emergence of Professionalism* (Lexington, Mass.: Lexington, 1977), 56.

36. Ibid., ix–x. See also Skolnick, *Justice Without Trial*, 235–43. {145}

37. On this broader conception of professionalization, see Skolnick's discussion of Durkheim in ibid., 235.

38. Richard A. Stauffenberger, ed., *Progress in Policing: Essays on Change* (Cambridge, Mass.: Ballinger, 1980).

39. Margaret Levi, *Bureaucratic Insurgency: The Case of Police Unions* (Lexington, Mass.: Lexington, 1977).

40. Wilson, *Thinking About Crime*, 100–102. Wilson does not mention community relations programs in his discussion of crime attack, but such programs are part and parcel of progressive policing. On crime attack, see also James Q. Wilson and Barbara Boland, *The Effect of the Police on Crime* (Washington, D.C.: National Institute of Law Enforcement and Criminal Justice, 1979), 3–4.

41. Wilson and Boland, *The Effect of the Police on Crime*, 20.

42. Ibid., 4.

43. Ibid., 19.

44. See, generally, Lee P. Brown and Hubert Locke, "The Police and the Community," in Stauffenberger, *Progress in Policing*, 85–102.

45. Wilson, *Thinking About Crime*, 102–3.

46. *New York Times*, 12 July 1982. See also an earlier article on the creation of a "new division to combat robberies," *New York Times*, 5 March 1981.

47. Wilson and Boland, *The Effect of the Police on Crime*, 12.

48. Ibid., 3.

49. Ibid., 18–19.

50. James Q. Wilson and Barbara Boland, "The Effects of the Police on Crime: A Response to Jacob and Rich," *Law and Society Review* 16, no. 1 (1981–82): 164.

51. Ibid., 168.

52. Herbert Jacob and Michael J. Rich, "The Effects of the Police on Crime: A Rejoinder," *Law and Society Review* 16, no. 1 (1981–82): 171.

53. Wilson and Boland compare cities to one another, while Jacob and Rich look at changes in robbery rates in 9 cities over about a 30-year period. The controversy can be traced through the pages of the *Law and Society Review* as follows: James Q. Wilson and Barbara Boland, "The Effect of the Police on Crime," *Law and Society Review* 12 (Spring 1978): 367–90; Herbert Jacob and Michael J. Rich, "The Effects of the Police on Crime: A Second Look," *Law and Society Review* 15, no. 1 (1980–81): 109–22; Wilson and Boland, "A Response to Jacob and Rich," 165–69; and Jacob and Rich, "A Rejoinder" 171–72.

54. Wilson and Boland, *The Effect of the Police on Crime*, 18. A more convincing demonstration of the positive effects of proactive tactics (particularly suspicion stops) on street crime (particularly robbery) appeared too late to be incorporated into my analysis. See Gordon P. Whitaker, Charles David Phillips, Peter J. Haas, and Robert E. Worden, "Crime and Aggressive Patrol: Further Evidence on Deterrence," (Chapel Hill: Institute for Research in Social Science, unpub., n.d.)

55. Wilson, *Thinking About Crime*, 102.

56. Silberman, *Criminal Violence; Criminal Justice*, 213.

57. An increase in suspicion stops does not necessarily lead to increased dissatisfaction with the police, according to research which was reported too late to be {146} incorporated into my analysis. Indeed, young black males, in particular, responded positively to a more proactive style. The more proactive style evaluated in this research entailed relatively few suspicion stops, however. "Some neighborhoods had almost no suspicion stops, while officers in other neighborhoods averaged almost four such stops per forty hours." In other words, the most proactive officers made less than one stop per day on average. Gordon P. Whitaker, Charles D. Phillips, and Alisa A. Pollitz, "Aggressive Patrol: A Search for Side Effects," (Chapel Hill: Institute for Research in Social Science, unpub., n.d.)

58. Muir, *Police*, 38.

59. Ibid., 44–45.

60. This discussion of the nature of team policing comes primarily from William G. Gay, Jane P. Woodward, H. Talmadge Day, James P. O'Neil, and Carl J. Tucker, *Issues in Team Policing: A Review of the Literature* (Washington, D.C.: National Institute of Law Enforcement and Criminal Justice, 1977), 51 pp.

61. Ibid., 9.

62. Ibid., 12.

63. Ibid., 15.

64. On the rather checkered character of the programs and the efforts at assessment, see William G. Gay, H. Talmadge Day, and Jane P. Woodward, *Neighborhood Team Policing:*

National Evaluation Program, Phase 1 Summary Report (Washington, D.C.: National Institute of Law Enforcement and Criminal Justice, 1977), 45 pp.

65. Silberman, *Criminal Violence, Criminal Justice*, 249.

66. Ibid., 250. Michael K. Brown discovered comparable problems in Los Angeles and attributed it to a breakdown of central control. It is unclear whether sufficient training was provided or whether the incentive structure was altered. *Working the Street: Police Discretion and the Dilemmas of Reform* (New York: Russell Sage, 1981), 301–2.

67. Ibid.

68. Gay et al., *Neighborhood Team Policing*, 35–37.

69. Ibid. On the weaknesses of the New York program, see 37 and 40.

70. Ibid., 29.

71. Walker, *Critical History of Police Reform*, 8.

72. Silberman, *Criminal Violence, Criminal Justice*, 251–52.

73. Michael J. Rich, Robert L. Lineberry, and Herbert Jacob, "Police Policies and Urban Crime," in Herbert Jacob, Robert L. Lineberry, Anne M. Heinz, Michael J. Rich and Duane H. Swank, *Governmental Responses to Crime: Crime and Governmental Responses in American Cities* (Washington, D.C.: National Institute of Justice, 1982), 58–59.

74. Ibid., 61. These figures are for 1958–78.

75. Ibid., 74–75. These figures are for 1958–78.

76. Ibid., 55.

77. Ibid., 55–56.

78. Ibid., 56.

79. Ibid., Fig. 3.6, p. 68.

80. Ibid., 86. {147}

81. Ibid., 65.

82. Joseph P. Viteritti, *Police, Politics, and Pluralism in New York City: A Comparative Case Study*, Sage Professional Paper No. 03–004, Vol. 1 (Beverly Hill, Calif.: Sage, 1973), 28.

83. Stephen C. Halpern, "Police Employee Organizations and Accountability Procedures in Three Cities: Some Reflections on Police Policy-Making," *Law and Society Review* 8 (Summer 1974): 561–82.

84. Samuel Walker, *Popular Justice: A History of American Criminal Justice* (New York: Oxford University Press, 1980) 241.

85. Peter C. Buffum and Rita Sagi, "Philadelphia: Politics of Reform and Retreat," in *Crime in City Politics* ed. Ann Heinz, Herbert Jacob, and Robert L. Lineberry (New York: Longman, 1983), 122–26; and Marlys McPherson, "Minneapolis: Crime in a Politically Fragmented Arena," in ibid., 174–78.

86. Viteritti, *Police, Politics, and Pluralism*, 35–40.

87. James Q Wilson, *Varieties of Police Behavior. The Management of Law and Order in Eight Communities* (New York: Athereum, 1970), 195.

88. Rubenstein, *City Police*, 44–45 and 69–123.

89. Goldstein, *Police Corruption*, 10–11; and Simpson, *Literature on Police Corruption*, 74–76.

90. Knapp Commission, *Report*, 210.

91. Wilson, *Varieties of Police Behavior*, 181.

92. Lipsky, *Street-level Bureaucracy*, 30.

93. Even under these extreme circumstances, a rank-and-file backlash may develop. Consider, for example, the reaction to Seattle's widely respected chief, Patrick Fitzsimons, who dismissed two veteran officers for randomly discharging their guns in a minority residential area while intoxicated. Both officially and unofficially, the rank-and-file rose in opposition to the chief's firm discipline. See *Seattle Times*, 26 April 1981.

94. James Q. Wilson and George L. Kelling, "Broken Windows: The Police and Neighborhood Safety," *Atlantic Monthly* (March 1982), 35.

6

Equity in the Criminal Courts

The criminal courts have been subjected to much heavier and more wide-spread criticism than have the police. At first glance, the critics seem to be united in their attack on the arbitrary and capricious practices of criminal courts and in their demands for more uniformity and predictability. Closer scrutiny, however, reveals strong differences between liberal and conservative critics, who disagree on both diagnosis and remedy. To my way of thinking, the premise of irrationality, from which virtually all critics begin, is mistaken, and so none of the proposals for reform, whether liberal or conservative, is particularly persuasive.

The basic purpose of this chapter is to clear up the extensive misunder-standings about the quality of justice provided by the criminal courts. In so doing, I offer an alternative view that suggests that criminal courts function in a fair and purposeful fashion. This conclusion leaves open the more funda-mental questions of how well the policies of criminal courts serve the broader objectives of crime control and criminal justice. To a minor degree, those questions emerge in this chapter's discussion of the differences between liberal and conservative critics of the criminal courts. But it is really in Chapter 7 that the basic policy choices are addressed, along with the impact of the politics of law and order on those choices.

The current tendency to exaggerate the faults of our criminal courts can be best understood as a kind of overreaction to an unrealistic image of the criminal courts that was only recently abandoned. Traditionally, we have thought of criminal courts in almost exclusively legal terms. The business of the courts was understood to be the application of the rules of the criminal code to particular acts, and the principles of adversary justice {149} were thought to prevail in determinations of guilt and innocence. Criminal courts were, in short, considered the domain of lawyers who acted, or were at least supposed to act, in accordance with legal doctrine. Even on those occasions when no formal trial took place, it was assumed that the legal principles gov-erning formal trials were somehow applicable.

Only within the last fifteen years has a different kind of imagery come to dominate our thinking about the criminal courts. It is now broadly conceded that the principles of exchange have about as much to tell us about the criminal courts as do the principles of law.[1] Until recently, officials of criminal courts regularly denied that cases were resolved by plea bargaining—in much the same way that police chiefs still tend to deny that traffic ticket quotas are imposed on police officers. It is now generally conceded that plea bargaining is routine and that leverage and compromise play an important part in the disposition of cases. Legal rules are by no means irrelevant, but outcomes are decisively influenced by the power and priorities of the bargaining partners—the prosecuting attorney, the judge, the defense counsel, and the defendant.

It is one thing to acknowledge bargaining practices and quite another to accept them as legitimate. The Supreme Court's efforts to provide convincing constitutional justification for plea bargaining have surely failed miserably.* But the mere fact that the principles of adversary justice are compromised in criminal courts does not mean that the courts are inequitable and erratic. While bureaucratic practices developed by criminal courts are difficult to square with constitutional standards, and are suspect in other ways as well, the problems are of a different magnitude and, in fact, are different in kind from what critics would have us believe.

Let us, then, begin by considering the misunderstandings that cloud public perceptions of criminal courts and lead to misguided recommendations for reform. The latter portions of the chapter are devoted to a more upbeat and realistic, although by no means uncritical, assessment of criminal courts. All of this is preliminary to an analysis in Chapter 7 of the {150} responsiveness of criminal courts to the substantial pressures for reform generated by the many critics of criminal courts.

---

* The Supreme Court offers a contractual defense of plea bargaining. "Plea bargaining flows from 'the mutuality of advantage' to defendants and prosecutors each with his own reasons for wanting to avoid trial.... Defendants advised by competent counsel and protected by other procedural safeguards are presumptively capable of intelligent choice in response to prosecutorial persuasion and unlikely to be driven to false self-condemnation" (*Bordenkircher* v. *Hayes* 434 U.S. 363 [1979]). It is difficult to square this conclusion with the facts of the *Bordenkircher* case. The defendant was told that if he did not plead guilty to the charge of forging an $88 check and accept the prosecutor's offer of a five-year sentence (!), the habitual criminal statute would be invoked. The habitual criminal statute carried a mandatory life term after a third felony conviction. Since the forgery conviction would have been the defendant's third, the life sentence would have been automatic had he chosen to go to trial and lost. This is just what happened. Thus, forcing defendants to play "you bet your life" in a minor forgery case hardly seems consistent with a contractual interpretation of plea bargaining. While the *Bordenkircher* case is not necessarily typical, the contractual interpretation is inconsistent with any realistic understanding of plea bargaining, as will become clear in the course of this chapter.

MISPERCEPTIONS OF CRIMINAL COURTS

Critics on the right and left agree with James Q. Wilson's complaint that "many sentences being administered are, in the strict sense, irrational—that is, there is no coherent goal toward which they are directed."[2] At its most extreme, the implication is that decisions are rooted in corruption or based on pure whim. The severest critics would be inclined to take as typical the New York city judge who apparently made determinations of guilt by polling spectators in the courtroom and chose among sentencing alternatives by flipping a coin.[3] The more substantial objection is that judges and other participants in criminal courts bring their own idiosyncratic, even if serious and conscientious, standards to sentencing, thus leading to intolerable disparity.[4] A companion concern is that inconsistency is the inevitable consequence of an overburdened system that is using a variety of shortcuts to cope with an unmanageable workload.[5]

Reform, therefore, according to critics of various persuasions, requires procedures that reduce discretion within the criminal courts. The keystone of the so-called justice model is determinate sentencing, which entails a legislatively mandated schedule of sentences to which all court personnel must adhere. Most, perhaps all, determinate sentencing plans include some flexibility to permit carefully circumscribed exceptions for mitigating or aggravating circumstances.[6] But the essential goal remains to make sentencing standards public, proportional, and uniform. Justice will be served, so the argument runs, if punishment is meted out in proportion to the harm done and in an evenhanded fashion.

Taken this far, the justice model can surely enlist widespread support, but this apparent consensus cloaks substantial disagreements. Liberals contend that discretion has been traditionally employed to coerce defendants into pleading guilty—putting them under irresistible pressure to give up their rights to trial and accept whatever punishment suits the purposes of the powers that be.[7] Conservatives, in contrast, object to what they perceive as a permissive process. As they see it, defendants and their lawyers have a great deal of leverage, which is used to force unwarranted sentence reductions from our overcrowded and overprotective legal system.[8]

There are, in short, different policy agendas hidden beneath the justice model. The liberal view that criminal courts are coercive suggests reforms that will strengthen the rights of defendants to protect themselves from the whims of callous and self-interested officials. Conversely, if as the conservatives believe criminal courts are permissive, the path of reform leads {151} to more severe sentencing practices. As I see it, critics on the right and on the left misperceive both the problems and their solutions.

The Permissive Critique

The permissive critique of the criminal courts is based on the assumption that it is the defendant, not the state, that has the upper hand. Part of the problem stems directly from the expansion of due process rights by the Warren Court. As a result, van den Haag and others point out that defendants have at their disposal a plethora of legal rights as well as attorneys who know how to use these rights to maximize the defendants' chances of acquittal on some legal technicality or other.[9] Chief Justice Burger, while still a court of appeals judge, made much the same point:

> We have eager and extraordinarily bright young men going into criminal law. They make every motion in the book. It is good to have them, and there has been a lot of good effects from them. But there is also the tendency of defense lawyers today to make a "federal case" out of every trial.... Defense counsel generally are clogging the system by an excess of zeal.[10]

This problem is further exacerbated by the belief that many jurisdictions have far more cases than can be handled in a careful fashion, much less taken all the way to trial. The final step along the road to permissive sentencing is taken by judges who, according to Wilson, do "not believe that jail" deters crime and are therefore reluctant to incarcerate.[11]

Given these premises, it follows that the criminal courts are going to be permissive in general and, as Wilson points out, particularly permissive in high-crime periods. If there are insufficient personnel to take many cases to trial, defendants and their counsel can gain concessions by threatening to go to trial. Moreover, if judges are reluctant to incarcerate, the counter-threat of a heavier sentence following conviction in a formal trial is simply not credible. The final irony is that as the crime rate rises, so too does the bargaining power of the defendant, because an increase in crime normally results in a greater number of cases to be processed by the criminal courts.

> Though congested dockets are not the only reason for this practice, an increase in congestion increases the incentives for such bargaining and thus may increase the proportion of lighter sentences. For those who believe in the deterrence theory of sentencing, it is a grim irony: The more crime increases, the more the pressure on court calendars, and the greater the chances that the response to the crime increase will be a sentence decrease.[12]

Thus, defendants are in a position to manipulate the criminal courts to reinforce the rewards rather than the penalties of crime.

The empirical data seem, at first, to support the permissive critique. Although van den Haag provides no source for his claim that only 1 percent {152} of the crimes committed lead to imprisonment, comparable data are available.[13] Figures for 1965, compiled by Charles Silberman, reveal that only about 2 percent of crimes committed lead to imprisonment, and only about 9 percent of those arrested are sent to prison.[14] Wilson further fuels the fire with scattered data suggesting that convicted felons with previous records are frequently granted probation. "In Los Angeles County, for example, the proportion of convicted robbers with a major prior record who were sent to prison in 1970 was only 27 percent."[15] Robbery is, of course, the classic predatory crime. For other crimes, the rate of probation was still higher, according to the studies cited by Wilson.[16] As to trends in the 1960s, Wilson provides only a single example: 'In Boston the average penalty in heroin cases fell during the 1960s—at the very time heroin abuse was rising."[17]

While the figures are accurate, the inference about lenient attitudes among criminal court officials is not really justified. Notice, first, that the most alarming numbers—only 1 or 2 percent imprisonment—are based on crimes committed. Since many crimes go unsolved, it is hardly appropriate to draw any conclusions concerning permissive attitudes by using the crime rate as a baseline. Clearly, the responsibility of the criminal courts begins only once an arrest is made. With respect to arrests, Silberman points out that jail time, often served under worse conditions than those found in prisons, should be included in determining the rate of incarceration. When the two are combined, it turns out that roughly 40 percent (rather than 9 percent) of those arrested, 55 percent of those charged, and 58 percent of those convicted are incarcerated.[18] But the sharpest challenge to the permissive complaint of leniency is provided by a study conducted by the Vera Institute of all felony arrests in New York City in 1971. Once again the familiar pattern of deterioration occurs. The incarceration rate was 27 percent with only 5 percent of those arrested sentenced to "felony time"—that is, over one year.[19] A closer look indicates, however, that the critical factor accounting for deterioration of felony arrests is a prior relationship between the offender and the victim. In crimes where the victim and the offender were unknown to one another—that is, in crimes involving predatory strangers—the incarceration rate jumped to 65 percent in robbery cases with 32 percent serving felony time.[20]

While it is still possible to conclude that sentencing should be more severe, the Vera Institute study demonstrates that deterioration does not stem from a reluctance to punish dangerous criminals.[21] Officials do, it is true, respond less punitively to prior relationship crimes, but only insofar as these crimes do not involve the kind of predatory behavior that constitutes a threat to the social order.

> Judges and prosecutors, and in some instances police officers, were outspoken in their reluctance to prosecute as full-scale felonies some cases that erupted from quarrels between friends or lovers.... Sometimes the prosecutor argues that {153} a jury would never convict in such a case; sometimes the judge felt that it would serve no purpose to imprison the defendant and possibly

disrupt the relationship permanently, or to penalize heavily what
was clearly an unpremeditated over-reaction to a personal griev-
ance—especially if the injury was minor or the crime unlikely to
recur.[22]

More fundamentally, the deterioration of prior relationship crimes has more
to do with victims than with officials of the criminal courts. "The reluctance of
the complainants in these cases to pursue prosecution (often because they
were reconciled with the defendants or in some cases because they fear the
defendants) accounted for a larger proportion of the high rate of dismissal
than any other factor."[23] In other words, the primary cause of deterioration in
prior relationships crimes is not the lenient attitudes of judges and prosecutors but the unwillingness of victims to prosecute.

Silberman's analysis casts doubt on two other aspects of the leniency
hypothesis. He finds, first, no indication of increased leniency, at least up
through 1965. That is, the 1965 figures on which his analysis of deterioration is
based "go back more than a decade; there is no evidence that the courts have
become more lenient."[24] Moreover, when the 1965 findings are compared with
data from the 1920s in Chicago, Kansas City, and St. Louis, the rate of incarceration appears to be lower in the earlier period: 15 to 19 percent as opposed
to the 23 percent in 1965.[25] While these findings are not conclusive, they certainly suggest that there is reason to doubt the conventional wisdom that
criminal courts became soft on crime during the 1960s. Nor, according to
Silberman, does the exclusionary rule appear to be a significant source of
deterioration, as the permissive critique would have us believe, except in drug
cases and other crimes where there is no complainant because nobody feels
victimized.[26] Regardless of how one might feel about "victimless crime" or
about constitutional constraints on the police, it is not violations of drug,
gambling, and prostitution laws that are primarily responsible for engen-
dering fear. It is no doubt true that drug dealing can reach sufficient proportions to threaten normal activity in particular neighborhoods. Still, these
crimes, which amount to business transactions, do not in themselves amount
to predatory intrusions into our lives.

The Coercive Critique

Abraham Blumberg has been one of the most persistent and widely read
liberal critics of the criminal courts. His basic objection is summed up graphically, albeit extravagantly, in an image he draws from Anglo-American legal
history.

[P]ersons have sometimes been burned at the stake, drawn and
quartered, or pressed to death. This last mode of execution was
an excruciating style of {154} death employed especially in cases

where the individual refused to plead guilty or not guilty to an indictment. Nothing so appalling or violent has been used in the contemporary administration of criminal law. But the basic over-riding concern is still *a plea*, rather than anything more elaborate.... The methodology employed to get that plea has undergone the kind of subtle refinement and elaboration that only the modern features of formal organization can provide.[27]

More concretely, the argument of Blumberg and other liberals is that once arrested, those accused of crime are presumed to be guilty and then subjected to virtually irresistible pressures to plead guilty.

Borrowing from Erving Goffman, Blumberg describes "the moral career of the defendant" as a way of characterizing the pressures imposed on accused persons to get them to plead guilty.

[T]he accused is confronted by definitions of himself which reflect the various worlds of [those who mediate between the accused and the criminal courts]—yet are consistent for the most part in their negative evaluations of him. [They] have seized upon a wholly unflattering aspect of his biography to reinterpret his entire personality and justify their present attitude and conduct toward him. Even an individual with considerable personal and economic resources has great difficulty resisting pressures to redefine himself under these circumstances. For the ordinary accused of modest personal, economic, and social resources, the group pressures and definitions of himself are simply too much to bear.[28]

I take Blumberg's point to be not so much that innocent people come to think of themselves as factually guilty but that they come to believe that it is fruitless to fight against the label of guilt applied to them. Accordingly, they simply try to make the best of a bad situation. It is rather like the undergraduate student who aspires to a career in law or medicine but is continually confronted with grade evaluations in the C– to C+ range. No matter how strong the personal call to medicine or law may be, it quickly becomes apparent that entry into a professional school is out of reach.

The pressures brought to bear on the accused can be characterized more specifically. The presumption of guilt begins with the police who make the arrest and, as W. Boyd Littrell points out, who control the flow of information to the prosecutor.[29] For most defendants without the resources to conduct an independent investigation of the legal and factual circumstances, the case made by the police and the prosecutor must be accepted as a given, according to the coercive view. The defendant can be further pressured by multiple charges that the prosecution threatens to pursue toward heavier sentences should the accused insist on going to trial. Typically, according to Blumberg, everyone with whom the defendants come in contact becomes a party to these pressures, including defense counsel and the defendants' families.[30] For Blumberg, the practice of defense law is too often a "confidence game" in which the lawyers are {155} "double agents" who give the appearance of assiduous defense of their clients but whose real loyalties are to the criminal courts.[31] The defendant, from this perspective, is only an episode in the attorney's enduring relationships with the prosecutors and judges whose goodwill is essential to a successful career in the defense bar.

Some quantitative data lend a preliminary plausibility to the coercive critique, but the empirical case does not really stand up under careful scrutiny. Blumberg infers coercion from the high percentage of guilty pleas from indicted defendants. Roughly 80 percent of defendants in King County Court of Brooklyn, New York, from which he draws his 1960 to 1962 data base, were adjudged guilty in one way or another.[32]

> It would appear at least tentatively that once one is caught up in the system as an accused individual, there is little chance of escaping conviction.[33]

Support for the coercive critique can also be inferred from data indicating that the poor and minorities, who are most vulnerable to coercive tactics, tend to be treated more punitively. Such were the findings, for example, of a study conducted by a team of investigative reporters working for the *Philadelphia Inquirer*. Among their findings, based on Philadelphia data in 1971 and 1972, was that white defendants convicted for committing violent crimes received probation 58 percent of the time. The corresponding figure for blacks was 36 percent. Similarly, only 49 percent of whites sentenced to jail received sentences of seven months or longer. The corresponding figure for blacks was 69 percent.[34] But neither Blumberg's argument nor the *Inquirer* finding is conclusive.

At least two aspects of Blumberg's argument are open to question. He acknowledges but does not explain the tremendous deterioration occurring at the preliminary arraignment. Almost 70 percent of those originally arraigned escape felony indictment because charges are reduced or dismissed.[35] Of course, since he "knows" that overcharging is a common way of bringing pressure to bear on defendants, he simply interprets deterioration as evidence of coercion rather than permissive practice.[36] The other thing that Blumberg and liberal critics of criminal courts "know" is that defendants who go to trial end up with heavy sentences. Defendants are thus coerced into pleading guilty and giving up their constitutional right to a formal trial. On this matter, the empirical record is not clear. The extensive data collected by Eisenstein and Jacob in Baltimore, Chicago, and Detroit for 1972 indicate that going to trial was only a very minor factor in accounting for the sentences received by defendants.[37] As Brereton and Casper point out, however, these data indicate that the decision to go to trial does have some risk. Their own findings, drawn from robbery and burglary data in three California counties between 1974 and 1978, reveal that it is regularly the case that a greater proportion of those who go to trial receive prison sentences than do those who plead guilty.[38] It {156} is difficult to know what to make of all these data, which are compatible with different interpretations. My own inclination is to conclude that the empirical research provides only marginal evidence of coercion and, in and of itself, hardly demonstrates the purposeful and relentless pressure on which the coercive critique rests.

The empirical evidence with respect to racial bias is also equivocal. For a long time, it was taken as pretty much of a given that the criminal process was systematically biased against minorities and the poor. If so, it seems reasonable to infer coercive practices within the criminal courts. In other words, it seems reasonable to assume that white, wealthy defendants do better in criminal courts because they are insulated by more aggressive legal representation from the coercive pressures routinely imposed on poor and minority defendants. The problem with this interpretation is that recent research casts considerable doubt on the assumption that criminal courts are biased according to race and class.

The evidence of sentencing disparity that initially led to conclusions of bias in criminal courts tends to melt away, but does not disappear altogether, when the data are examined more closely. It turns out that it is not so much race and class as the nature of the crime and the past record of defendants that account for differential treatment. In other words, once comparisons are not simply between black and white or rich and poor defendants but, for example, between black and white defendants with comparable criminal records who have committed the same crime under similar circumstances, the result is substantial equality of treatment, at least with respect to race, on which there is the greatest amount of data. Typical of this line of research are the conclusions drawn by Eisenstein and Jacob: "We found race to have little effect on any portion of the felony disposition process that we studied."[39]

Nevertheless, Spohn, Gruhl, and Welch found that while blacks did not receive longer sentences than whites, blacks were substantially more likely to be imprisoned than whites. "Even after controlling for both legal and extra-legal factors, black males still were sentenced to prison five percent more often than white males."[40] The authors argue that this discrepancy is not negligible, in part because the stakes are so high for those who suffer the discrimination, but also because the 5 percent differential actually means that blacks are about 20 percent more likely to be imprisoned.

> Twenty-nine percent of convicted blacks, but only 24 percent of convicted whites, were sent to prison. Thus, black defendants are 20 percent more likely than white defendants to be incarcerated.[41]

Taken together, these data on bias in criminal courts suggest, once again, a much less coherently coercive system than Blumberg and others who embrace the coercive critique would have us believe. {157}

Summary

The data clearly indicate that criminal courts are not so crudely arbitrary as their critics charge. There is certainly no real evidence of the progressively lenient sentencing trends that were supposed to explain the rising crime rates of the 1960s and early 1970s. Similarly, the record clearly shows that the factors that influence the decisions of criminal courts are, for the most part, reasonable: the offense, the defendant's record, the circumstances of the crime. We have a much more acceptable system than critics on either side are willing to acknowledge.

The available findings therefore severely weaken the cases that can be made for both the permissive and the coercive critiques. It is true that partisans of the two critiques can still point to indications of permissiveness and coercion. Some deterioration in prior relationship crimes is, in fact, due to the unwillingness of judges and prosecutors to crack down. Similarly, there is quantitative (as well as qualitative) evidence that heavier sentences are levied against those who are unwilling to plead guilty. A certain amount of irresponsible behavior of both the coercive and permissive varieties can, no doubt, be found and may even be the norm in certain places and times. Nonetheless, the permissive and coercive critiques, in the final analysis, inappropriately transform worst-case scenarios into descriptive generalizations.

But what stands out most about the quantitative record is how inconclusive it is. Eisenstein and Jacob's research suggests, moreover, that the problem may not simply be a matter of getting better and more comprehensive data. The quality of their data seems very high indeed, and their methods were carefully worked out and applied. Yet, they graphically reveal that much of the variation in the criminal courts they studied remains unexplained.[42] The conclusion I am inclined to draw is that the complexity of the criminal courts is resistant to quantitative analysis. In the next section, I offer my own view of criminal courts, a view that is consistent with the quantitative data but not derived from them. Instead, I want to focus on what we know about the values and interests of the various participants in criminal courts.

BUREAUCRATIC JUSTICE

The coercive and permissive critiques are flawed by unrealistically unidimensional understandings of criminal court decision making. Does it really make sense to assume that judges, prosecutors, and defense counsel are doggedly determined to impose a plea of guilty on defendants, irrespective of the circumstances of the case, or are perfectly willing to allow dangerous criminals to escape punishment? Only with a remarkably simple or cynical sense of personal motivation and organizational and political forces can one respond affirmatively to those questions. {158}

The reality of the criminal courts seems a good deal more complex, as is strongly suggested by the quantitative data just considered. It is, moreover, a reality that is not nearly so bleak as the critics charge. I have always been struck by the considerable agreement between empirical researchers of the criminal courts and insiders who operate the system. The insiders seem to believe that criminal courts function in a responsible, if imperfect, fashion. This conclusion corresponds closely to the quantitative picture, which reveals neither erratic performance in general nor systematic coercion or mindless leniency in particular. My analysis discloses a coercive bias, but one that is different in kind and degree from the pure repression of the coercive critique. I am also inclined to believe that the shortcomings of criminal courts are more accurately viewed as symptoms of basic social problems than as institutional weaknesses as such—a position developed at the conclusion of this section.

The concept of bureaucratic justice worked out by Littrell provides the most persuasive account of how the participants in criminal process reconcile legal and bureaucratic forces. "Bureaucratic justice unites the presumption of guilt with the operational morality of fairness."[43] The presumption of guilt, an idea first introduced by Herbert Packer, is now accepted by virtually all observers as a definitive force in the operation criminal courts.[44] The operational morality of fairness is less widely understood and accepted. Its derivation can be traced at least back to David Sudnow's work on "normal crimes."[45] The precise formulation is, however, Littrell's own contribution, I believe. Each of these ideas and their operative implications are explored in detail and provide the structure for this section. Suffice it to say for the time being that, contrary to accepted adversarial principles, all participants in the criminal process behave as if a person who is arrested is probably guilty. Nevertheless, the coercive thrust of the presumption of guilt is softened somewhat by the operational morality of fairness that leads the participants to make certain that defendants get neither more nor less than is coming to them—that defendants, in other words, get their due.[46]

The one ingredient missing from Littrell's interpretation of criminal courts is the political accommodation that must be made by judges and prosecutors. Accommodations to the political mandate are, of course, central to the study of the politics of law and order and are considered in the next chapter. First, let us reinterpret the criminal courts as an exercise in bureaucratic justice.

The Presumption of Guilt

The presumption of guilt is the key concession made by the participants in criminal process to organizational exigencies. "The center of gravity for

{159} the process" is, in this way, shifted to "the early administrative fact-finding stages" and the more cumbersome "adjudicative fact-finding is reduced to a minimum."[47]

> The supposition is that the screening processes operated by the police and prosecutors are reliable indicators of probable guilt. Once a man has been arrested and a determination has been made that there is enough evidence of guilt to permit holding him for further action, then all subsequent activity directed toward him is based on the view that he is probably guilty.[48]

Indeed, "all subsequent activity" is directed at obtaining a guilty plea and thus avoiding a trial. Given the predominance of guilty pleas in criminal courts across the country, the presumption of guilt seems to serve its purposes, as Packer sees them.

The array of organizational interests served by guilty pleas is so imposing that it is easy to understand why the practice of plea bargaining tends to prevail over even very insistent currents of reform. Plea bargaining reduces uncertainty, which weighs so heavily on everyone in criminal process, including defendants. Neither the time spent in trial nor its outcome can ever be predicted in advance with any real sense of assurance. Plea bargaining substitutes the routine for the indeterminate, and as Eisenstein and Jacob point out, attorneys who mislead or do not keep their promises are punished.[49] Of course, plea bargaining also saves time and does so in a way that reconciles the ostensibly competing interests of all the parties. The prosecutor gets a high conviction rate and/or avoids losses. Pressure is taken off the judge's calendar, thus providing more time for the most problematic cases. Defense counsel spend less time on each case—an advantage to the overworked public defender as well as to most private attorneys, who can charge more modest fees to their not particularly affluent clients. Defendants are served insofar as the guilty plea results in a lesser sentence than might have been handed out following a formal trial. Even the police are served by guilty pleas. Because they are the primary source of information and understand the legal formalities, the police "make the cases"—that is, they exercise effective control over the bargain that is finally struck.[50] Plea bargaining, in short, allows cases to be handled more predictably, expeditiously, and harmoniously.

The presumption of guilt and legality are not mutually exclusive, although the quality of law that emerges is clearly suspect. Legal standards and procedures are built into the institutional structures of criminal courts and are reinforced by the fact that these structures are controlled by legal professionals as well as by the possibility that cases may be appealed. Legal standards are clearly compromised, however, by the presumption of guilt, which creates what Littrell refers to as a "bureaucratic inversion of legal authority."[51] One way to get a sense of the "quasi-legal" character of plea bargaining is to think in terms of a legal continuum with the police {160} encounter at one end and the formal trial at the other. Plea bargaining tends to fall near the mid-point of this continuum.

The proceedings leading up to a guilty plea are conducted in a setting that is both better structured and more legalized than the typical police encounter. Charges are filed, and evidence presented by the police is screened by the prosecution and is open to scrutiny by the defense. Negotiations are removed in terms of both time and place from the original confrontation between the police officer and the suspect. The protagonists are represented by agents who are lawyers and are experienced at routinizing conflict. Finally, the possibility of a formal trial casts a legal shadow over the proceedings. At the least, then, law plays a role in cooling the conflict and channeling it into regularized procedures.

On the other hand, the professionals do not define their roles in strictly legal fashion—that is, in adversarial terms. The formal trial institutionalizes such principles of adversary justice as judicial and jury neutrality, argument and conflict between opposing counsel, and strict evidentiary standards. Co-operation and efficiency are subordinated to the tedious practices of adversary justice. Bureaucratic justice, in contrast, involves opposing counsel working in concert, often together with the judge, in a fashion that short-circuits adversary principles and evades the complications of a formal trial.[52]

The inversion of legal authority, which is, according to Littrell, the hall-mark of bureaucratic justice and a natural consequence of the presumption of guilt, lodges authority at the bottom rather than at the top of the legal hierarchy. Prosecutors screen cases, but in a pro forma sort of way with very limited objectives. "Prosecutors were more concerned with trial readiness ...than with a full review of the work of lower levels of the organization of prosecution."[53] Review is primarily directed at establishing legal guilt: will the case stand up in court? Littrell does not consider the role of defense counsels, but it is safe to say that they have neither the time nor the resources to conduct an independent investigation and generally acquiesce in the prosecu-torial assessment of the facts.

It would be wrong to write this lowering of legal standards off to bureau-cratic expediency, as the coercive critique implies. Screening is circumscribed by the widely shared "truth" that the overwhelming majority of defendants are actually guilty. I do not think that one can overemphasize the strength and influence of this consensus. But regardless of the purity of the motives that sustain the presumption of guilt, we are still entitled to ask whether it is justified and what impact it has on the quality of justice. But before drawing any conclusions, let us consider the second component of bureaucratic justice, the operational morality of fairness. {161}

The Operational Morality of Fairness

Standing alone, the presumption of guilt serves the organizational in-terests of criminal courts very nicely, in that everyone seems to benefit from maximizing the number of guilty pleas. But the presumption of guilt also lends some credence to the critics' charge that the whole process is arbitrary. Because it meets everyone's needs so well, in other words, there is an obvious danger that the guilty plea will become an end in itself. Would there not be a strong temptation to do whatever is necessary to avoid a trial, even if that meant coercing or coddling defendants?

The presumption of guilt does not stand alone but is tempered by the operational morality of fairness. Sudnow explains just how fairness is incor-porated into bureaucratic justice.[*]

> Both the P.D. and D.A. are concerned to obtain a guilty plea whenever possible and thereby avoid a trial. At the same time, each party is concerned that the defendant "receive his due." The reduction of offense X to Y must be of such a character that the new sentence will depart from the anticipated sentence for the original charge to such a degree that the defendant is likely to plead guilty to the new charge and, at the same time, not so great that the defendant does not "get his due."[54]

Both the research record and the logic of the situation indicate that there is such a search for fairness. Working out a fair sentence serves both individual values and organizational interests. On the one hand, attention to fairness allows the parties to assuage their personal and professional consciences; it provides reassurance that they are behaving in a responsible fashion. On the other hand, the process of determining fairness is, as we shall see, routinized in a way that promotes predictability and stability in the criminal courts.

What standards of fairness are employed? Those who offer the permissive critique complain that the punishment should fit the crime, and they charge that bureaucratic justice goes astray in tailoring the punishment to the criminal. There is some truth to this charge, but *not* to the inference drawn from it that sentencing is arbitrary.

The search for fairness involves attention to both crime and criminal. The seriousness of the crime is an important factor, although it is more the in-trinsic quality of the criminal act than the legal definition that guides the par-ties.[55] Still the calculation seems pretty straightforward.

---

[*] Of course the first step in being fair to defendants is to establish procedures that promote reliable determinations of guilt and innocence, but as I have indicated, the presumption of guilt reflects, for better or worse, the faith that the professionals have in existing pro-cedures.

Officials regarded bad acts that involved violence or the threat of violence against persons to be the most serious form of misconduct.... A less serious {162} category of offenses consisted of crimes (1) against persons in which the possibility of violence was remote and (2) that involved relatively large amounts of property.... The least serious crimes were technically indictable offenses that officials believed involved relatively benign bad acts. Shoplifting was such an offense, even though the value of stolen property might be a few hundred dollars.[56]

More complex and elusive is the second determinant of a fair sentence: "the sinisterness" of the offender's character. If the offender is really a "bad guy," a heavy sentence is warranted. If the offender is only a guy "headed for trouble," a lighter sentence is deemed reasonable. Finally, there are the "basically good people in trouble.... The primary concern of officials who dealt with these benign characters," Littrell discovered, "was to impress upon them that they were truly in criminal trouble where they did not belong." Accordingly, verbal warnings were deemed sufficient.[57] The line between character and crime is somewhat blurred since there is a tendency to make character judgments, in part, on the circumstances of the crime. Was it accidental in some measure? Was there gratuitous violence? Generally speaking, however, character judgments are based primarily on the offender's demeanor and past record.[58]

Taking both crime and character into account, a sentence is then worked out. While Littrell offers a more elaborate and systematic presentation of this process than do most other researchers, there is general agreement on the outlines of the process. Indeed, it is a kind of common-sense solution to the problems of sentencing and can be described in a much less formal fashion. Judge Justin Ravitz of Detroit, interviewed in a study by Willard Gaylin, puts it this way:

I've gotten into situations where perhaps I've given some minimal time to a junky who's not assaultive, but he's got four or five previous arrests; he's been on probation; he violated probation. Obviously, if he has proven unresponsive to more sensible programs, then I might give some sentence. I'll try to give him house time as opposed to prison time.... Then I'd put him on probation and add some probationary conditions, hoping to jolt him so he'll be more receptive toward treatment. But that's the persistent violator of property. The persistent violator of people, the person of violence, and so on, I put away. To protect society I'd put that person away.[59]

There are, at least, a couple of interesting things about this formulation. One sees, first, the same balancing of crime and character discussed by Littrell, along with roughly the same standards of judgment: distinctions between petty and serious crimes, based largely on whether and to what extent violence against people was involved, and parallel distinctions on whether the offender seemed incorrigible, dangerous, or both. It is also worth noting that although Judge Ravitz's approach to sentencing is fairly typical, he is an avowed Marxist, thus suggesting a wide range of agreement among judges on sentencing principles. {163}

But agreement on principles does not necessarily preclude disparity in practice. It is, for example, possible to agree on the circumstances that justify a heavy sentence but disagree on the dividing line between heavy and light sentences. Gaylin discovered just such problems in his intensive interviews with a wide variety of judges from different sections of the country, with different ideological preferences, working in different parts of the judicial hierarchy. He was clearly appalled by the way these differences were reflected in sentencing standards. The conclusion he understandably drew from this research was that there is an "awful inequity inherent in our current sentencing system."[60]

Gaylin's findings cannot be taken at face value, however, largely because of the wide variety of judges he chose to interview. At most, his research suggests that there is disparity among jurisdictions, but this neither confirms the charges that sentencing practices are arbitrary nor leads to the conclusion that reforms should be undertaken. As Silberman points out, "disparity is an inevitable consequence of the fact that each state (and in many states, each community) has its own autonomous system of courts with jurisdiction over state and local crimes. That autonomy, in turn, means that sentences will reflect different state and local attitudes."[61]

Conversely, there seems to be relatively little disparity within jurisdictions, and what is more, there do seem to be informal norms operative. "Sentencing disparities within cities are not," according to Eisenstein and Jacob, "a fundamental problem."[62] The informal norms, Silberman tells us, allow the professionals to work in a predictable environment.[63] Consider also Littrell's findings:

> One chief of detectives admitted that there were unforeseeable factors that might alter cases. However, he estimated that he could accurately predict the outcome of "about 90%" of the cases he sent to the prosecutor's office.[64]

And is this not precisely what is to be expected, given the organizational incentives that support plea bargaining? The whole point is to develop a relatively efficient system for processing cases, and only widely shared principles and practices are consistent with that objective. Without informal guidelines, known to the professionals and generally adhered to, each case would become the occasion for lengthy bargaining. With such guidelines, routine cases may be treated expeditiously, and a bargaining framework is provided for the problematic cases.

But if informal and reasonably equitable norms exist, how are we to account for the failure of quantitative researchers to identify the key variables that explain sentencing decisions? While quantitative research seems to have established reasonably well that class and race do not explain much of the variation in sentences, this research sheds very little light on how sentencing decisions are constructed. As I have written elsewhere about Eisenstein and Jacob's research: "Time and again the {164} authors find themselves able to account for only a small portion of the variation in the outcomes they analyze."[65] Douglas Maynard, after looking broadly at the available research, comes to the same conclusion. "[W]hen researchers do find variables which have a significant effect, they do not explain much variance in sentencing out-comes."[66] What are we to make of all this? Are the insiders just kidding them-selves? If not, why has the quantitative research proven so inconclusive?

Maynard argues that statistical models that specify a laundry list of variables and test for their significance are much too mechanical. They "posit actors who are 'cultural dopes,' not active agents who engage in judgmental work as they produce decisions."[67] In assessing the character of the defendant, race, class, or both may be deemed relevant, but so too may be family status or fluency in English. Then, there are the various biographical details that provide insight into, for example, the meaning of, and the justification for, punishment in the lives of defendants. Moreover, "neither demographic nor biographical details stand alone," Maynard tells us; "they are contextually interrelated."[68] I take this to mean that the negotiations themselves define the context that enables everyone to make sense out of the demographic and bio-graphical details. Given the subtlety and complexity of this process, it stands to reason that insiders familiar with the rules of the game would find senten-cing predictable and equitable, while quantitative researchers working with discrete demographic variables would not make much headway.[69]

However one might feel about this way of doing things, it seems clear that sentencing practices are in no sense of the term irrational—that is, without rhyme nor reason and disparate almost by definition. Sentences are, instead, based on reasoned decisions rooted in understandings of right and wrong that are widely shared by criminal court professionals working in their respective jurisdictions. And these understandings become rather like un-written rules for the criminal courts.

The Interstitial Biases of Bureaucratic Justice

Perhaps the biggest challenge in a discussion of the shortcomings of bur-eaucratic justice is to maintain a sense of proportion. My own position is that while criminal courts are not *systematically* biased along lines of class or race, there is a marginal and idiosyncratic bias against the lower strata of the society. At the heart of my argument are three simple propositions: (1) "Mistakes" can occur both when guilt is determined and when sentencing decisions are made; (2) these mistakes stem, in part, from social and cultural discontinuities that tend to work against the lower strata; (3) financial resources play an important role in determining which defendants are able to resist the carrots and sticks of the criminal courts, {165} thus influencing the likelihood that errors will be corrected. Each of these points is developed in the pages just ahead, but this entire discussion rests on the premise that mistakes are the exception, not the rule, and it is for this reason that I see bias as marginal and idiosyncratic rather than central.

The *presumption of guilt* lends a pro forma quality to the initial phases of bureaucratic justice, which must answer three distinct but related questions.

1. Is the defendant factually guilty? Factual guilt turns on the behavior of the defendant and, more specifically, on whether it corresponds to the claims of the police.

2. Is the defendant legally guilty? Legal guilt focuses on the circumstances of the arrest and, more specifically, on whether they meet legal and constitutional standards.

3. How strong is the prosecutor's case? Here the problem is one of marshalling sufficient evidence to convince a judge or jury beyond a reasonable doubt.

The first two questions have to do with what actually happened, and answers depend, in part, on judging the credibility of the police and defendants. The third question looks ahead to an assessment of courtroom tactics and strategy. Only the third question is subjected to careful scrutiny, and therein lies the problem.

Criminal court professionals believe that the overwhelming proportion of defendants are factually guilty; the professionals are, moreover, inclined to accept the police account of the circumstances of the arrest. It is also true that criminal court professionals think that it is a simple matter to separate the "dead bang" cases, which should be quickly pleaded, from the "reasonable doubt" cases, which require more attention and perhaps a trial.[70] Even Jerome Skolnick, a generally critical observer of criminal courts, has expressed great confidence in the "expert estimates" of defense counsel to make this crucial distinction.

> It may not be so easy to predict the outcome of a game between the Green Bay Packers and the Chicago Bears, but it does not require an expert to know either the Bears or the Packers could defeat the Harvard eleven on any given afternoon. Many criminal cases are of this order of predictability before trial.[71]

Thus, as Skolnick and most defense counsel see it, the presumption of guilt and the resultant pressures to plead develop only when they are warranted.

But in what sense are defense counsel, or prosecutors for that matter, experts at determining what actually happened during the crime or in the course of the arrest? It is primarily legal expertise that lawyers have at their disposal—the kind of expertise that enables them to evaluate the strength of the case against the defendant and predict the outcome of a trial. Both {166} prosecutors and defense counsel have an interest in enhancing this kind of expertise, and it is understandable that they focus their energies on this point in criminal process. But the strength of the case is ultimately tied to the facts, which are the province of the police, who have a stake in making the arrest stick. Lawyers are ordinarily without an independent assessment of the facts when they sort out the "dead bang" and "reasonable doubt" cases. Indeed, an independent inquiry into the circumstances of the case will be undertaken only *after* it has been decided that there is a reasonable doubt about the defendant's guilt.

The crucial expertise on which attorneys rely, then, is the expertise required to size up the reliability of the defendant and the police officers involved in the case. If a mistake is made at this stage, the attorney's legal expertise becomes largely irrelevant; he is likely to undertake at most a halfhearted defense of an insistent client or, as is more likely, to convince the client to capitulate. There is no way of knowing conclusively how reliable attorneys are at sizing up defendants and their cases. The only research I have seen, a participant observation study of the Seattle Public Defender's office, indicated that the initial assessment of defense counsel was wrong in twelve of the fifteen cases investigated.[*] I am reluctant to base any conclusions on this one unreplicated bit of research and am inclined to concede a considerable measure of expertise to experienced defense attorneys.

Nonetheless, without facts at their disposal, defense counsel have to make their determinations on impressions made by the defendants. These impressions may well be influenced by misunderstandings that are a function of the social distance that separates middle-class professionals from the lower strata of society. Consider, for example, the mistrust and deception frequently encountered by public defenders among their clients, who believe that you only get what you pay for. Their suspicion of free legal services may well turn out to be a self-fulfilling prophecy as the attorney responds in kind to the client's indifference or hostility.[72] The whole setting is pregnant with the possibility of misunderstanding rooted in problems of communication and cultural stereotyping.

---

[*] This study was made by a law student, Albert J. Velarde, temporarily employed as an investigator in the Public Defender's office. He conducted detailed investigations—checking on the circumstances, interviewing witnesses, and so on. Of fifteen cases deemed "losers" by the public defender after the initial interview, "[t]en cases resulted in dismissals before trial, two were acquitted after trial, one was convicted and two pled guilty to reduced charges." "The Defense Investigator in an Adversarial System" (unpub. 1976), 35.

The operational morality of fairness opens the door even more widely to the same kind of problems. There is, it is true, nothing pro forma about efforts to work out the correct disposition of cases and assign the appropriate sentence. These decisions, as the Vera Institute research indicates, frequently lead to a dismissal or reduction of charges. But {167} regardless of how sincere and conscientious their efforts may be, criminal court professionals are at this stage making decisions that may easily be biased by misunderstandings, preconceptions, or both.

Determinations of the seriousness of the crime and the character of the offender are based, in part, on values that may not be shared by all segments of the society and on assumptions about the offender's motivation that are not easily accessible across the social boundaries that often divide lawyers from their clients. Mather, for example, reports a sentencing dispute that turned on whether the defendant "was 'a professional burglar' as the D.A. claimed," in which case the state prison was appropriate, or "'just an old drunk' as his attorney argued," and thus better suited to the county jail.[73] More generally, Sudnow tells us that sentencing decisions are keyed to understandings about "modes of criminal activity, ecological characteristics of the community, patterns of daily slum life, psychological and social biographies of offenders, criminal histories and features; in sum, practically tested criminological wisdom."[74]

The point is not that these are necessarily inappropriate ways to assess sentences. On the contrary, I am inclined to agree with Feeley and Maynard that these kinds of decisions are necessary in order to do justice, and an argument to this effect is presented in Chapter 8.[75] There is, however, no particular reason to believe that lawyers have any special expertise at making judgments that may rather easily be biased by discontinuities in the society.

Bias against the lower strata is compounded by their vulnerability to the pressures of criminal process. The faith that insiders have in administrative fact-finding may be at least partially attributable to the wishful thinking of professionals who have a stake in maximizing the number of guilty pleas. Defendants who can afford to hire top-notch attorneys need not partake of that faith. Affluent clients are in a position to demand and pay for an independent investigation of the circumstances of the crime. They need not acquiesce in the presumption of guilt. It is also reasonable to believe that defense attorneys who frequently employ an adversarial response are less likely to be influenced by the prevailing "criminological wisdom" in sizing up their clients and bargaining for sentences. The point I am making, it should be underscored, has at least as much to do with the equity of bureaucratic justice as with its reliability. Even if the presumption of guilt and the operational morality of fairness were beyond reproach, it would still remain true that defendants from the lower strata would benefit from a lesser measure of protection than those who can afford the best hired gun available.

But if criminal courts are really biased against the lower strata, why does this bias not appear more clearly in the massive body of empirical research accumulated in recent years? I suppose the first point to be made in answer to that question is that there are some signs of bias. If the {168} research record is weak and equivocal on these matters, it is because, as I suggested at the outset of this discussion, the biases are marginal and idiosyncratic rather than central and systematic.

Consider the issue of legal representation, which I have suggested accounts for much of the bias against the lower strata of society in criminal courts. While it is, generally speaking, true that the poor are not as well represented as those who can afford private counsel, there are exceptions and perhaps compensatory factors as well. Leaving aside the relatively few legal luminaries who can be regularly expected to resist the presumption of guilt in an aggressive manner, there is probably not a great deal of difference between public defenders who serve the poor and most private attorneys.[76] Indeed, my own impression is that a higher proportion of public defenders may be sensitive to cultural cleavages and therefore better able to monitor the character tests that are integral to the operational morality of fairness. It is, of course, essential that defense counsel understand their clients well enough to protect them against invidious cultural stereotyping.[77] It may also be the case that some lower-status defendants who mistrust their attorneys may be sufficiently experienced in the ways of criminal courts to drive relatively hard bargains on their own, as, for example, Casper's respondents, who claimed that as a result of his wheeling and dealing he had "made out like a bandit."[78] Such bias as is to be found in criminal courts may simply vary in quality, direction, and intensity in ways that confound the efforts of quantitative researchers to document its presence.

More fundamentally, only if we were to think of criminal courts as an overt conspiracy against the poor and minorities would it make sense to expect bias against the lower strata to play a central role in the disposition of cases. My argument has been that criminal courts are oriented toward bureaucratic efficiency and have a significant commitment to doing justice. Singling out the have-nots in society for preemptory treatment would serve neither purpose.[79] The injustice of such practices is, of course, manifest. Bureaucratically, the problem is to find an efficient way of sorting out defendants. Since such a large portion of the defendants are drawn from the lower strata, the distinction between haves and have-nots would not be particularly useful as a sorting device. Once again, this is not to say that there is no bias in the criminal courts. The point is simply that criminal courts are a good deal more benign than their critics would have us believe.

THE POLITICS OF LAW AND ORDER

There are really two dimensions to the critique leveled against criminal courts by proponents of the justice model.[80] The ostensible complaint is that the discretionary setting of criminal courts has led to unequal treatment and hence to injustice. It is clear, however, that the dispute {169} between criminal courts and their critics has at least as much to do with *values* as with *justice*. How else are we to explain the conflict between liberals, who believe criminal courts are too tough on defendants, and conservatives, who detect untoward permissiveness? This dispute simply mirrors different understandings of the causes and consequences of crime that divide the mainstream.

So far, my rejoinder to the critics has been entirely to the charges of injustice that rather tenuously unify liberals and conservatives. Whatever may be their faults, criminal courts, I have argued, make a conscientious effort to ascertain guilt and levy equitable sentences. Within the constraints of an inherently discretionary process, criminal courts function in an essentially predictable and equitable fashion. Given the several policy options and the infinite variety of circumstances surrounding each case, efforts to impose uniformity seem more likely to undermine than to advance the cause of justice in criminal process. If justice involves treating like cases alike, then discretion is an essential condition of justice.

In the next chapter, policy issues are taken up more directly, and the problems of injustice recede into the background. The main focus is on the substantial impact of justice model reforms on operative policy. While not inherently punitive, it should come as no surprise that the law-and-order political climate has pushed the justice model in practice in a distinctly punitive direction. State legislative reform in the 1970s, for example, combined reduced discretion with tougher sentences.[81] More surprising is the permeability of criminal courts to these punitive pressures. There is, after all, no reason to believe that insiders have been sympathetic to the reforms associated with the justice model. Quite the contrary. Resistance to changes in established practices can be taken pretty much for granted, as I argued with respect to the police. The justice model is, moreover, particularly unwelcome because it restricts discretion and is based on the mistaken impression that criminal courts are irresponsible and inequitable. Nonetheless, the extensive overcrowding of prisons and jails throughout the country provides ample, if impressionistic, evidence of the impact of punitive pressures on operative policies. It is now time to consider why and with what consequences criminal courts have yielded to the politics of law and order.

NOTES

1. Malcolm M. Feeley, "Two Models of the Criminal Justice System: An Organizational Perspective," *Law and Society Review* 7 (Spring 1973): 407–25.

2. James Q. Wilson, *Thinking About Crime* (New York: Vintage, 1977), 184.

3. *New York Times*, 29 May 1982. See, more generally, Howard James, *Crisis in the Courts*, rev. ed. (New York: McKay, 1971). {170}

4. Willard Gaylin, *Partial Justice: A Study of Bias in Sentencing* (New York: Vintage, 1975).

5. For a review of this argument, see Malcolm M. Feeley, *The Process Is the Punishment* (New York: Russell Sage Foundation, 1979), 244–47.

6. Andrew von Hirsch, *Doing Justice: Report of the Committee for the Study of Incarceration* (New York: Hill & Wang, 1976).

7. Abraham S. Blumberg, *Criminal Justice: Issues and Ironies*, 2nd ed. (New York: New Viewpoints, 1979), Chap. 9.

8. Ernest van den Haag, *Punishing Criminals* (New York: Basic Books, 1975).

9. Ibid., 289.

10. Donald McDonald, "Criminal Justice," in *The Establishment and All That* (Santa Barbara, Calif.: Center for the Study of Democratic Institutions, 1970), 175.

11. Wilson, *Thinking About Crime*, 185.

12. Ibid., 186.

13. Van den Haag, *Punishing Criminals*, 163.

14. Charles Silberman, *Criminal Violence, Criminal Justice* (New York: Random House, 1978), 258–59.

15. Wilson, *Thinking About Crime*, 194.

16. Ibid., 184.

17. Ibid., 185.

18. Silberman, *Criminal Violence, Criminal Justice*, 260–61.

19. Vera Institute of Justice, *Felony Arrests: Their Prosecution and Disposition in New York City's Courts*, rev. ed. (New York: Longman, 1981), 1.

20. Ibid., 68.

21. Silberman, *Criminal Violence, Criminal Justice*, 265.

22. Vera Institute, *Felony Arrests*, 136.

23. Ibid., 135; italics added.

24. Silberman, *Criminal Violence, Criminal Justice*, 136.

25. Ibid., 261–62.

26. Ibid., 264. In crimes involving sellers and buyers rather than victims and victimizers, the police are more likely to engage in illegal activity because arrests are so difficult without a complainant.

27. Blumberg, *Criminal Justice*, 190; italics in the original.

28. Ibid., 202–3.

29. W. Boyd Littrell, *Bureaucratic Justice: Police Prosecutors, and Plea Bargaining* (Beverly Hills, Calif.: Sage, 1979), 173. See also Herbert L. Packer, *The Limits of the Criminal Sanction* (Stanford, Calif.: Stanford University Press, 1968), 160.

30. Blumberg, *Criminal Justice*, 203.

31. Ibid., 242–46.

32. Ibid., 189. Silberman's national figures for 1965 indicate an even higher proportion, 95 percent. See his *Criminal Violence, Criminal Justice*, 259.

33. Blumberg, *Criminal Justice*, 173.

34. Donald L. Barlett and James B. Steele, *Crime and Injustice: A Series on the Breakdown in Criminal Justice—the Jailing of the Innocent, Freeing of the Guilty* (Philadelphia: Philadelphia Inquirer, 1973), 5.

35. Blumberg, *Criminal Justice*, 189. {171}

36. Ibid., 194.

37. James Eisenstein and Herbert Jacob, *Felony Justice: An Organizational Analysis of Criminal Courts* (Boston: Little, Brown, 1977), 270.

38. David Brereton and Jonathan D. Casper, "Does It Pay to Plead Guilty? Differential Sentencing and the Functioning of Criminal Courts," *Law and Society Review* 16, no. 1 (1981–82): 56–61.

39. Eisenstein and Jacob, *Felony Justice*, 284. See also the excellent review article by John Hagan, "Extra-legal Attributes and Criminal Sentencing: An Assessment of Sociological Viewpoint," *Law and Society Review* 8 (Spring 1974): 357–83.

40. Cassia Spohn, John Gruhl, and Susan Welch, "The Effect of Race on Sentencing: A Re-Examination of an Unsettled Question," *Law and Society Review* 16, no. 1 (1982–82): 85.

41. Ibid., 83.

42. Eisenstein and Jacob, *Felony Justice*. See figures on pp. 296, 236, 240, 242, 277 and 283. The authors are seldom able to explain more than half the variation and frequently able to explain around 20 percent or less.

43. Littrell, *Bureaucratic Justice*, 153.

44. Packer, *Limits of the Criminal Sanction*, 160.

45. David Sudnow, "Normal Crimes: Sociological Features of the Penal Code in a Public Defender's Office," *Social Problems* 12 (Winter 1965): 255–76.

46. My impression is that Littrell, *Bureaucratic Justice*, sees this combination as a good deal more coercive than I do, and his overall analysis may be seen as part of the coercive critique. While I am far from uncritical of the presumption of guilt and the operational morality of fairness, whether considered individually or in combination, the problems are less systematic and more elusive and subtle than is implied by the coercive critique.

47. Packer, *Limits of the Criminal Sanction*, 162.

48. Ibid., 160.

49. Eisenstein and Jacob, *Felony Justice*, 27–28.

50. Littrell, *Bureaucratic Justice*, 169–78.

51. Ibid., 162.

52. George F. Cole, *The American System of Criminal Justice* (North Scituate, Mass.: Duxbury, 1975), 141–45.

53. Littrell, *Bureaucratic Justice*, 169.

54. Sudnow, "Normal Crimes," 262.

55. Littrell, *Bureaucratic Justice*, 134–35.

56. Ibid., 135–36.

57. Ibid., 137–41.

58. See Lynn M. Mather, *Plea Bargaining or Trial? The Process of Criminal-Case Disposition* (Lexington, Mass.: Heath, 1979), 141–42.

59. Quoted in Gaylin, *Partial Justice*, 51–52.

60. Ibid., 43.

61. Silberman, *Criminal Violence, Criminal Justice*, 287.

62. Eisenstein and Jacob, *Felony Justice*, v.

63. Silberman, *Criminal Violence, Criminal Justice*, 291; italics added.

64. Littrell, *Bureaucratic Justice*, 175.

65. To be more specific, I wrote that Eisenstein and Jacob "can account for only {172} about 20% or less of the variance in nine of the 18 tests of dependent variables. In only six tests can they account for...50% or more. Looked at another way, for only one dependent variable—length of sentences—is it possible to explain more than 50% of the variance in all three cities. Thus, we are left in the dark when it comes to accounting for variance in such important matters as conviction rates and the incidence of jail terms for convicted defendants." Stuart A. Scheingold, review essay in *Criminology* 15 (August 1977): 270–71.

66. Douglas W. Maynard, "Defendant Attributes in Plea Bargaining: Notes on the Modeling of Sentencing Decisions," in *Social Problems* 29 (April 1982): 348.

67. Ibid., 352.

68. Ibid., 354.

69. On the problem of quantitative research, see ibid., 354–55; and Feeley, *The Process Is the Punishment*, 123–25.

70. Mather, *Plea Bargaining or Trial!* Chap. 3.

71. Jerome Skolnick, "Social Control in the Adversary System," *Journal of Conflict Resolution* 11 (March 1967): 68.

72. Jonathan D. Casper, *American Criminal Justice: The Defendant's Perspective* (Englewood Cliffs, N.J.: Prentice-Hall, 1972), esp. Chap. 4.

73. Mather, *Plea Bargaining or Trial?* 204.

74. Sudnow, "Normal Crime," 275.

75. Maynard, "Defendant Attributes in Plea Bargaining," 357; and Feeley, *The Process Is the Punishment*, 283–90.

76. Skolnick, "Social Control in the Adversary System," 64–67.

77. For an insightful and more extended discussion of an analogous point having to do with formal trials, see W. Lance Bennett and Martha S. Feldman, *Reconstructing Reality in the Courtroom* (New Brunswick, N.J.: Rutgers University Press, 1981), 173.

78. Casper, *American Criminal Justice*, 65.

79. At least one researcher has uncovered a process of compensatory bias. In the Atlanta criminal courts, "anti-black judges are balanced by pro-black judges." James L. Gibson, "Race as a Determinant of Criminal Sentences: A Methodological Critique and a Case Study," *Law and Society Review* 12 (Spring 1978): 475.

80. On the justice model, see pp. 150–51.

81. Anne M. Heinz, *Governmental Responses to Crime. Legislative Responses to Crime: The Changing Content of Criminal Law* (Washington, D.C.: National Institute of Justice, 1983), 95–97.

7

The Politics of Criminal Court Reform

The debate among the critics provides a useful starting point for an inquiry into the politics of policy making in the criminal courts. Hidden beneath the charges and countercharges are different policy preferences that reflect the full range of mainstream thinking about the nature of crime.[*] The permissive critique is supported by conservatives, who favor either a purely punitive response to crime or a more moderate policy of deterrence. The coercive critique is the work of liberals, who prefer rehabilitation or due process policies for the criminal courts.

From neither perspective is bureaucratic justice satisfactory because it temporizes among policy choices. As we learned in the previous chapter, the professionals who run criminal courts have developed discretionary practices that are, from the critics' points of view, ideologically insufficient. The presumption of guilt is too coercive for liberals, but conservatives object to the due process leverage remaining to defendants. The operational morality of fairness, according to available data, seems to be generally consistent with deterrence in that the punishment ordinarily fits the crime. Allowances are, however, made for the character of the defendant, thus providing professionals with an opportunity to depart from deterrence and move toward punishment or rehabilitation when warranted by the circumstances. Criminal court professionals have, in short, chosen to embrace an eclectic mélange of sentencing principles. {174}

From the outside looking in, this may all seem like, and is certainly portrayed as, a kind of bureaucratic conspiracy against justice and crime control. I am more inclined to see it as a sensible effort by the professionals to cope with an extremely difficult situation. For at least two good reasons, they are unwilling to narrow their options as liberals and conservatives demand.

---

[*] Marxism is not directly germane to this debate because the Marxist critique leads to revolutionary transformation rather than policy reform. While Marxists would undoubtedly think of criminal courts as coercive, they do not really get involved in the policy debate as such. It is therefore understandable that the Marxist judge discussed in Chapter 6 would employ rather conventional sentencing practices.

First, when considered dispassionately, it must be acknowledged that each of the policy choices is linked to a legitimate objective. The simple fact is that in this society, criminal penalties are expected to serve a variety of largely incompatible social purposes: deterrence, incapacitation, retribution, rehabilitation, and due process. The intensity of the debate within the mainstream indicates how deeply divided the society is on these matters. A blanket endorsement of one or another of these policies would be unlikely, therefore, to still the political controversy swirling around the criminal courts. Nor, as I argue subsequently, can a conclusive crime-control case be made on behalf of any of these policies. There is therefore no principled or practical reason that criminal court professionals should identify exclusively with one of the several legitimate purposes of sentencing policy.

Second, the only chance for reconciling the incompatible objectives of sentencing policy is to tailor sentences to the circumstances of particular cases. In some cases, the argument for incapacitation may be irresistible—the incorrigibly violent offender, for example. In other cases, rehabilitation may be a realistic possibility. On those frequent occasions when there is no obvious choice, professionals are understandably tempted to juggle two or more objectives in the fashion of Judge Ravitz, who was quoted in the previous chapter.[1] In other words, although the several objectives of sentencing policy may be incompatible in the abstract, they can sometimes be effectively harmonized in the programs of individual offenders. This particularization does not, moreover, threaten equity, which requires only that *like* cases be treated in the same way. Indeed, stubborn adherence to a particular policy, independent of the distinctive circumstances of the case at hand, would be indicative of a foolish consistency inappropriate for effective policy making.

In the next section, a single case study is discussed to convey as vividly as possible the strong temptation to tailor sentences to the circumstances of particular crimes. This case study also demonstrates, however, that particularization does not necessarily lift the burden of the excruciatingly difficult choices involved in sentencing decisions. Still, from the insider's point of view, particularization seems a necessary, if not a sufficient, condition for just and sensible policy making.

Be all that as it may, criminal courts are at the center of a significant political controversy and have proven permeable to the punitive pressures of the politics of law and order. This permeability, resulting from legal and {175} electoral links between criminal courts and the political process, is considered in a later section of this chapter along with the unpromising prospects of punitive reform as an effective tool for controlling violent street crime.

THE DILEMMAS OF SENTENCING

Sentencing practices engage participants in criminal courts on at least three levels. At its most mundane, sentencing is simply a job to be done as quickly and as efficiently as possible. But sentencing decisions also tend to arouse strong feelings because the freedom and well-being of individual human beings, both offenders and their victims, are at stake. Finally, there is what I call the ideological dimension of sentencing—the way in which sentencing decisions can be said to rest on basic assumptions about the nature of crime, social relations, and political legitimacy. These different aspects of sentencing have all been touched on; it is now time to incorporate them into a systematic analysis of the determinants of sentencing.

The Job of Sentencing

There was a time, as observers began to abandon the legal model, when it was generally accepted that we could learn just about everything we wanted to know about sentencing if we simply considered it as a job. Blumberg provides a subtle and insightful treatment of this approach to sentencing.[2] The essential idea is that all professionals are exclusively interested in expediting the disposition of cases for their own selfish reasons. Defendants have other concerns, but they are, as Blumberg sees it, excluded from the dispositional process. Accordingly, bargains are struck at the defendants' expense. For those like Wilson, who believe that defendants have a great deal of leverage, the job perspective leads in a permissive direction, but the motivation of the professionals is no different. According to this way of thinking, the defendant is, in effect, the squeaky wheel that gets greased with a lighter sentence in return for a guilty plea. Professionals, in other words, are once again seen as simply following the line of least resistance—acting on the basis of expedience rather than principle.[3]

The more we learn about criminal courts, however, the clearer it becomes that the job perspective provides only a partial explanation of sentencing practices. Indeed, the job perspective itself has come to mean more than simply an effort by professionals to get more bang for the buck. Stuffing as many defendants through the system as quickly as possible {176} would have serious drawbacks for the professionals because the process would become wildly arbitrary with outcomes depending solely on the bargaining resources that could be marshaled by individual defendants. We know now that this kind of indeterminacy is disquieting to professionals, who seek predictability as well as efficiency.

More fundamentally, the job perspective seems gratuitously cynical. Criminal court professionals, like other professionals, are not just interested in getting the job done but also in doing it well—according to whatever standards they acknowledge as appropriate. While lawyers working in criminal courts certainly look for shortcuts that make their jobs easier, their search, for the most part, is for respectable shortcuts that will result in a job well done. In order to get a sense of the standards that criminal court professionals bring to their work, it is necessary to understand something about the strong feelings aroused by sentencing decisions, as well as the way in which personal and professional values shape the sense of what constitutes legitimate sentencing practice.

Interpersonal Conundrums

Interpersonal dimensions of sentencing decisions intrude very insistently but rather inconclusively into the calculations of criminal court professionals. What tends to escape the rest of us but is unmistakably clear to the professionals is that the fates of individual human beings—offenders, victims, and others—are in their hands. What is more, it is probably very seldom that a decision seems fair to all those immediately involved. From the outside looking in, we see a one-dimensional conflict between good and evil, an understanding anchored in our preconceptions and fueled by the brief and inflammatory versions of crime and criminal trials generally provided by the media. But the situation is much more complex for the insider, who must confront flesh-and-blood human beings.

In order to convey these interpersonal conundrums with their strong emotional overtones, I want to focus on the plight of a young assistant district attorney, Steven Phillips, dealing with a straightforward case of predatory street crime. In an article he wrote about the case, the prosecutor described the crime as follows:

> He was on his way home from a schoolyard pickup basketball game, dribbling his ball down Arthur Avenue in the Bronx, when a white teenager walked up and stabbed him once in the abdomen. The black boy was dead before he hit the ground. The assailant turned and fled, leaving his victim sprawled face upward on the side-walk. From start to finish, the killing took no more than five seconds.[4]

Except for their race, the victim and the killer were much alike. Both were in their late teens, and both were from families of modest circumstances {177} living in the Bronx. Each of them was a good student, although the black youth was especially promising. They were complete strangers to one another, and the killing was completely random.

Once the killer had been tracked down, the police were able to build an ironclad case against him. "From the very beginning ... I knew no defense attorney would risk taking it to trial." On what, then, could plea bargaining be based? As far as the prosecutor was concerned, there were no grounds on which to bargain:

> I had close to an airtight case, one that was bound to lead to a murder conviction. The crime itself was both shocking and sense-less, and the defendant, then 18 years old, would be treated as an adult rather than a juvenile. I saw no reason why I should not take a very hard position.[5]

But a number of factors weakened the prosecutor's resolve.

The defense attorney brought in a psychiatrist's report that provided an explanation for the murder and concluded that the killer could be completely rehabilitated. The explanation was complex but can be boiled down to two problematic features of his relationship with his peers. First, there were tensions between the boy and his parents. His parents were immigrants; they were also elderly. His mother was overprotective, while his father was "a stern disciplinarian" who had "attempted to install...his own rather rigid set of values." Life at home, therefore, gave the boy relatively few resources for coping with the peer pressures of street life.[6] His second problem with his peers was that he was small, frail, and physically immature. He was frequently taunted because he was unable to meet teenage standards that emphasized "being both sexually and physically powerful." While deploring the murder, the psychiatrist wanted to underscore the compulsive forces working on the killer.

> [I]t must be understood that [the boy] acted as he did out of a kind of neurotic desperation, from a terrible need to win accept-ance from his peers, and to rebel against the strict morality of his parents. In [his] mind, the grotesque action of taking a baking knife and stabbing a strange black boy in the presence of his friends became a means of showing them, and himself, that he could outdo any of them in both violence, and at least sym-bolically in sexuality. The use of the knife as a chosen weapon is significant, for it is a phallic substitute, and was used to assuage doubts that he had developed about his own masculinity.[7]

The point of this explanation was not to excuse but to lay a basis for a psych-iatric prognosis and for a plea that the boy not be sent to prison.

> [I]t is my strong feeling and my professional judgment that with continued care [this young man] will become a well adjusted and valuable member of society. I view with horror the prospect of his going to prison. Such an eventuality would hopelessly undermine all hopes of effective treatment, would exacerbate his problems, and would most likely destroy him as an individual.[8] {178}

While prosecutor Phillips was inclined to doubt a report prepared at the defendant's expense, the psychiatrist's view also "seemed both thoughtful and sincere."

The other side of the case was forcefully made by the victim's father, whose family was being destroyed by the murder.

> Their son's death had just about killed his wife. The death had made her old before her time and he knew she would never be the same again.

> And then there was their younger son. He had been doing really well in school, almost as well as his dead brother.... But ever since the murder, the knowledge that his brother's killer was free [that is, out on bail] had been eating at him.... He was turning bitter, neglecting his studies, and for the first time had begun to get into trouble with the law.[9]

The father made it clear that "'that white boy' had to go to jail for a long time and the longer the better."[10]

There was also, of course, a racial dimension, which the father pointed out. "He knew damn well that if the tables were turned his son, or any black boy, would be rotting in jail facing a certain life sentence." Mail and editorial comment to this effect also rained down on Mr. Phillips. Here, then, were other messages that could not be ignored.

> [T]he failure to punish the white killer severely was a clear signal to other white youths with similar inclinations that black life was cheap and could be taken with impunity. Similarly, it told someone in the black community that there was no justice in the courts, and that recourse to justice in the streets was a wiser alternative.[11]

In this way, the potential consequences of the sentencing decision were expanded beyond those immediately involved to the society at large.

What had seemed initially like an open-and-shut case was transformed into a real puzzle, for which Phillips unsuccessfully sought help from several quarters. The judge's response to Phillip's proposal that the decision be made judicially was short and to the point. "What, are you out of your mind? You want me to stick my neck out all alone on a case like this? No way!" Even his colleagues, to whom he turned for counsel and who were not being asked to stick out their necks, could only advise that he should "do the right thing, and don't worry."

> The trouble, of course, was that I did not know what the right thing was, and I could not stop worrying. I wanted to reach a just result, but justice, I quickly came to realize, was a relative thing. It all depended upon your perspective. Justice for an emotionally disturbed boy, gripped by psychological forces partially beyond

his control, or for his aged parents, faced with the loss of their only son? Justice for the dead boy, senselessly cut down in his youth, or for his family grief-stricken and embittered by their loss, and by the seeming indifference of the judicial process? Society needed justice too. But what kind? {179} Stern justice to clearly show that racial violence would not be tolerated? Or a more humane justice that sought to heal and rehabilitate rather than punish?[12]

The recommendation the judge accepted was for a fifteen-year prison term with eligibility for parole after three years. "Two months after the sentence, the white youth's father suffered a stroke. He is now an invalid. The dead boy's brother is now under indictment, charged with armed robbery. There has been no noticeable decrease in the amount of crime or racial violence in the Bronx."[13]

Phillips does not explain the calculation that led to the final sentencing recommendation. We do know that it was not based exclusively on his *feelings*, despite the important part they played in the way he sized up the situation. He was fully aware of the range of social purposes that sentences are supposed to serve, but that understanding did not prove particularly helpful.

> Each one was based upon a different assumption.... For example, if the purpose of punishment was retribution, then the very seriousness of the boy's offense...required harsh punishment. But if the idea was rehabilitation rather than retribution, then I had a boy who most probably could be transformed through sympathetic and therapeutic, i.e. lenient, treatment into a valuable member of society.
>
> If, on the other hand, punishment was designed to be exemplary, if it was to teach and to deter, then harsh treatment was necessary to demonstrate that racial violence would not be tolerated.
>
> Retribution, rehabilitation, and deterrence, they all have a certain validity, and I could not easily choose between them. Besides, I was haunted by the images of two families and concerned about the impact of my decision upon all of those decent and innocent people.[14]

Clearly, the final decision was some sort of eclectic compromise. The sentence was heavy enough to send the defendant to prison. There, according to the defense counsel, the best that could happen was that the effeminate boy would be raped and turned into a homosexual. Just as likely, he would have his throat slit once the black and Hispanic inmates, who are in the overwhelming majority, discovered what the boy's crime was. Perhaps it was these concerns that led to a sentencing recommendation that made the boy eligible for parole in three years—a long way from the wishes of the victim's father, who wanted him imprisoned "for a long time and the longer the better."

But we are still left in the dark about why Phillips struck the compromise as he did. I would suggest that the factors so far considered tell us only why professionals are driven toward compromise: because of irreconcilable conflicts posed by personal feelings and social purpose. How they calculate those compromises depends on the hierarchy of values that {180} they bring to sentencing, and it is to this essentially ideological issue that we now turn.

Sentencing and Ideology

Four distinct sentencing options face the criminal court professionals: incapacitation, deterrence, rehabilitation, and retribution. The tendency is to discuss and defend these policies in crime-control terms, but they are better understood in ideological than in instrumental terms. While crime-control cases can be made, none is empirically compelling. It is therefore more realistic to think about these policy preferences as articles of faith, resting on premises about the nature of society and the proper structures of authority. If, in other words, we are to understand the policy choices of criminal court professionals, we must familiarize ourselves with the values that they bring to those decisions.[15]

The professionals tend to divide, ideologically speaking, along the same lines as other Americans, but their legal training and organizational responsibilities tend to complicate their value systems. There are, in the first place, both liberals and conservatives to be found among the criminal court professionals. In addition to these *political* values, the professionals also tend to think more seriously about appropriate structures of authority than do most Americans, thus subdividing liberals and conservatives in the manner indicated in Figure 7.1.

This diagram presents a simplified view of the complex world of sentencing. Criminal court professionals do not, as has been pointed out, identify exclusively with one or another of the policy choices. Nevertheless, {181} the diagram does help us understand how particular convergences of political and institutional values would incline professionals in one direction or another. Moreover, the problematic cell at the convergence of liberal and legal values suggests the special dilemma confronting due process liberals and also sheds some interesting light on the politics of sentencing reform.

According to the conservative view presented in Chapter 1, criminals *choose* to violate the law. They should therefore be punished for several reasons. There is, first, the issue of fairness: punishment amounts to the just deserts of criminals and should be meted out in proportion to their offenses. Punishment is, additionally, seen as a way of preventing and/or deterring

		POLITICAL VALUES	
		Liberal	Conservative
INSTITUTIONAL	Legal	?	Deterrence-Retribution
VALUES	Managerial	Rehabilitation	Incapacitation

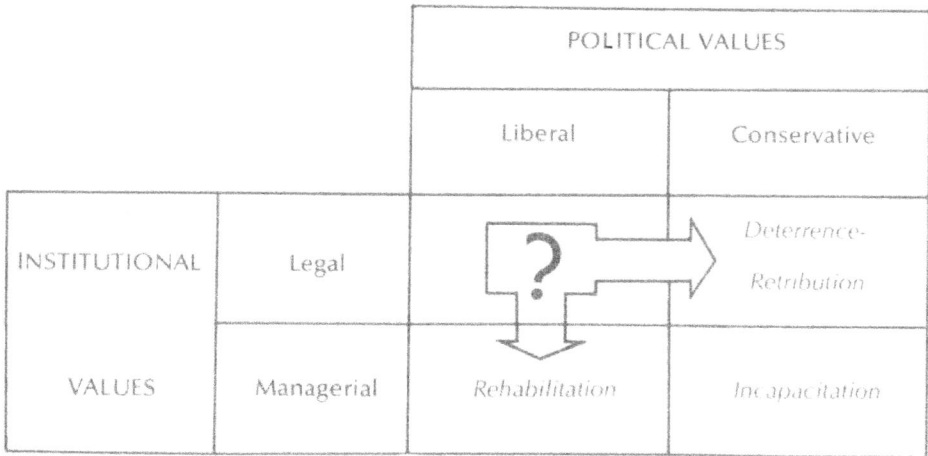

FIGURE 7.1 The Criminal Courts: Ideology and Policy.

crime. While offenders are incarcerated, they cannot commit crime. In addition to its incapacitative effects, punishment also stands, according to this way of thinking, as an object lesson that will deter others who might be tempted by crime if it was sufficiently profitable. While most conservatives would generally accept these ideas, there is at the least a substantial difference in emphasis between what were identified in Chapter 1 as punitive and moderate conservatives.

Punitive conservatives have a deeply pessimistic view of human nature and are uneasy with legal constraints on criminal process. As they see things, criminals are immoral and irrational—responsive to fear perhaps, but to little else. Accordingly, the first priorities of criminal courts are to convict these predators and punish them severely. The only way to be certain that predators will not commit crimes is to keep them in jail, and the longer they are incarcerated, the better off the rest of us will be. Beyond *incapacitation*, heavy sentences are probably also seen by punitive conservatives as serving, albeit in a secondary fashion, the cause of deterrence. Those who have already committed crimes may be frightened away from additional offenses, and some of the rest of us with suspect moral standards may be similarly frightened away from the temptations of crime.

Given this orientation, punitive conservatives tend to be very uneasy with legal values. Equality before the law, generally, and due process guarantees, in particular, are objectionable because they are inconsistent with the feelings of punitive conservatives that criminals are really a breed apart. "Rights are for decent people, not for bums like you," is the way a tough cop in a TV drama put it. While crudely expressed, this invective does capture the sentiments of hard-line conservatives, who are inclined to think of many criminals as unconscionable threats to the social order. But punitive conservatives have instrumental as well as expressive objections to legal values.

The instrumental objections to due process are obvious. It is not sufficient, according to due process standards, that defendants be factually guilty. They must be legally guilty as well. Consider, for example, the {182} prohibition against illegal searches that may well turn up completely reliable evidence. To the punitive conservative, the stakes of crime control are just too high to allow a guilty predator to go free because the evidence, while factually sound, is legally tainted. Due process guarantees can make it more difficult to convict criminals.

Finally, the logic of incapacitation is inimical to the basic legal value of equality before the law and is, instead, responsive to what I call in Figure 7.1 managerial values. According to legal values, impersonal rules are to be applied in a uniform manner, irrespective of the outcome. The focus is on consistency and neutrality. Managerial decisions, in contrast, are result oriented and responsive to particularities of person and circumstance, irrespective of established rights or rules. This is a distinction I borrow from Lon Fuller:

> To act wisely, the economic manager must take into account every circumstance relevant to his decision and must himself assume the initiative in discovering what circumstances are relevant. His decisions must be subject to reversal or change as conditions alter. The judge, on the other hand, acts upon those facts that are in advance deemed relevant under declared principles of decision. His decision does not simply direct resources and energies; it declares rights, and to be meaningful must in some measure stand firm through changing circumstances.[16]

Sentencing is responsive to legal values insofar as we are judged by what we *have done* in accordance with established rules. But incapacitation requires that we pick and choose among offenders on the basis of predictions about what they *will do*. While past acts of the offender may provide some evidence on which incapacitative predictions will be made, such predictions inevitably lead away from impersonal rules. Many murderers, like the young defendant considered earlier in the chapter, are unlikely to become repeat offenders, but it is necessary to pry into personality in order to sort out the good risks from the bad ones. In so doing, we move away from formal equality, which is so intrinsic to legal values.[17]

Moderate conservatives have a somewhat less pessimistic view of human nature. According to this way of thinking, criminals are certainly immoral, but they are not irrational. They can therefore be conditioned to respond to a fairly administered punishment system, one that reliably and expeditiously separates the guilty from the innocent and that, also expeditiously, punishes in proportion to harm. At the heart of this position are the cases for general and individual deterrence. General deterrence is based on the proposition that if the costs of crime are raised above the benefits, would-be predators in the general population, despite immoral inclinations, will forego criminal activity. As for individuals who commit crimes, they will be deterred from repeat offenses by the punishment experience and by the fact that repeat offenders will be treated ever more {183} harshly with each new offense. In this way, an incapacitative note is struck at the margins because the society is protected from repeat offenders for increasingly long periods of time.

The deterrence policies preferred by moderate conservatives are generally consistent with legal values. Equality before the law is preserved by fitting the punishment to the crime rather than the criminal. People are punished for what they did rather than who they are. Even the incapacitative undercurrent of repeat offender sentencing is anchored to past acts rather than predictions about future behavior based on personality assessment. With respect to due process guarantees, the fit between deterrence and legal values is more problematic. Unlike punitive conservatives, moderate conservatives are not interested in terrifying offenders but wish instead to appeal to their reason by establishing reliable procedures. Due process rights must be protected, therefore, insofar as they promote factual accuracy and institutional integrity. On the other hand, moderate conservatives are likely to be just as uneasy as are punitive conservatives with due process guarantees that elevate legal guilt over factual guilt. In allowing offenders to escape on "technicalities," these stricter standards of due process stand in the way of predictable punishment for offenders and thus undermine the deterrent force of sentencing policy.

Liberals find it much more difficult than conservatives to settle on a sentencing policy. According to the liberal view of the world, crime is the product of basic social forces, and criminals are primarily victims of circumstance rather than immoral or irrational free agents. Because of their disadvantaged social position, people at the bottom of the society have relatively few legitimate opportunities, and so they turn to crime in disproportionate numbers. Given these premises, liberal reformers are likely to see criminal process and sentencing as largely superfluous and to look instead to social programs that alter the distribution of wealth and opportunity within the society. Liberals also believe that the disadvantaged must be protected, not only from a hostile social milieu, but also from the potentially repressive power of the criminal process. When finally they turn their attention to sentencing policy and criminal process more generally, liberals tend to be wary and distrustful—more concerned with controlling authority than with purposeful action.

Rehabilitation is modestly but problematically attractive to liberals. It is attractive because treatment is substituted for the "crime of punishment."[18] Vocational and emotional assistance are provided to enable offenders to make better use of legitimate opportunities and thus avoid returning to a life of crime. So far, so good. Here is a humane plan, based on helping offenders to help themselves. Of course, rehabilitation, with its focus on individual criminals rather than social problems, can provide only symptomatic relief. Nonetheless, there is some reason to think of rehabilitation as a step in the right direction—at least until it is considered more carefully. {184}

Note, however, that rehabilitation is a managerial strategy that relies on correctional personnel to remake individual human beings subjected to the power of the state for an indefinite period of time. Sentences are tailored to individual idiosyncrasies and are thus inconsistent with the principle of equality before the law. Rehabilitation can also be viewed as "an invitation to personal tyranny and [a] denial of human rights. Once a prisoner is placed in the hands of the doctor to be cured before he is released, there is no one who can predict how long the cure will take, nor control the autonomy of the doctor's judgment."[19] Rehabilitation is, finally, expected to occur despite the brutal and dehumanizing conditions of most American prisons. For all its humane intentions, rehabilitation has an arbitrary and coercive bias.

In the abstract, liberals might be expected to look with some favor on retribution, which is anchored in a desert-based concept of justice and sternly limits the powers of the state to intervene in offenders' lives. Martin Golding summarizes the Kantian case for retribution as follows:

> Coercion under the conditions of law in order to prevent a breach of rights...is morally right. Such coercion is a "hindrance to a hindrance" of legitimate freedom and is therefore justifiable. Freedom is limited for the sake of freedom itself.[20]

The guilty, and only the guilty, are to be punished; and they are to be punished according to what they have done and in strict proportion to the harm they have inflicted and their personal culpability for that harm.[21] The state is justified in punishing lawbreakers because they have overstepped the agreed upon patterns of mutual forbearance on which our freedom ultimately rests. At the same time, state power is circumscribed by narrow and rather precise principles of punishment and by procedural guarantees that contribute to the factual reliability of criminal process.

In the final analysis, however, the case for retribution is at best only mildly persuasive to liberals. The threshold problem is that, as Golding puts it, retribution has a "bad press."

> The very term connotes retaliation and revenge. Some opponents of the position go so far as to call it the "vindictive" theory, a theory that believes in pain for pain's sake.[22]

While this imagery is misleading, I do not think that its impact on liberal thinking should be taken lightly. There are more fundamental reservations about retribution, however. Consider, to begin with, that retribution offers no plan for crime control. The sole justification for retribution is that it is morally correct. "Crimes are moral wrongs and they deserve punishment" is the way in which Golding capsulizes the case for retribution.[23] But the moral warrant to punish criminals is, according to the liberal view of the world, very weak.

After all, criminals who are seen primarily as victims of {185} circumstance do not really deserve punishment because they are not fully responsible for their criminal behavior. It also seems likely that liberals would clash with retributive thinking on due process issues. Given the determination of liberals, particularly legalistic liberals, to curb the potentially abusive power of criminal process, they are inclined toward an expansive interpretation of due process protections. Retribution, in contrast, requires that all who have committed crimes be punished—leading, therefore, toward a more restrictive conception of due process. Retributivists, like advocates of deterrence, would be committed only to those due process protections that contribute to factual reliability.

At the level of overall policy, there is therefore no sentencing option that is consistent with both liberal and legal values. Those criminal professionals who think in liberal-legal terms—primarily defense attorneys and some judges —will find it hard to get beyond maximizing the rights of defendants to protect them from all forms of coercion, whether in the name of incapacitation, deterrence, rehabilitation, or retribution. When it comes to sentencing policy as such, legalistic or due process liberals are likely to steer clear of any general commitment to either rehabilitation, which compromises legal values, or retribution and deterrence, which compromise liberal values. Due process liberals, even more than other professionals, are thus forced into case-by-case determinations based on the responsibility and correctability of particular defendants. Regardless of which direction they go, however, due process liberals will be inclined to choose the least onerous and most humane sentences.

Conservatives have much less trouble making policy commitments. Moderate conservatives, whom I would expect to find well represented among judges and prosecutors, will be comfortable with deterrence and retribution, which are basically compatible with one another in practice despite their theoretical differences. Both of them, that is to say, are consistent with predetermined sentences based on the seriousness of the crime and the offender's record. In principle, deterrence looks ahead to the impact of sentencing on the future behavior of the offender and others, while retribution looks back to the harm done and the culpability of the offender.[24] In practice, these differences are not likely to be terribly significant. Punitive conservatives, some of whom may be found among the ranks of judges and prosecutors but are more likely to appear within police departments, will pretty consistently favor heavy sentences that will strike fear in the hearts of would-be offenders and will keep those who have committed crimes off the streets for long periods of time. Overall, I would say that conservatives, like liberals, have a good deal in common; but, unlike liberals, conservatives approach sentencing with few qualms and a willingness to make unequivocal policy choices. {186}

Policy and Politics

In one sense, this inquiry into the dilemmas of sentencing is merely a prelude to the main business of the chapter: the politics of criminal court reform. We now understand how criminal court professionals approach the job of sentencing, absent the direct external pressures generated by the politics of law and order. Having established this baseline, we can in the next section analyze the basic character and the policy consequences of the political permeability of the criminal courts. There are, however, interesting political implications to the sentencing dilemmas just considered. To understand these sentencing dilemmas is to gain insight into two important aspects of the politics of criminal court reform.

First, it is important to understand that the insiders' view of sentencing policy is politically relevant in its own right. The three special features of the insiders' view set criminal court professionals apart from the general public—even, I would contend, from the informed public. Because sentencing is the insiders' job, they develop routines that both make the job easier and provide defenses against the pain and suffering that they witness and, indeed, inflict with their sentencing decisions. Second, insiders are immersed to a significant degree in the trials and tribulations of victims and defendants. Insiders, therefore, react more to real people in concrete situations and less to the abstractions and symbols to which the public generally responds. Finally, the ideological inclinations of professionals are closely linked to institutional values that are of relatively little concern to outsiders.

In coming to appreciate the gap that ordinarily separates criminal court professionals from the general public, the character and intensity of the political controversy that embroils the criminal courts becomes a little clearer. Consider, for example, the furor over the successful use of the insanity defense by President Reagan's would-be assassin, John Hinckley, Jr. What seems to have escaped most people's attention is that the final decision was made by a jury of citizens, not by professionals. Perhaps it is just that we believe that these good citizens were hoodwinked by lawyers or trapped in outmoded rules and therefore conclude that the jury was of only marginal importance to the final disposition of the case. There is another way to look at things. The jury system is one of the few social institutions that liberates citizens from the easy abstractions of the myth of crime and punishment, thus closing the gap between the public and the professionals. One conclusion to be drawn is that if the public were better informed, the intensity of the political controversy over sentencing policy might be significantly reduced. The more fundamental point is that outsiders and insiders inevitably bring different understandings to the assessment of social institutions. In this sense, the political conflict in which the criminal courts are embroiled is inescapable, once the public turns its attention to sentencing practices. {187}

The value conflicts that trouble the insiders provide a second and more direct link to the political debates over sentencing policy. The empty cell in the upper-left-hand corner of Figure 7.1 provides some insight into the increasing support in recent years for determinate sentencing plans that provide fixed terms for offenders and restrict prosecutorial and/or judicial discretion.[25] Once rehabilitation was discredited, for reasons already discussed, liberals were left without a crime-control policy for the criminal courts—indeed without any sentencing policy at all. They tended to take refuge in due process, for which a modest crime-control case has sometimes been made. It is argued that expanded due process protections impose higher standards on criminal process professionals, who can no longer rely, for example, on coerced confessions, which are notoriously unreliable. Be that as it may, it is disingenuous and ultimately unpersuasive to sell the due process "obstacle course" as a crime-control measure. For both principled and practical reasons, then, due process oriented liberals have been attracted to determinate sentencing reform. The deterrence message of fixed terms for specified crimes has the practical appeal of crime control, and fitting the punishment to the crime is consistent with the principle of equality before the law. Due process liberals and moderate conservatives, therefore, have tended to make common cause in behalf of determinate sentencing. The coalition is fragile, as Jonathan Casper, David Brereton, and David Neal have pointed out in connection with the California Determinate Sentencing Law.

> Due process liberals who supported the bill with reservations have found one of their fears borne out: once legislators get into the business of setting prison terms there is little to stop them from raising them substantially. Terms have been raised several times already, and many new probation disqualifiers have been introduced since the 1976 passage of the DSL.[26]

As we see in the next section, it is not only in California that determinate sentencing has taken a punitive turn. In any case, the tension between liberal and conservative values makes the coalition on which determinate sentencing rests inherently unstable.

THE POLITICS OF LAW AND ORDER

Up to this point, no explicit connection has been made between politics and policy. Indeed, the analysis so far tends to imply an autonomous criminal court organization functioning in accordance with its own internal needs. Certainly the major complaint of the critics is that the irrationality of criminal courts is rooted in the whims and convenience of court professionals. While I have offered a much less pejorative interpretation of sentencing decisions, my emphasis has clearly been on constructing an insiders' view of criminal courts.

The criminal courts are, however, {188} politically permeable, and it is now time to sort out the links between politics and policy and, more particularly, to assess the policy consequences of the politics of law and order.

Political Permeability

The rather limited body of available literature suggests that criminal courts are well insulated from direct electoral pressures—at least in the short run. Under normal circumstances, Martin Levin tells us in his pioneering study of the politics of the criminal courts in Minneapolis and Pittsburgh, policy reflects the prevailing political style of a city rather than the ebb and flow of elections.[27] Even in extraordinary circumstances, criminal courts seem to be well insulated from transient forces. This is the message I take from Isaac Balbus's splendid research on the way in which the criminal courts in Los Angeles, Detroit and Chicago dealt with the black ghetto protests of the 1960s.[28] Over the longer haul, however, a certain responsiveness to sustained electoral pressure can be inferred from other research findings that are available. Since the politics of law and order seem to have considerable staying power, it is reasonable to hypothesize some permeability, albeit a permeability influenced and circumscribed by two substantial layers of insulation.

Levin's research is particularly useful because he contrasts Minneapolis and Pittsburgh policy choices in terms directly assimilable to the policy diagram in Figure 7.1. In Pittsburgh, the judges were benevolent and willing to make exceptions according to the circumstances of individual defendants.

> The Pittsburgh judges generally are oriented toward the defendant rather than toward punishment or deterrence. Their decision-making is nonlegalistic in that it tends to be particularistic, pragmatic, and based on policy considerations; their sentencing decisions are lenient.[29]

Minneapolis sentences, on the other hand, were "severe" and uniform. "Minneapolis judges typically tend to be oriented more toward 'society' and its needs and protection than toward the defendant.... Their decisionmaking is legalistic and universalistic."[30] Thus the managerial liberalism of the rehabilitative approach seemed to prevail in Pittsburgh, while Minneapolis judges pursued a policy of deterrence.

The differences between the two cities can be traced directly to politics, but not in the form of policy signals from the electorate. As Levin sees it, the two cities were characterized by different political styles reflected in the kinds of judges who served on the criminal court bench and ultimately in the sentencing practices they adopted. Minneapolis, with a reform style of politics, drew their judges from among lawyers engaged in {189} private legal practice, and the recommendations of the local bar association were taken seriously by the electorate and by the governor, who made a great many interim judicial appointments.[31] As a result, judges were drawn primarily from the middle class and came to the bench with strong preferences for legal consistency and business values. These preferences translated into uniformity and severity in sentencing practices. Pittsburgh's politics were machine-style rather than reform, and the judges presiding over criminal courts were recruited through the party system and came mostly from "minority ethnic and lower-income backgrounds."[32] Pittsburgh's judges were therefore more understanding of defendants' problems and more comfortable with discretionary decision making.

> In Pittsburgh, the pre-judicial careers of most judges in political parties and government, and their ethnic minority and lower-income backgrounds, seem to have contributed to the development of a characteristic common to many successful local politicians—the ability to understand the motives of other people by entering empathetically into their feelings. Their political experience and their relative lack of legal experience seem to have influenced the highly particularistic and nonlegalistic character of their decision-making, their emphasis on policy considerations, and their use of pragmatic criteria.... [T]heir predominant orientation toward, and tendency to empathize with, many of the defendants, and their readiness to act as a buffer between the law and the people upon whom it is enforced seem to make leniency "natural."[33]

Paradoxically, then, the criminal courts are insulated from ephemeral pressures by a more fundamental kind of accommodation to the political process.

Evidence of a more genuine kind of autonomy can be derived from Balbus's research on the ghetto protests of the 1960s. He found that differences of political style among the three cities he investigated were of little help in predicting responses to the flood of cases generated by the breakdown of social order in the ghetto.

> [I]ntercity variations in ... the structural relationship between court system and the local polity were relatively insignificant determinants of the court response to major revolts.[34]

Nor did the criminal courts yield to pressures for punitive responses to the disorder. Indeed, Balbus discovered "an *inverse relationship between the magnitude of revolts and the severity of court sanctions*."[35] At least in crisis periods, it would seem, therefore, that criminal courts are able to resist effectively both policy and structural forms of political accommodation.

The lenient sentencing policies were instead a response to internal needs, which were in part managerial and in part legal. The managerial problems are obvious, and the solution chosen equally obvious. Surely Wilson would have predicted that the response of the criminal courts to a massive increase in caseload would have been lenient treatment in order to {190} speed up the processing of defendants. But it was not only these organizational problems with their expediential solutions that account for the permissive response of the criminal courts to ghetto protests. If speed had been the only concern, the defendants might have been peremptorily incarcerated. But cracking down in that manner would have entailed significant violations of the law—particularly given the dragnet arrest procedures adopted by the hard-pressed police in their efforts to regain control of the streets.

> [A]lthough normal prosecution gate-keeping was largely abandoned, arrestees *were* prosecuted rather than simply detained without charges, and standard charges were employed in an effort to assimilate the riot activity under the general rubric of predefined, formally proscribed acts. Although bail was set at higher levels than normally, bail *was* set, and the Writ of Habeas Corpus was not formally revoked. Finally, in all three cities a concerted effort was undertaken on the part of court authorities to adhere to normal statutory deadlines. In short, the ordinary criminal process *was* set in motion rather than abandoned in favor of ad hoc procedure.[36]

The amended version of bureaucratic justice that emerged during ghetto protests I take as an indication of the resilience of established procedures and a further indication of the partial autonomy of the criminal courts.[*]

So far, the emphasis has been on insulation rather than permeability, but that is only part of the story. There is some research indicating that criminal courts are responsive to long-term policy pressures and, in fact, that Levin's conclusions may exaggerate the policy stability of criminal courts. Still, the ground covered to this point remains important in that it clarifies the kinds of resistance to policy initiatives that are likely to be encountered in criminal courts.

Eisenstein and Jacob's study of the criminal courts in Baltimore and Chicago offers some confirmation of Levin's basic argument, but their research also indicates a more fluid policy setting that is directly relevant to assessing the impact of the politics of law and order. In Chicago, the only city for which they expressly address the question, Eisenstein and Jacob found the same pattern of long-run dependency on the prevailing political style, or

---

[*] This autonomy is ultimately dependent on the forbearance of the political authorities. In *The Dialectics of Legal Repression* (see note 28), Balbus explains that the political authorities acquiesce in these constraints on their prerogatives in order to reinforce the legitimacy of the regime: "American political authorities...pay a price for their effort to adapt normal sanctioning mechanisms to the challenge of collective revolts, the price being minimal deprivation inflicted on the participants. But this price is willingly paid, since the use of ordinary sanctioning mechanisms permits political authorities to define revolts as 'ordinary crimes'" (255).

political culture, as they call it, combined with substantial insulation from electoral politics. {191}

> The strong hold of the Democratic organization insulated court-
> rooms and sponsoring organizations from the influence of out-
> side organizations. Several organizations in Chicago held intense
> opinions about the courts' operations. These included militant
> black organizations, civil libertarian groups, and other groups
> that held pro-defendant views.... None of these groups, however,
> exerted effective influence despite their efforts.[37]

Notice that Chicago, the prototypical machine city, seems to be operating in a punitive mode, and the same was apparently true in Baltimore.[38] In other words, the connection between machine politics and a pro-defendant bias can hardly be taken for granted. By the same token, Detroit, a reform city with a professional pattern of recruitment, followed felony disposition policies that tended to be responsive to the plight of black defendants.[39] Levin's mistake was it seems to me to treat policy choices as if they were solely a function of the institutional values identified in Figure 7.1. Discretionary styles are compatible with both liberal and conservative values; the same is, of course, true of legalistic styles.

This modification of Levin's argument suggests that as the political values of a city change, so too will the policies pursued in its criminal courts—even without a transformation of political styles. As Figure 7.1 indicates, value shifts in either a liberal or conservative direction imply a change in policy. More concretely, Detroit treated black defendants more sympathetically because blacks became more influential and their values and interests more important in getting the votes required to gain and retain elective office. The values and interests of the white middle class in Minneapolis were given priority for the same basic reason. Since street crime has been a political issue for a relatively long period of time, and given the powerful anxieties associated with the fear of crime, it seems reasonable to believe that the politics of law and order would have a sufficiently marked impact on the local scene to lead to policy change within the criminal courts.

The available data provide two different kinds of circumstantial confirmation of this supposition. Jacob and Lineberry have discovered significant increases in the politicization of crime through the 1960s and 1970s (see Table 7.1). The magnitude of these changes suggests the development of a political climate that may well move policy in a punitive direction, although Jacob and Lineberry make no effort to pursue the argument in that direction. More concretely, it turns out that the 1970s were a punitive period in which the rate of incarceration in state penal institutions went up sharply from 86.2 to 130 per 100,000 of population—an increase of slightly more than 50 percent.[40]

Of course, had the crime or arrest rate been increasing apace during this time, it would be inappropriate to infer more punitive sentencing practices.

But such was not the case. On the contrary, the rate of violent {192} crime, especially violent crime committed by predatory strangers, leveled off during latter part of the 1970s. "[T]he overall rate at which...violent crimes committed by strangers over the 1973–1979 period shows no upward trend."[41] There are also data indicating that arrest rates stabilized, beginning in the year 1975.[42] How, then, are we to account for the higher rates of incarceration at the end of the 1970s? I say it is reasonable to infer that the punitive message of the politics of law and order was getting through to the criminal courts—an inference strengthened by the increasing salience of crime in local elections during the late 1970s, as shown in Table 7.1.

TABLE 7.1 Salience of the Crime Issue in Local Election Campaigns

City	1948–62	1962–74	1974–78	1948–78
Atlanta (N = 4)	1.00	3.50	5.00	3.25
Boston (N = 4)	5.50	4.00	4.00	4.75
Houston (N = 7)	1.50	1.00	5.50	2.57
Indianapolis (N = 7)	3.67	2.67	6.00	3.57
Minneapolis (N = 7)	3.50	4.33	3.50	3.86
Newark (N = 3)	3.00	5.00	6.00	4.67
Oakland (N = 5)	1.50	1.00	4.00	1.80
Philadelphia (N = 5)	1.67	1.00	6.00	2.40
Phoenix (N = 8)	4.50	2.00	3.50	3.63
San Jose (N = 4)	1.00	1.00	4.00	1.75
For All Ten Cities (N = 54)	2.87	2.61	4.62	3.20

Key: 1 = crime was not a salient election issue at all.

7 = crime was a very salient election issue.

SOURCE: Herbert Jacob, Robert L. Lineberry, with Anne M. Heinz, Janice A. Beecher, Jack Moran, Duane H. Swank, *Governmental Responses to Crime: Crime on Urban Agendas* (Washington, D.C.: National Institute of Justice 1982), 32.

Crime Control

The ostensible objective of law-and-order policies is crime control. Whether formulated in the measured tones of deterrence and retribution or the heated claims of incapacitation, the underlying message is that the only way to control crime is to crack down on it. Criminals and would-be criminals must learn that there is a price to be paid for committing crimes—the assumption being that to the extent this is understood, they will be discouraged from criminal activity. The more punitive members of the law-and-order constituency would go further and maximize the length {193} of sentences in order to keep criminals out of circulation as long as possible.

From the law-and-order point of view, criminal courts are the villains of criminal process. In pursuing permissive policies, criminal courts have recycled dangerous criminals back into society and given the wrong message to would-be criminals (i.e., that crime does pay). Wilson is typical of this line of thought.

> As crime became a popular and eventually a political issue, more attention was devoted to the police than to any other part of the criminal justice system. The frequency with which perpetrators of predatory crime are arrested, however, should have alerted us to the possibility that, though the police need improvement, they are not the crucial agency in the system. Of far greater importance are those agencies that handle persons once arrested and that determine whether, how soon, and under what conditions they will be returned to the communities from which they came. These agencies are the criminal courts and the correctional institutions.[43]

Wilson makes it altogether clear that the return of criminals to the communities is too quick and under the worst possible conditions. Moreover, given what we know about public attitudes on crime and punishment, most Americans probably agree with Wilson's general sentiments—if not necessarily with his moderate program of deterrence.

Nevertheless, there is no reason to believe that Wilson's approach nor that of the more punitive elements in the law-and-order coalition would work to reduce crime. In a small measure, my skepticism about the conservative responses is based on the weakness of the case *against* current practices and *for* deterrence and incapacitation, but the crux of the matter is elsewhere. Wilson simply seems misguided in trying to direct attention to the criminal courts. The problem of protecting the society from predatory strangers is, according to the data, located at a stage of criminal process well before the lawyers enter the picture. Thus, a detailed analysis of the crime-control capabilities of punitive policies is not necessary, but a brief consideration of the cases for incapacitation and deterrence will provide a useful point of departure.

The case for incapacitation appears, at first glance, irrefutable. "For as long as it lasts, the incapacitation of detained offenders protects society from them."[44] Moreover, if it is true, as seems likely, that most serious crime is committed by repeat criminals, for each offender incarcerated, substantial numbers of crimes are being prevented.[45] Conservatives like van den Haag, as well as liberals like Silberman, point out that all this cannot be taken at face value, however.

> The temporary or even the permanent incapacitation of convicts reduces the crime rate only if there is no compensating increase of crime by others. Often there is.[46] {194}

Incarceration may also harden offenders and increase the chances of recidivism.[47] Indeed, prison life may so brutalize individuals as to increase their propensity for violent crime.[48] Even with all these caveats, a persuasive case can be made for incarceration as a means of protecting society, at least temporarily, from the street crime it fears.

The case for deterrence is somewhat more problematic but still plausible. Most advocates of deterrence agree that the research indicates that certainty rather than severity accounts for the deterrent effects of punishment.[49] Accordingly, it is important to distinguish the punitive versions of deterrence that are unlikely to be effective from Wilson's more moderate proposals that are consistent with the available data.

> [E]very conviction for a nontrivial offense would entail a penalty that involved a deprivation of liberty, even if brief. For many offenses the minimum sentence might be as low as one week, and even that might be served on weekends. For most offenses the average sentence would be relatively short—perhaps no more than six months or a year—but would be invariably applied. Only the most serious offenses would result in long penalties.

> "[Deprivation of liberty" need not, and usually would not, entail confinement in a conventional prison. After the deprivation of liberty is decided upon, a decision would be made as to whether it would involve confinement at night and on weekends, while allowing a person to work during the day; enrollment in a closely supervised community-based treatment program; or confinement in a well-guarded prison.[50]

Interpretations of the data, and more specifically of the research of Isaac Ehrlich, differ.[51] Wilson finds the case for deterrence convincing, while Silberman is very skeptical. To some extent, their differences boil down to a dispute over whether the cup of deterrence is half empty or half full. Silberman's common-sense belief is that punishment "deters at least *some* crime."[52] The data are, however, inconclusive, according to Silberman. "We simply do not know enough to predict with confidence how much crime will be deterred by any given change in punishment, or even whether stepped-up punishment will have any effect at all."[53] Wilson, while conceding some problems with the deterrence data, finds them to be very encouraging. Still, his conclusions are couched in rather negative terms. "There is scarcely any evidence to support the proposition that would-be criminals are indifferent to the risks associated with a proposed course of action."[54] My inclination is to see the case for deterrence as no better or worse than cases that can be made for other policy alternatives. Nonetheless, the politics of law and order seem unlikely to serve any useful crime-control purposes.

The first problem, as Silberman points out, is that the law-and-order position assumes that criminal courts are not already punishing in proportion to the severity of the crime. Wilson's complaint is typical: {195}

> To an astonishing degree, judges and prosecutors have used their discretion to minimize the incapacitative value of prisons.... What is remarkable is that so few knowledgeable persons, especially among the ranks of many professional students of crime, are even willing to entertain the possibility that penalties make a difference.[55]

But we have seen that bureaucratic justice calculates punishment according to the seriousness of the offense and the dangerousness of the offender. Even the Marxist judge quoted in Chapter 6 was willing to incarcerate the really dangerous offender. "The persistent violator of people, the person of violence, and so on, I put away. To protect society I'd put that person away."[56] The Vera Institute study provides systematic confirmation that punishment is forthcoming for the predatory stranger.

The second problem emerges directly from the aggregate data. The real obstacle to effective crime control is to be found in arrest figures rather than sentencing practices. In 1979, for example, only about 25 percent of robberies were cleared by arrest. The figures were much higher for murder and rape—about 75 and 50 percent, respectively—while much lower for burglary, roughly 15 percent.[57] Keep in mind, however, that murder and rape are frequently prior relationship crimes. Generally speaking, then, predatory *strangers* have good reason to believe when they commit a crime that their chances of getting caught are relatively small. Obviously, criminals who are not arrested will not be incapacitated. Similarly, a low rate of arrest will weaken the deterrent effect of even the most predictable sentencing policy. Indeed, for criminals who do not believe they are going to be caught, sentencing policies are beside the point.

Punitive sentencing policies occasioned by the politics of law and order are therefore unlikely to serve the purposes of crime control. Indeed, for reasons to be considered in the concluding section, such policies may well do more harm than good.

Recall that the politics of law and order, as it concerns the criminal courts, comes to us flying two flags: the hard-line flag of punitive conservatives and the justice flag waved by moderate conservatives. Ordinarily, political candidates offer *both* a tougher and a fairer—that is, a less discretionary—system. Either way, we would expect the increased incarceration revealed by the available data. Therefore, these data do not tell us whether reform is moving in a purely punitive direction or is seriously embracing legal values.

My guess is that the principal impact has been punitive, although the nature and extent of the punitive drift has probably varied considerably depending on the prevailing political culture. In reform cities, punitive {196} pressures have probably been guided by legal values toward retribution and deterrence, along the lines of the Minneapolis courts described by Levin. Machine cities, with a taste for discretionary decision making, have in all likelihood emphasized incapacitation. In both settings, however, the net effect has been punitive, and the basic character of the system has remained unchanged.

It is, in the first place, a good deal easier to tighten the screws than to restructure the existing system of bureaucratic justice. After all, bureaucratic justice makes good sense to criminal court professionals. Heumann has written persuasively of the socialization of young lawyers who came to the criminal courts with fundamental objections to plea bargaining.[58] Similar things are likely to happen to crusading candidates, once they are confronted with the realities of the criminal courts. Not the least of these realities will be the resistance of insiders to changes in established practices. But I also believe that as erstwhile critics become insiders, they will gain a greater appreciation for the merits of bureaucratic justice.

The justice model is, moreover, never going to live up to its advance billing. Punishment will never be strictly fitted to the crime. Once prior record is taken into account, as Wilson and others argue it must be, sentencing is already being adapted in some measure to the criminal. Of course, there are more or less discretionary ways of reading that record, but the underlying principle is already weakened. As a matter of fact, sentencing guidelines based on the crime and the prior record boil down to a formalization and codification of the informal norms of bureaucratic justice. The resemblance is further increased by the allowance, regularly included in determinant sentencing plans, for departures from the guidelines in exceptional cases, albeit with the requirement of a formal justification.

But even if by some magic a rigid plan could be imposed, there is good reason to believe that this would not so much end discretion as transfer it from the sentencing decision to the charging decision.

> Since the offense for which offenders were convicted would largely determine the sentence they received, prosecutors would become the sentencing authority through their control of the charging process.[59]

Indeed, if Littrell is correct about the bureaucratic inversion of legal authority, the end result of an effective determinate sentencing policy would be to put much of the discretion in the hands of the police, who exercise so much influence over charging.

It is nowhere near so complex an undertaking to increase the harshness of sentences. Indeed, in a punitive political climate, tougher sentencing amounts to the line of least resistance. The judge or prosecutor who gets a reputation for lenient sentencing is a vulnerable target at election time. {197} Although I know of no systematic research on the subject, there is no reason to shrug off as an aberration the case of two liberal Seattle judges who were successfully targeted for defeat by the Seattle Police Officers' Guild and some citizen groups.[60] Under such circumstances, other candidates are likely to get the message. Given a law-and-order climate, even liberal candidates can be expected to move in a punitive direction. Witness the example of Elizabeth Holtzman's 1981 campaign for district attorney in Brooklyn, New York, as reported by the *New York Times.*

> Miss Holtzman, a legislator with a liberal record, is stressing such issues as stronger penalties for serious crime, saying that fighting crime has become paramount for the people of Brooklyn.[61]

Such promises are also more difficult to evade than commitment to structural change. Sentencing decisions are public, and the media are unlikely to allow it to go unnoticed when a serious crime is committed by someone who received probation or a suspended sentence. Under such circumstances, an understandable tendency to err on the punitive side is likely to develop.

If so, the results are likely to be increases in the already stiff sentences being handed out to predatory strangers and perhaps heavier penalties inflicted on those who have committed minor crimes—especially prior relationship crimes because these are the cases most likely to be "solved" by the police. Elliot Currie reports that "increasingly, the prisons are swollen because of an influx of property criminals, not violent ones."[62] To increase the sentences of predatory strangers could have some additional incapacitating and deterrent effects, although for reasons already considered, these benefits are likely to be rather limited. Scapegoating minor criminals is at best irrelevant and at worst self-defeating insofar as their prison experiences harden them and make them more prone to violent crime on release. All told, then, a purely punitive drift in sentencing policy is hardly a step in the right direction.

NOTES

1. See p. 162.

2. See pp. 153–55.

3. It is, incidentally, not strictly true that Wilson embraces the job perspective. As he sees it, permissive sentences can be, in part, traced to "the growing belief among some judges that since prisons apparently do not rehabilitate, it is wrong to send criminals to them." In

other words, these judges, however mistakenly, actually believe in what they do. See James Q. Wilson, *Thinking About Crime* (New York: Vintage, 1977). 186

4. Steven Phillips, "Justice for Whom?" *Psychology Today* (March 1977), 70. {198}

5. Ibid., 72.

6. Ibid., 74–75.

7. Ibid., 75.

8. Ibid.

9. Ibid., 85.

10. Ibid.

11. Ibid.

12. Ibid., 86.

13. Ibid., 88.

14. Ibid., 86–88.

15. This is, I take it, the essential point of John Hogarth's superb study of Canadian magistrates, although he is inclined to trace the magistrate's "penal philosophy" back beyond personal values—or "the social purposes of a magistrate," as he puts it—to a "deeper level of personality." See John Hogarth, *Sentencing as a Human Process* (Toronto: University of Toronto Press, 1971), 92.

16. Lon L. Fuller, *The Morality of Law* (New Haven: Yale University Press, 1964), 172.

17. John Schaar has argued that formal equality is a way of defending the remaining remnants of individualism in a political climate that is distinctly hostile to this eighteenth-century ideal. "In the huge heterogeneous polities of today...each of us must...live much of his life among virtual strangers, and no man can safely endure or morally accept judgments of his worth made by strangers. No man can turn himself over for moral judgment to others who do not share his hopes and fears, his code of righteousness, his loves and hates. In the constitutionalist polity, with its postulate of equality, each of us in effect is under a contract of strictly limited public liability. This is probably the only technique which can protect any meaningful liberty and personal integrity in the giant states of today." Thus, for Schaar, rule-of-law ideals are not simply a historical curiosity, the vestigial remnants of an earlier era's quest for freedom, but one of the necessary conditions contemporary freedom. See John H. Schaar, "Some Ways of Thinking About Equality," *Journal of Politics* 26 (November 1964): 877.

18. Karl Menninger, *The Crime of Punishment* (New York: Viking, 1969).

19. Rudolph J. Gerber and Patrick D. McAnany, "Punishment as Reflected in Prevailing Ideologies," in *Crime and Justice: The Criminal in the Arms of the Law*, Vol. 2, rev. ed., Leon Radzinowicz and Marvin E. Wolfgang (New York: Basic Books, 1977), 71.

20. Martin P. Golding, *Philosophy of Law* (Englewood Cliffs, N.J.: Prentice-Hall, 1975), 91.

21. Ibid., 92.

22. Ibid., 84.

23. Ibid., 93.

24. Ibid., 91–92.

25. Malcolm M. Feeley, *Court Reform on Trial: Why Simple Solutions Fail* (New York: Basic Books, 1983), 142–47.

26. Jonathan D. Casper, David Brereton, and David Neal, *The Implementation of the California Determinate Sentencing Law: Executive Summary* (Washington, D.C.: National Institute of Justice, 1982), 45. {199}

27. Martin A. Levin, *Urban Politics and the Criminal Courts* (Chicago: University of Chicago Press, 1977).

28. Isaac D. Balbus, *The Dialectics of Legal Repression: Black Rebels before the American Criminal Court* (New Brunswick, N.J.: Transaction, 1977).

29. Levin, *Urban Politics and Criminal Courts*, 5–6.

30. Ibid., 6.

31. Ibid., 49–50.

32. Ibid., 142.

33. Ibid., 6.

34. Balbus, *The Dialectics of Legal Repression*, 240.

35. Ibid., 250; italics in the original.

36. Ibid., 235; italics in the original.

37. James Eisenstein and Herbert Jacob, *Felony Justice: An Organizational Analysis of Criminal Courts* (Boston: Little, Brown, 1977), 122.

38. Ibid., 78–80 and 92.

39. Ibid., 140–41 and 161.

40. Timothy J. Flanagan, David J. van Alstyne, and Michael R. Gottfredson, eds., *Sourcebook of Criminal Justice Statistics—1981* (Washington, D.C.: Bureau of Justice Statistics, 1982), 471.

41. Bureau of Labor Statistics, *Bulletin*, (April 1982), 1. The rate for violent crime committed by nonstrangers has risen only slightly between 1973 and 1979.

42. Flanagan et al., *Sourcebook of Criminal Justice Statistics—1981*, 364.

43. Wilson, *Thinking About Crime*, 182.

44. Ernest van den Haag, *Punishing Criminals: Concerning a Very Old and Painful Question* (New York: Basic Books, 1975), 51.

45. Wilson, *Thinking About Crime*, 225.

46. Van den Haag, *Punishing Criminals*, 52. See also Charles Silberman, *Criminal Violence, Criminal Justice* (New York: Random House, 1978), 196.

47. Van den Haag, *Punishing Criminals*, 52.

48. Ramsey Clark, *Crime in America: Observations on Its Nature, Causes, Prevention and Control* (New York: Simon and Schuster, 1970), Chap. 13.

49. Wilson, *Thinking About Crime*, 195.

50. Ibid., 202.

51. Isaac Ehrlich, "The Deterrent Effect of Criminal Law Enforcement," *Journal of Legal Studies* 1 (June 1972): 259–76.

52. Silberman, *Criminal Violence, Criminal Justice*, 78; italics in the original.

53. Ibid., 195.

54. Wilson, *Thinking About Crime*, 197'.

55. Ibid., 194 and 196.

56. See p. 162.

57. Flanagan et al., *Sourcebook of Criminal Justice Statistics—1981*, 368.

58. Milton Heumann, *Plea Bargaining* (Chicago: University of Chicago Press, 1978).

59. Silberman, *Criminal Violence, Criminal Justice*, 295.

60. *Seattle Sun*, 26 May 1976 and 27 October 1976. See also *Seattle Post-Intelligencer*, 23 September 1976.

61. *New York Times*, 21 August 1981.

62. Elliot Currie, "Fighting Crime," *Working Papers 9*, no. 4 (July/August 1982): 19.

Part IV

Criminal Justice

{Page 203}

8

Beyond the Politics of Law and Order

Conflict is the key to understanding the complex interaction of politics, crime, and criminal process—and not just the conflict between lawbreakers and the law-abiding, as the mainstream would have us believe. At each step along the way—defining crime, grass-roots and official reactions to it, and the workings of criminal process—the underlying reality has been segments of society pursuing their own values and interests. Although softened by accommodations and cooperation, the clash of values and interests typifies the criminal process.

This is not a reality that most Americans are prepared to recognize. We prefer to think about crime as a battle between the evil few and the virtuous many. At the same time, we impose unrealistic standards and expectations on the criminal process. As long as we oversimplify things in this way, both our hopes and our fears are likely to get out of hand. We hope for, and in fact come to expect, decisive action by agencies of the criminal process. When we discover, instead, equivocating policies and a rising crime rate, we grow desperate and vindictive. The increase in crime seems a clear sign of moral deterioration and a mounting physical danger—not simply evidence of the inevitable tensions of a divided society with much of the victimization confined within segments, as conflict criminology teaches. And if the agencies of criminal process are unable or, for some perverse reason, unwilling to nip crime in the bud, the chances of coping with crime seem ever more remote as crime grows further out of hand. Understandably we become convinced that only draconian measures will succeed and that if we do not act quickly, it may be too late even for them.

Our unwillingness to acknowledge the complex reality of crime and {204} criminal process is rooted in powerful cultural forces. The myth of crime and punishment, with all its oversimplifications concerning good and evil and its naive faith in punitive responses to crime, has deep historical roots. Moreover, its message is constantly reiterated in virtually all our cultural forums. We welcome this message, not simply because it is familiar and therefore seems to make sense, but also because it serves our personal needs well. It is comforting to believe that our traditional values are secure and that there is a simple solution to the crime problem. The attraction of punitive policies is a flight from the complexity and uncertainty of contemporary society more than a primitive drive for revenge.

Whatever may be the sources of our oversimplification of crime, the unfortunate consequence in recent years has been to politicize street crime and move operative policy in a punitive direction. Some perverse consolation may be taken from the strongly symbolic quality of politicization. To a significant degree, the politics of law and order is just so much sound and fury—useful to politicians for establishing electoral alliances and mobilizing support at the grass roots, but of limited effect when it comes to working out concrete policy. Policy change tends to be inhibited by the vested interests and entrenched values of criminal process professionals, who are themselves in conflict with one another. Still, some of the law-and-order pressure gets through, and this punitive drift works at cross purposes to the most promising reforms of progressive policing and tends to lead the criminal courts toward an indiscriminate and self-defeating crackdown on offenders.

The obvious question posed by this analysis is whether there is a better way of doing things. I have asked myself this question many times, and it has surely been posed to me with great insistence by students. With some trepidation, I will close by considering and, in fact, advocating "neighborhood justice" as an encouraging approach to reform.

Neighborhood justice is rooted in the idea of a partial decentralization of criminal process, along the lines of neighborhood team policing discussed in Chapter 5. My trepidation reflects how little we know about how neighborhood justice actually works. All we have to go on are a few modest and inadequately evaluated pilot projects. It is also true that crime is an intractable problem, and policy reforms must be thought of in ameliorative terms.

I do not, however, propose to devote this chapter to a condemnation of neighborhood justice by faint praise. On the contrary, I propose to make a principled case for neighborhood justice as the appropriate response to crime, given the premises of conflict criminology on which this book is based and the inherently discretionary character of criminal process as it has emerged from our analysis of the police and the criminal courts. I also defend neighborhood justice against some serious objections that may reasonably be raised against it. As the team policing example {205} makes clear, the decentralization that is at the heart of neighborhood justice means that different neighborhoods may well be responding in distinctive ways to crime and criminals. Movement in this direction obviously runs counter to cherished American legal values, which call for equal application of uniform rules. A strong case can nonetheless be made for neighborhood justice.

In short, I am less interested in extolling the virtues of neighborhood justice *in practice* than in looking critically at the principled arguments for and against it. It is impossible at this experimental stage to know how well neighborhood justice will work, and the political climate is, in any case, not currently conducive to such reforms. My emphasis, therefore, is on threshold concerns that might stand in the way of giving neighborhood justice a fair try at some time in the future when the public and the politicians are more receptive to serious reform.

FORMS AND PRINCIPLES OF NEIGHBORHOOD JUSTICE

Strictly speaking, neighborhood justice is a term applicable only to informal dispute settlement centers set up throughout the country in recent years. These experimental programs differ considerably from one another, but, as Roman Tomasic and Malcolm Feeley point out, they have quite a bit in common.

> [T]hey are designed as alternatives to courts; handle both criminal and civil grievances; rely on voluntary participation by the disputants; and employ techniques of mediation and compromise rather than compulsory formality and the winner-take-all approach of courts. Proponents of neighborhood justice centers argue that these features of these new institutions, along with their community base, enhance the likelihood that root causes of grievances can be explored and effective settlements reached.[1]

Neighborhood justice centers thus pursue an adaptive approach to dispute resolution. The terms of settlement are established consensually by the parties rather than imposed in accordance with prior rules; due process protections, like other legal formalities, are largely disregarded.

Tomasic and Feeley see neighborhood justice centers as part of a current of general law reform that emphasizes "delegalization, simplification, and informality."[2] Considered from this broader perspective, the principles on which neighborhood justice centers are based are to be found in reforms proposed for each stage of criminal process. It is, in effect, these reforms that define the concept of neighborhood justice as it is used in this chapter—that is, reforms stressing informality and responsiveness to neighborhood diversity.

To be more specific, neighborhood justice is rooted in the complementary {206} principles of community development and responsive institutions. Neighborhoods in which crime is a serious problem are, generally speaking, neighborhoods in which community norms and the networks sustaining those norms have broken down. The first objective, then, is to reverse the process of community disintegration. Second, because neighborhoods are likely to have their own special characteristics, it is important that the agencies of criminal process become responsive to these particularities. Only if the two processes go forward together is neighborhood justice likely to work effectively. If, in other words, the agencies of criminal process are unresponsive to the norms and needs of individual neighborhoods, there will be little basis for community development. Conversely, if neighborhood life is in chaos, to whom and to what are agencies of criminal process to respond?

The objective of this section is to explore these two fundamental principles of neighborhood justice in the broader context of social and legal theory. This exploration is preliminary to the case for neighborhood justice that I make in the next section. First, however, let us get a more concrete sense of what neighborhood justice is all about.

Forms of Neighborhood Justice

There are a number of variants of neighborhood justice. While each of them includes provisions for community development and for more responsive institutions, the mix differs markedly from plan to plan. Moreover, since there are neighborhood justice schemes for each stage of criminal process, the mechanisms of neighborhood justice also vary widely.

At one end of the continuum are delinquency prevention programs that seek to bypass formal agencies of criminal process and focus almost entirely on community development. The objective of such programs is to make the community itself the source of service and support to troubled youth. Consider an apparently successful Puerto Rican program founded by Sister Isolina Ferre, as described by Charles Silberman:

> The premise...was that the most effective way to change juvenile behavior is to change adult behavior—and that the most effective way to change adult behavior is to create a structure that enables people to assume roles that require responsibility in and to their own community. For in the last analysis it is the disorganization of the community at large—the evidence on all sides that their parents are unable to control their own lives, unable to impose sanctions on people who threaten their own or their community's well-being—that persuades the young that the cards are hopelessly stacked against them...thereby allowing crime to seem a rewarding alternative.[3]

While the immediate focus is therefore on the "delinquent," community development is seen as the more fundamental objective and the companion {207} consequence of enlisting the energies of neighborhood residents and local groups to provide support for those who are in trouble.

At the other end of the continuum is neighborhood team policing. The emphasis of team policing is much more on responsiveness than on community development. With semiautonomous neighborhood teams taking over primary policing responsibility, it is assumed that responsiveness will be increased simply by the proximity of the police to the neighborhood—at least as long as there is a departmental incentive structure that rewards community service. Neighborhood team policing also includes provisions for activating community networks through things like blockwatch teams and police advisory councils. But, at least as I see it, these community outreach programs are secondary to institutional decentralization, which is the principal instrument of reform.[4]

A much more even mix between institutional responsiveness and community development can be found in programs for keeping neighborhood conflicts out of the formal court system. As with team policing, neighborhood dispute resolution remains in the pilot program stage, and there is considerable variation among the plans that have been tried.[5] Generally speaking, the emphasis is on such misdemeanors as assault, larceny, and vandalism, although some programs have tackled *prior relationship* felonies.[6] Neighborhood dispute resolution is supposed to enhance the responsiveness of the criminal process through neighborhood decentralization, informal procedures, and, in some programs, through the use of lay members of the community, trained in mediation techniques, as hearings officers.[7] Referral of cases by the police and the criminal courts further accentuates the basic message of responsiveness. Inclusion of local citizens in the hearing process can also be seen as a step toward community development. The balance swings farther toward community development when neighborhood organizations are responsible for initiating and operating the program and when active efforts are made to encourage neighborhood residents to bring their problems directly to the justice centers.[8] It is clear, in any case, that neighborhood settlement both depends upon and seems capable of evoking a sense of community. As Sally Merry puts it:

> Particularly in areas where substantial differences in class, lifestyle, and values divide residents, the inevitable conflicts of daily life are exacerbated by misunderstanding and, often, group and ethnic prejudice. Disputants in these situations may deal with their differences through avoidance, endurance of a state of ongoing conflict, or "lumping it," while conflict swells feelings of ethnic hostility. Mediation could provide a valuable means to counteract this social isolation by providing a mechanism for

people to communicate with each other, breaking down hostilities founded on misunderstanding.[9]

The agencies of criminal process, for their part, must allow neighborhood norms to take precedence over the rules and procedures of formal law {208} enforcement. Of course, should neighborhood norms fail, it is understood that the criminal courts will be invoked.[10]

Community-based corrections entails a similarly even balance between responsiveness and community development. The assumption is that the rehabilitation of offenders is more likely to occur in a setting that maintains their contacts with, rather than isolating them from, their own communities.

> [T]he task of corrections involves the reconstruction or construction of ties between the offender and the community through the maintenance of family bonds, obtaining education and employment, and finding a place for the offender in the mainstream of social life.[11]

Community-based correctional plans may involve either decentralized residential facilities or probation plans. Either way, the offenders participate in community life by holding jobs or attending school and through volunteer programs that call on community residents to take an interest in, and serve as lay counselors for, individual offenders.[12] The community is therefore involved in a variety of ways in community-based correctional programs. Offenders reside in the community and are provided education and employment, but the volunteer program is at the heart of community development. As Martha Wylie, director of Project Start, a Detroit program, put it:

> The volunteers remain one of the best recruitment, training, and public information resources. For those who have really gotten "hooked" it has become a cause—that is, they know that there is something an individual can do about "the crime problem."[13]

The objective is, in short, to encourage the community to take a significant share of the responsibility for reintegrating offenders.

This brief summary of the several forms of neighborhood justice does no more than scratch the surface. Each plan could be described in much more detail, and what is known about their successes and failures could be considered. Given the tremendous number and diversity of neighborhood programs, such an inquiry would, however, inevitably get out of hand. The available evaluation research is, moreover, spotty and inconclusive. Accordingly, having provided a sketch of the institutional forms of neighborhood justice, I prefer to shift from its practice to a more careful look at the two principles on which it rests: community development and responsive institutions.

Community Development

The most cogent statement of the thinking that lies behind the community development aspects of neighborhood justice is to be found in Peter Berger {209} and Richard Neuhaus's work on "mediating structures."[14] Although Berger and Neuhaus do not address themselves to crime or neighborhood justice, their ideas have been adapted to delinquency and other areas of public policy.[15] The original statement by Berger and Neuhaus remains the best source for understanding one of the premises on which neighborhood justice ultimately rests, while Robert Woodson's delinquency study clarifies the links between mediating structures and neighborhood justice.

The theory of mediating structures focuses on the alienating quality of modern life in which individuals, particularly the poor, tend to be caught between the oppressive certainty of large-scale bureaucracies—the "megastructure" of business, labor, and government, as Berger and Neuhaus put it—and the contingent existence of private life. Individuals depend on megastructures for services and employment but find them impersonal, unresponsive, and intrusive.[16] On the other hand, "in private life the individual is left very much to his own devices, and thus is uncertain and anxious."[17] Mediating structures, it is argued, can reduce "both the anomic precariousness of individual existence in isolation from society and the threat of alienation to the public order."[18]

But how is it that mediating structures can attenuate the powerful forces of modernity? Indeed, just exactly what is it that Berger and Neuhaus mean by mediating structures? The examples they provide—neighborhood, family, church, and voluntary association—help us begin to answer both questions. Individuals learn and affirm their values through participation in mediating structures. Without such structures, values can be imposed only by the alienating power of the large-scale bureaucracies.

> [M]ediating structures are the value-generating and value-maintaining agencies in society. Without them, values become another function of the megastructures, notably of the state, and this is a hallmark of totalitarianism. In the totalitarian case, the individual becomes the object rather than the subject of the value-propagating processes of society.[19]

Mediating structures are, then, part of an organic and distinctly pluralistic image of society. "Within one's group—whether it be racial, national, political, religious, or all of these—one discovers an answer to the elementary question, 'Who am I?', and is supported in living out that answer."[20] Thus, mediating structures allow us to seek out and live our own lives rather than have lives imposed on us by impersonal megastructures.

A social policy consistent with the integrative potential of mediating structures therefore goes well beyond simple decentralization, which reduces the scale of the delivery system but maintains policy uniformity. The autonomy of the mediating structure—be it the family, the neighborhood, the church, or a private association—must be preserved. But this is possible only if the diversity of values is respected by the state. Neighborhoods must, for example, be allowed to determine "their own chosen life {210} styles and values."[21] At the very least, government policy must not undermine mediating structures. More positively, mediating structures should serve as a kind of conduit through which government services are expanded and adapted to the diverse needs of a genuinely pluralistic society.[22] The vision is, then, one of unity growing out of diversity with mediating structures as the essential, non-coercive integrative mechanism of modern society.

Woodson explicitly employs the ideas of Berger and Neuhaus to argue in behalf of delinquency prevention programs that utilize community resources in preference to programs of criminal process professionals—be their inclinations coercive or therapeutic. The key to Woodson's thinking is the neighborhood functioning as a kind of surrogate family.

> Functionally, the institution of the family has been society's basic support system for the development of personally adequate individuals, oriented to appropriate social values and capable of sustained socially appropriate behavior.[23]

Given a breakdown of nuclear and extended families, "neighborhood youth development projects" become, in effect, the surrogate family.

> The "family" lives in its own familiar neighborhood, where it can make maximum use of available human and material resources. Thus, an individual member of this unit is brought into direct relation through the family with the larger community structure, becoming actively involved with *community development* as an aspect of his own development.[24]

Woodson's discussion of several programs that have put these principles into practice emphasizes the way in which the ideal of service to others has been nurtured among both community volunteers and restive youth. "In the end, child saving is also neighborhood revitalization in a profound way."[25]

It might seem at first glance as if mediating structures would be about as controversial as Mom and apple pie, but Berger and Neuhaus readily concede that objections can and will be raised by those at the liberal center of American politics.

> [T]he great concern [of liberals] is for the individual...and for a just public order, but anything "in between" is viewed as irrelevant, or even an obstacle, to the rational ordering of society....
>
> ...Private rights are frequently defended *against* mediating structures—children's rights against the family, the rights of sexual

deviants against neighborhood or small-town sentiment, and so forth.[26]

A companion objection is that pluralism, which lies at the heart of mediating structures, will prove divisive and thwart social progress.[27] The controversy over school busing provides in instructive example of the tensions between the prerogatives of family and neighborhood, on the one {211} hand, and the claims of racial justice and a unified society, on the other. Mediating structures do pose some serious problems.

Insofar as criminal process is concerned, the central problem is whether mediating structures are compatible with legal authority. Is it possible to incorporate a profusion of neighborhood priorities into the criminal law without undermining the moral force of the law through relativistic thinking that compromises society's fundamental values? Before responding to this question, let us first look at the second principle on which neighborhood justice rests: responsive institutions.

Responsive Institutions

Our legal system, including the criminal law, tends to operate rigidly and formalistically and therefore responds sluggishly to society's problems. This is the guiding premise of Philippe Nonet and Philip Selznick's provocative call for a more responsive law.[28] Their essay is based on a developmental model of law, according to which our system of "autonomous law" is itself a reform of an earlier style of "repressive law." The "responsive law" they advocate can, then, be seen as the third and highest stage of a developmental cycle. The history and details of Nonet and Selznick's developmental model are only marginally relevant to neighborhood justice. The developmental model, however, does have a strong reform bias. Insofar as Nonet and Selznick demonstrate that each stage serves the peculiar needs of its era, the clear inference is that it is both desirable and inevitable that the law adapt to the society.[29] More to the point is the interesting correspondence between responsive law and neighborhood justice.

The problem that Nonet and Selznick detect in the currently prevailing "autonomous" style of law is that it puts too much emphasis on "accountability."[30] In historical or developmental terms, the emphasis on accountability is understandable and is, in fact, a corrective of repressive practices. Under a repressive regime, law and politics are virtually indistinguishable, and legal rules are infinitely manipulable and always at the service of those in power. Repressive law "is a pliable tool, readily available to consolidate power, husband authority, secure privilege, and win conformity."[31] The major contribution of legal autonomy, then, is to put limits on those who wield power and, more particularly, control *"rampant official discretion."*[32] These limits take the form of an elaborate system of rules that obligates government officials as well as the general public.

There is, however, a distinctly seamy side to accountability. The primacy of rules was, in the first place, part of "a historic bargain" that traded substance for procedure. "*Legal institutions purchase[d] procedural* {212} *autonomy at the price of substantive subordination.*"[33] The distinction between procedure and substance is elusive, but the basic point is that the constraints of the law are focused less on what officials do than on how they do it—less on official objectives than on methods. It is rather like the old wisecrack about France where, so the saying goes, you can do anything just as long as you pronounce it correctly. In dealing with capital punishment, for example, the Supreme Court has tended to steer clear of judgments about the wisdom of that way of responding to crime and has focused instead on whether it works in a racially biased fashion.[34] In addition, since accountability is anchored in official adherence to rules, all the rigidity of rule following is incorporated into our autonomous style of law.

> Accountability is most readily maintained when performance can be measured by determinate standards; at the same time, the demand for accountability fosters insecurity and a search for bureaucratic havens where responsibilities are narrowly defined and easily met. In other words, accountability breeds formalism and retreatism, rendering institutions rigid, incapable of coping with new contingencies.[35]

These and other shortcomings of autonomous law have led to a crisis of legal authority, and out of that crisis Nonet and Selznick hope and expect the development of a responsive style of law.[36]

As would be expected, the objective of responsive law is to replace the rigidity, formalism, and caution of autonomous law with a more open and adaptable system. As Nonet and Selznick get more specific, the correspondence between responsive law and neighborhood justice becomes clearer. The legal order must, first, soften its penchant for uniform rules and become "more receptive to cultural diversity, less prone to brutalize the deviant and the eccentric."[37] Second, the law must come to see problems of public order less in terms of rule following and more in terms of problem solving.

> This posture assumes that the terms of public order are not rigidly fixed but, rather, open to renegotiation so that they will take better account of affected social interests.... That paradigm invokes a pluralistic model of the group structure of society, thus underlining the reality and reaffirming the legitimacy of social conflict.[38]

Responsive law thus has the capacity to learn from social crisis and be open to the possibility that substantial problems with disobedience of legal rules should be seen as a symptom of that crisis rather than its cause. The necessary corollary of this recognition is a willingness to adapt the rules to the plural-istic particularities of the society.

Nonet and Selznick are not very explicit about the kinds of institutional adaptations required by a responsive law, but what they do say suggests the community-based reforms summarized at the beginning of this section {213} would be altogether acceptable. The one thing that is clear from their presen-tation is that responsive law necessarily entails discretionary decision making. "Openness...presumes wide grants of discretion, so that official conduct may remain flexible, adaptive, and self-corrective."[39] The danger is that rampant discretion will lead backward to repressive law rather than forward to respon-sive law. But it is precisely at this point that neighborhood justice and re-sponsive law converge.

> Discretion does not necessarily foster unrestrained authority. It is most likely to do so when power is isolated from social structure and therefore removed from the moderating effect of community involvement.[40]

Of course, each of the neighborhood justice schemes institutionalizes com-munity participation to a significant degree, and this participation becomes the primary vehicle for adapting the presumptive uniformity of criminal process to the social realities of our pluralistic society.

The message of Nonet and Selznick's inquiry into legal theory is, then, not simply that the institutional changes associated with neighborhood justice are acceptable but that they are necessary if the authority of the law is to be maintained. Of course, as they readily concede, responsive law, like any re-form, has its dangers and costs as well as its benefits. As law becomes more caught up in purpose and thus draws closer to politics, a regression toward repressive law is, for example, always possible. Must we not also ask what we are giving up in exchanging the principle of equality under law for variable standards derived from neighborhood values? Is responsive law not, in other words, inherently unjust and open to discriminatory bias insofar as the prin-ciple of equality under law is abandoned?

Forms and Principles in Sum

The roots of neighborhood justice are, I have been arguing, apparent in some very fundamental problems of contemporary American society and in the shortcomings of our political and legal institutions. The politics of law and order may therefore be seen as just one aspect of a much broader malaise, and the primary virtue of neighborhood justice is that crime and criminal process are dealt with in the context of, rather than in isolation from, the problems of our pluralistic and stratified society. It must be quickly added, however, that neighborhood justice leaves untouched the fundamental economic inequalities of the society, and it is largely for that reason that I suggested at the outset of this chapter that neighborhood justice is no panacea.[41]

But this consideration of the underlying principles of neighborhood justice has left us with two more immediate questions about the possible pitfalls of reform. {214}

1. Is it possible to incorporate a variety of value systems into criminal process without yielding to an ethical relativism that will erode the moral force of the law?

2. Is it not discriminatory in principle and dangerous in practice to grant discretionary authority to apply the law differently to different segments of the society?

These serious and challenging questions are considerably less troubling when we measure the reforms of neighborhood justice against the real world of criminal process, as it has been presented in this book, rather than against the idealized system that most of us tend to embrace.

MAKING A CASE FOR NEIGHBORHOOD JUSTICE

In its idealized form, criminal process applies general rules in an impersonal and equal fashion. The proscriptions of substantive criminal law are addressed to everyone, and the rights provided for defendants are designed, at least in part, to assure equal and unbiased application. The reality of criminal process is something else. Everyone who works in criminal process knows that discretion is inevitable; at least in unguarded moments, people will acknowledge as much. But they continue to embrace uniformity and equal treatment as the only appropriate, if ultimately unattainable, measures of justice. The choice they make is to work to minimize the ostensible injustice of discretion—a reasonable enough position in an imperfect world.

But departures from uniform rules and formal equality should not be so readily associated with injustice. In a heterogeneous society marked by disparities of wealth, opportunity, and influence, as well as by great cultural variation, to treat all individuals alike will compound rather than mitigate injustice. Similarly, to the extent that all segments of society do not share the values and interests embodied in each provision of the criminal code, no moral lesson is communicated by the enforcement process. Certainly the research considered in this book suggests that departures from strict standards of uniformity and formal equality are regularly associated in the minds of officials with justice and morality. These perceptions are, no doubt, sometimes faulty, and discretionary authority is frequently abused—perhaps maliciously, perhaps as a result of insensitivity. That does not mean, however, that reform requires more assiduous pursuit of uniformity and formal equality. Far better to develop modes of differentiation that will be more reliably sensitive to cultural diversity and socioeconomic inequality, and that is what neighborhood justice is all about. In short, departures from uniformity and formal equality do not make neighborhood justice an unjust reform, nor will they rob the criminal law of its moral force. {215}

Justice and Injustice

Standards of uniformity and formal equality have never really been widely honored. The demands of proponents of the so-called justice model that we "return" to the traditional values of criminal process have a hollow ring to them. As we have seen, conscientious judges, police, and prosecutors are frequently tempted to base their decisions on the traits, motivations, and predispositions of the individuals and groups involved.[42]

Why is this the case? Equality before the law is one of our most cherished ideals. Yet there is a pervasive tendency to turn away from it. It is tempting to attribute the whole problem to human frailty—a willingness to sacrifice principle to expediency. Certainly, civil libertarians point just this kind of condemnatory finger at the police officer who takes shortcuts through a defendant's rights. But if expediency means taking the easy way, then particularization is hardly the expedient solution. Ordinarily, the easy way leads toward a mechanical application of the general rule. Indeed, our stereotype of the officious bureaucrat is the indolent time server who is unwilling to take the trouble to understand the problems of individual citizens.

No, it is simply *justice* that tempts officials to subvert the standards of formal equality. Particularization is guided by a strong sense of doing justice—a feeling that only cases that are actually comparable should be treated alike. The blindfold required by formal equality cuts decision makers off from relevant information bearing on comparability. Even more important, it becomes difficult to formulate the right response under the circumstances, since many of the circumstances are deemed out of bounds. In other words, to the extent that justice has to do with giving all persons their due, formal equality is not the solution but the problem.[43]

Formal equality might suffice in a homogeneous society composed of autonomous individuals bound together by a strong and pervasive commitment to a common set of values—a traditional village, for example. To the extent that the substantive criminal law crystallized a social consensus and that individuals competed with one another on roughly equal terms, it would perhaps be sufficient to let the punishment fit the crime. All persons would have comparable alternatives to criminal behavior. Given these two preconditions, there would, in the first place, be less discrepancy between formal equality and social circumstance. At the same time, because citizens would acknowledge the moral authority of a law that embodied widely shared values, the intrusions of criminal process would be more easily understood and accepted.

Even in this ideal setting, the particularity of individual and situational circumstances would put considerable pressure on uniformity and formal equality. In our heterogeneous society composed of many segments, each nurturing distinctive life styles, rooted in its own "behavioral patterns" and "normative systems," uniformity and formal equality become even {216} more problematic as standards of justice. Levin's study of urban criminal courts in Minneapolis and Pittsburgh provides a concrete illustration of the difficulties posed by social cleavage. Because "two cultures exist in our cities—a lower-class as well as a dominant middle-class...the criminal courts will," according to Levin, "have to ignore either the rule of law or the realities of urban life."[44]

But it is one thing to acknowledge this tension and another to embrace neighborhood justice. Levin would prefer to simply accept the tension as one of the inescapable dilemmas of urban criminal process rather than endorse the exercise of discretionary authority. In part, his objection to discretionary authority is the classic one: discretion and justice are incompatible, even when discretion is exercised in a compassionate way. We must choose, as he and many others see it, between the "benevolent" judges of Pittsburgh committed to the "values of individuality and desert" and the Minneapolis practice of justice, which "requires equal treatment of equals according to precise rules and different treatment or distinctions...only made according to rules."[45]

My argument runs in a different direction. While it may be appropriate to associate *a* conception of justice with formal equality, uniformity, and precise rules, we need not think of this as the *only* conception of justice. And we certainly need not think of a desert-based conception of neighborhood justice as unjust. Indeed, given a society divided, whether between cultures or among segments, the case for a discretionary form of justice becomes compelling. Under such circumstances, it is inappropriate and unrealistic to think of individuals in the terms implied by formal equality—as equally free agents facing essentially the same choices. It makes better sense to acknowledge that we all function within socially imposed constraints; that these constraints are experienced differentially; and that there are, accordingly, a variety of justifiable responses to the same social stimuli.

Neighborhood Justice and Social Morality

We are sometimes inclined to think of criminal law and criminal process in narrowly instrumental terms—solely in connection with preventing, reducing, and deterring crime by catching, convicting, and punishing (or rehabilitating) criminals. But as was argued in Chapter 3 and as Levin reminds us, the criminal law has "declarative" and "condemnatory" functions as well:

> Criminal law is in large part intended to be a list of acts that society wishes to "declare" inappropriate rather than a list of acts against which it wishes full enforcement.[46] {217}

The criminal law can be seen as an affirmation of our moral order. Levin worries, however, that discretionary decision making tends to lessen the moral force of the law inasmuch as society's norms are not consistently re-affirmed in criminal process. My argument, on the contrary, is that a measure of discretionary justice is required if the law is to transmit an effective moral message.

Levin seems to be saying that even when discretion is exercised prudently, as in Pittsburgh, the moral message tends to get lost as rules are bent around the particularities of individuals and situations. Conversely, the Minneapolis judges who stick more closely to the written rules tend to reinforce the declarations and condemnations of the criminal law:

> The Pittsburgh judges generally are oriented toward the defendant.... Their decision-making is nonlegalistic in that it tends to be particularistic, pragmatic, and based on policy considerations; their sentencing decisions are lenient. The situation in Minneapolis...is strikingly different—here sentencing decisions are severe.... This study indicates that the Minneapolis judges typically tend to be oriented more toward "society" and its needs and protection than toward the defendant.... Their decision-making is legalistic and universalistic.[47]

Thus, Levin senses moral reaffirmation in the work of the Minneapolis judges but detects "moral relativism" among the Pittsburgh judges, particularly insofar as they respond to the "two cultures" of the urban setting.[*]

Levin's objections to discretionary authority raise serious issues. Discretionary decision making attuned to the divisions within society could lead to moral relativism and toward the notion that all persons cannot or should not be equally law-abiding. After all, once we put ourselves in the shoes of the offender and come to understand why a choice has been made to violate the law, does it not follow that this understanding should, or at least could, be accepted as a justification for lawless acts? If not, how are we to protect the pluralism that provides the social rationale for neighborhood justice? Without

---

[*] Says Levin (see note 44), "The existence of these two cultures affects both the behavior of criminal-court judges and our methods of evaluating their performance in other ways as well. Since the "rediscovery" of poverty in America in the early 1960s, we have become increasingly aware of these two cultures. This awareness, the long and divisive Vietnam war, continued poverty in an age of unparalleled affluence, the transfer of the civil rights movement and the race problem to the previously "morally superior" North, have all contributed to making the past two decades an age of moral uncertainty and moral relativism" (205–6).

wishing to minimize either the conceptual or institutional difficulties of responding to these questions, I think that answers can be provided.

To begin with, the society in whose name Minneapolis judges ostensibly act is complex and divided. As Levin's "two cultures" argument suggests, and as the theories of conflict criminology presented in Chapter 1 {218} detail, these Minneapolis judges do not speak for a moral consensus but for the morality of the "dominant middle-class." If a moral lesson is to be conveyed in a divided society, it is necessary and proper that the social context be taken into account.

Second, the criminal law does not deliver a fixed, consistent, and consensual moral message. Nor is there a discrete behavioral referent for each provision of the criminal code. Only insofar as the level of generalization is high is this static and consensual view of criminal law serviceable. Thou shalt not kill, steal, rape! These proscriptions are more or less immune to differences of opinion and divisions in society. Moreover, at this level there is relatively little ambiguity when it comes to matching criminal acts to the criminal law.

The bulk of the criminal code is a good deal more elusive, both as it is promulgated and as it is applied. Consider the very refined calibrations of even the most basic postulates of criminal law. Murder: in what degree? Assault: felonious or simple battery? What about all those provisions of the criminal code not grounded in the basics of the Ten Commandments: laws against gambling, marijuana, and other victimless crime? Then there is the slippery distinction between civil and criminal liability.

When these matters were taken up in Chapter 1, it was argued that crime is best thought of as the politicization of social conflict:

> Systems of stratification develop as conflict becomes routinized and certain segments of society gain the upper hand.... Conflict in the work place is over wages, profits, and working conditions. Political conflict is over the rules of the game, with the politically powerful establishing rules that favor their interests and values. Those who fail to conform are, by definition, criminals.[48]

Moreover, the enforcement decisions of police, prosecutors, and judges are fraught with discretion, which will necessarily be informed by moral and political judgments. To suggest that this discretion be exercised with an eye to variations in standards of right and wrong in our pluralist society is hardly to jeopardize some immanent moral order.

On the contrary, and this is the crux of the matter, formal equality, not neighborhood justice, threatens the moral force of the law. Formal equality will not suffice because it cuts criminal process off from the moral context of criminal activity. Put in slightly different terms, formal equality assumes a moral consensus and, more specifically, assumes that the moral consensus that sustains the biblical core of criminal law can, or at least should, nurture the entirety of the criminal law. But, as I have just argued, it would seem unrealistic and even inappropriate to expect that in our heterogeneous society an unequivocal moral message would emerge from the morass of subtle distinctions and controversial proscriptions that comprise the bulk of our criminal law.

If our goal is that the criminal law should function as a device for {219} transmitting and nurturing standards of right and wrong, as Levin's analysis implies, we must be prepared to scrutinize and act upon the moral conflicts that are *sometimes* at the heart of criminal offenses. The alternative approach, inherent in formal equality, gives us criminal law as command—the simple imposition of criminal prohibitions on the citizenry rather than the establishment of channels of communication capable of building a viable moral order. On those matters for which no moral consensus exists, it is more appropriate, as I said earlier, to think of lawbreaking as a symptom rather than a source of social decomposition. If we are prepared to think in those terms, neighborhood justice becomes a learning device. As Nonet and Selznick put it: "*social pressures* [should be seen] *as sources of knowledge and opportunities for self-correction.*"[49] The simple suppression of these symptoms is self-defeating because it leads us to ignore the clues that violations of the law can provide to alternative moral perspectives and changing values.

Insofar as criminal law is seen as an opportunity for transmitting a moral lesson to the offender and society, to that extent the agencies of criminal process are engaged in a process of social communication.[50] Rather than take for granted the moral force of criminal law, neighborhood justice has as its goal establishing lines of communication, which are the prerequisite to delivering a moral message. Accordingly, our efforts should be directed at making those lines as reliable as possible. This is the basic thrust of neighborhood justice, which promises to enhance the legitimacy of the criminal law and reinforce the moral fabric of society by helping us compose (rather than suppress) social conflict.

Neighborhood justice provides a promising alternative to both the conservative and the liberal versions of criminal process. Unlike the conservative approach, neighborhood justice is sensitive to social stratification and is conciliatory rather than inflammatory. Unlike liberal views, neighborhood justice seeks neither to suppress discretion nor conceal it, but to make discretion more reliably and publicly sensitive to cultural diversity and socioeconomic inequality. Neighborhood justice therefore promises a more humane and adaptive criminal process.

There are some uncertainties about neighborhood justice. We do not, at this point, know for sure just how effective a tool of crime control neighborhood justice will turn out to be. On the basis of pilot project research, however, there is no reason to believe that neighborhood justice will be any *less* effective than traditional policies or the reforms engendered by the politics of law and order.[51] Similarly, we cannot be certain that community development and responsive institutions will ensure the responsible exercise of discretionary authority. But at least neighborhood {220} justice has a principled plan that goes beyond rigid and unrealistic efforts to squeeze discretion out of criminal process.

Nonetheless, some modest, piecemeal reforms seem much more likely than does an acceptance of neighborhood justice. We may, for example, turn away from punitive sentencing, but this will have more to do with the prohibitive costs of building prisons and providing for prisoners than with an overt repudiation of the politics of law and order. Similarly, police departments, at least in progressive cities, may become more responsive, but this will be the incidental consequence of legal pressures for affirmative action hiring, for example, rather than identification with the principles of team policing. Yet another possibility is that the interstitial biases of bureaucratic justice, of which I complained in Chapter 6, may be moderated if appellate review of sentencing is introduced.[52] But, once again, this reform will be the by-product of law-and-order inclinations to suppress discretion and not a recognition, a la neighborhood justice, that discretion is to be encouraged as long as it is exercised responsibly and in a fashion consistent with our pluralistic society. Such piecemeal reforms are possible because they do not challenge our fundamental understandings about crime and criminal process. Neighborhood justice is another matter entirely.

Quite independent of its merits, the prospects for neighborhood justice are not particularly bright for the simple reason that it calls for unsettling departures from established practices and beliefs. In part, this is the old question of vested interests. Criminal process professionals are simply going to be reluctant to share their authority with the neighborhoods. More fundamentally, neighborhood justice is symbolically suspect. Especially in a law-and-order political climate, the public and the professionals will seek symbolic reassurance that our traditional norms and values are intact and that those who jeopardize the fabric of society are unequivocally considered to be outcasts. Accordingly, the conciliatory tone of neighborhood justice becomes, in and of itself, a disabling defect. Indeed, even in a less hostile political climate, because neighborhood justice runs across the grain of so many of the mainstream premises discussed in Chapter 1, it will take a serious educational effort to persuade the public and the professionals to give neighborhood justice a fair try.

NOTES

1. Roman Tomasic and Malcolm M. Feeley, "Introduction," in *Neighborhood Justice: Assessment of an Emerging Idea*, ed. Roman Tomasic and Malcolm M. Feeley (New York: Longman, 1982), x.

2. Ibid.

3. Charles E. Silberman, *Criminal Violence, Criminal Justice* (New York: Random {221} House, 1978), 435. For more on this and other such programs, see Robert L. Woodson, *A Summons to Life: Mediating Structures and the Prevention of Youth Crime* (Cambridge, Mass.: Ballinger, 1981).

4. Programs for "community control" of the police imply a heavier emphasis on community development because community councils are given final responsibility for establishing police policy including hiring, promotion, and discipline of police officer. Needless to say, community control has made no headway in the real world of policing. See, generally, Alan A. Altshuler, *Community Control: The Black Demand for Participation in Large American Cities* (New York: Pegasus, 1970), 151–73.

5. For an excellent overview, see Tomasic and Feeley, *Neighborhood Justice*.

6. Daniel McGillis, "Minor Dispute Processing: A Review of Recent Developments," in ibid., 65–66. Neighborhood dispute resolution also deals with civil matters, which are the major focus of these informal mechanisms.

7. Ibid., 72.

8. Ibid., 70.

9. Sally Engle Merry, "Defining 'Success' in the Neighborhood Justice Movement," in Roman Tomasic and Malcolm Feeley, *Neighborhood Justice*, 187.

10. Richard Danzig, "Towards the Creation of a Complementary, Decentralized System of Criminal Justice," in Tomasic and Feeley, *Neighborhood Justice*, 16–17.

11. Quoted in George F. Cole, *The American System of Criminal Justice* (North Scituate, Mass.: Duxbury, 1975), 423.

12. Silberman discovered that residential programs are, in practice, frequently unresponsive and rigidly authoritarian—simply urban versions of traditional correctional facilities. See Silberman, *Criminal Violence, Criminal Justice*, 329–30.

13. Personal correspondence, 6 September 1981. On volunteer programs, see also *Instead of Prisons* no. 12 (Spring 1981). This is a newsletter of the Michigan Coalition for Prison Alternatives published by the American Friends Service Committee of Ann Arbor, Michigan. I am grateful to Ms. Wylie for her help and also to Tom Teicher who tried to set up a comparable program in the New York City area.

14. Peter L. Berger and Richard John Neuhaus, *To Empower People: The Role of Mediating Structures in Public Policy* (Washington, D.C.: American Enterprise Institute for Public Policy Research, 1977).

15. Woodson, *A Summons to Life*, deals with delinquency. This book is part of a series, published by Ballinger under the auspices of the American Enterprise Institute, dealing with such matters as health care, housing, welfare, and education.

16. Berger and Neuhaus, *To Empower People*, 2.

17. Ibid.

18. Ibid., 3.

19. Ibid., 6.

20. Ibid., 41.

21. Ibid., 15.

22. Ibid., 6–7.

23. Woodson, *A Summons to Life*, 40. {222}

24. Ibid., 42; italics added.

25. Ibid., 87.

26. Berger and Neuhaus, *To Empower People*, 5; italics in the original.

27. Ibid., 42.

28. Philippe Nonet and Philip Selznick, *Law and Society in Transition: Toward Responsive Law* (New York: Harper Colophon Books, 1978).

29. Nonet and Selznick's embrace of the developmental perspective is both equivocal and circumspect. They do not see themselves caught up in any sort of historical determinism, nor do they think of the three stages as descriptive of historical sequences. One model is, however, "prior" to another in the sense that a given society can and will move from one stage to another in response to an "inner dynamic" of institutional failure and regeneration. Thus, what they have sought to do is "to identify *potentials for change*" in each era, including our own. See ibid., 23; italics in the original.

30. Ibid., 76.

31. Ibid., 51.

32. Ibid.; italics in the original.

33. Ibid., 58; italics in the original.

34. *Gregg* v. *Georgia*, 428 U.S. 153 (1976).

35. Nonet and Selznick, *Law and Society in Transition*, 76.

36. Ibid., 4–8.

37. Ibid., 91.

38. Ibid., 92–93.

39. Ibid., 76.

40. Ibid., 15.

41. Cf. Michael K. Brown, *Working the Street: Police Discretion and the Dilemmas of Reform* (New York: Russell Sage Foundation, 1981): "[W]e ought to recognize that the contradictions of police work are rooted in the broader structural contradictions and conflicts of American society: the pervasive inequality among social classes, the intransigence of racism, and the deeply divided conceptions of morality" (303).

42. While disregard of uniformity and formal equality has probably not increased very much, it is true that only recently has that disregard been openly acknowledged and defended. Roberto Unger, among others, has noted the tendency of welfare state law, for example, "to turn from formalistic to purposive or policy oriented styles of legal reasoning." See Roberto Mangabeira Unger, *Law in Modern Society: Toward a Criticism of Social Theory* (New York: Free Press, 1976), 194. The current sense of crisis probably has more to do, therefore, with the emergence of discretion from the closet or with the liberal bias to which the public forms of discretion have been put in criminal process—for example, in juvenile justice and rehabilitative sentencing.

43. Craig Carr has made a formal analysis of both the distributive concept of justice which is inherent in neighborhood justice and the alternative of justice as equality. Carr's argument is that justice as equality (or comparative justice, as he calls it) is derivative of

distributive justice (or personal justice, as he calls it). His conclusion is that equality is not a satisfactory standard of justice. See Craig Carr, "*The Concept of Justice*" (Ph.D. dissertation, University of Washington, 1978), Chap. 1. {223}

44. Martin A. Levin, *Urban Politics and the Criminal Courts* (Chicago: University of Chicago Press, 1977), 205.

45. Ibid., 201–2. With respect to controlling crime, whether through rehabilitation or deterrence, Levin finds little to choose between the two approaches, although, on balance, he concludes that "justice" is slightly more effective than "benevolence." See ibid., 159–80 and 199–201.

46. Ibid., 160.

47. Ibid., 5–6.

48. See p. 22.

49. Nonet and Selznick, *Law and Society in Transition*, 77; italics in the original.

50. This notion of criminal process as communication is drawn from John Wilson's concept of equality. In discussing the approach of an egalitarian to conflicts with enemies, Wilson argues as follows: "Apart from self-defense, his treatment of them will always be such as to educate them to communicate. He will use only such methods which increase their self-awareness and hence the rational scope of their wills." See John Wilson, *Equality* (New York: Harcourt, Brace, & World, 1966), 163.

51. See Elliot Currie, "Fighting Crime," *Working Papers* 9, no. 4 (July/August 1982): 24–25.

52. On the case for appellate review of sentencing, see Malcolm M. Feeley, *Court Reform on Trial: Why Simple Solutions Fail* (New York: Basic Books, 1983), 151–55.

9

The Politics of Criminal Process

As its title suggests, one objective of this book has been to explore the politicization of crime that has occurred over the past twenty years. At the same time, an effort has been made to identify some of the criminal process "constants" that transcend the era of law and order. In closing, it would seem appropriate to sort out the enduring from the ephemeral, and in this way to look systematically at the conclusions that can be reasonably drawn from this study.

Conflict theory is the key to understanding both the politics of law and order and the character of criminal process. The divisions within the society and the struggle over scarce resources that are at the heart of conflict theory explain long-run tensions within criminal process, analogous tensions between criminal process and the "outside world," and apparent anomalies in the public's reaction to crime. In other words, this research must inevitably stand or fall on the persuasiveness of conflict theory.

To oversimplify a bit, I have argued that the divisions within society produce two distinctly different kinds of conflicts. Obviously, there are conflicts over available benefits: status, power, and material well-being. In addition to these conflicts of *interest*, there are *value* conflicts. On matters of right and wrong, we may not be entirely at odds, but significant moral differences exist within the society.

Taken together, these two dimensions of social conflict generate cleavages that are difficult to bridge. Although interests can generally be subdivided and compromised—as happens all the time in labor-management relations—conflicts of interest nonetheless generate considerable discord. Values are still more difficult to compromise because they tend to emerge as absolutes: conflicts between good and evil. To yield on {225} such matters seems like a retreat from virtue, and so value conflicts tend to be particularly intense. Moreover, insofar as segments of the society develop distinctive patterns of values and interests—their own subcultures, in other words—it actually becomes difficult to communicate and even harder to compose differences. Subcultures produce separate world views, and the resultant communication problems add to the difficulties of resolving conflicts over interests and values.

Precisely this sort of cleavage characterizes criminal process, as well as the politics in which it has been embroiled over the last couple of decades. Ultimately, these conflicts are accommodated. Policy emerges and implementation is affected. But policy never becomes a purposeful and concerted response to crime because the various parties to criminal process perceive crime so differently and because crime control is only one of their concerns—and not necessarily the most important one.

The principal parties to the politics of criminal process are the public, politicians, and criminal process professionals. Each brings to criminal process a distinctive set of values and interests, and the ostensible objective of crime control is largely overshadowed by the competing perspectives and purposes of the participants. Conflicts among the parties—for example, between the public and criminal court professionals over plea bargaining—are compounded by a variety of "internal" tensions, such as those between police managers and the rank-and-file, who divide according to their organizational responsibilities. The compromises struck within this fragmented decision-making process, as in American politics more generally, have much more to do with bargaining leverage than with purposeful policy making.

The public's participation in criminal process policy making tends to fluctuate dramatically. Because this book has focused on a period of heightened concern about crime, it may leave the mistaken impression of consistently intense public involvement. In fact, the public's concern with crime tends to be episodic and unpredictable.[1] The recent twenty-year period is extraordinary and perhaps unprecedented.

Under "normal" circumstances, the public is content to leave crime control pretty much to the professionals, who must of course accommodate to the politicians, and vice versa. By and large, public detachment was the rule during the two decades following World War II.[2] As long as crime remains in the background, the influence of the public on criminal process tends to be indirect. Each city develops policies and practices consistent with its basic character—its size, its demographic composition, its socioeconomic structure, and its political style. But the public ordinarily remains pretty much oblivious to the everyday workings of the police and the criminal courts, except for brief periods of attention at the time of some aberrant event like a corruption scandal, an explosive racial incident, or a particularly abhorrent crime.

Yet, the public has been intensely and punitively preoccupied with {226} crime and criminal process on and off for the past twenty years. How is this heightened concern to be explained? It might seem at first that the explanation is obvious, since politicization began to develop as the crime rate took off in the mid-1960s. But law-and-order rhetoric at that time extended beyond crime to the social turmoil stemming from the Vietnam war and urban racial traumas. It is also true that politicization has continued well beyond the plateauing of crime in the mid-1970s. Accordingly, the politicization of crime, and especially the public's punitive predispositions, are best understood in broad cultural terms that are only tangentially linked to the actual incidence of crime.

By and large, the public learns about the nature of crime and appropriate responses to it from culture rather than from experience. Our cultural images of crime are particularly alarming. We are led to consider as typical the rarest and most frightening crimes—crimes of violence committed by predatory strangers against women and the elderly. It is, then, understandable that those living in rural areas, who have the least direct experience with crime, are the most punitive. The simple truths of the myth of crime and punishment are, in other words, most likely to appeal to those who are sheltered from the complexities of crime and the vagaries of criminal process.

Crime is, moreover, a convenient symbol for focusing more general concerns about unwelcome changes in the social order. Given a broad social malaise, crime draws our attention because of the consoling lesson provided by the culture, which teaches us that punishment is a necessary and sufficient response to a fundamental problem. Punitive responses are liberating because they are so simple. We yearn to believe that seemingly intractable social and personal problems are actually responsive to direct and forceful action. The attractions of punishment are more expressive than instrumental.

By contrast, the concrete involvement of politicians and criminal process professionals makes them much less predictably punitive. In some respects politicians are in a position very much like that of the general public. Politicians are, of course, immersed in the culture, and since they are from the upper strata of the society, they are more likely to be familiar with crime in the abstract—that is, with the cultural life of crime. Once politicians decide to run for office, however, their personal predilections become much less important than the concrete problems of gaining votes. Should crime strike them as a promising issue, politicians are likely to take a punitive stance because, as I have argued, an aroused public is a punitive public. But the politician's ardor is unlikely to outlive the public's anxiety. In addition, once elected, politicians confront increasingly concrete problems because the cooperation of criminal process professionals is required to implement policy initiatives. Criminal process professionals are, for their part, sharply divided on the advisability of punitive policies and are, {227} in general, resistant to changes in established patterns. And for the professionals, even more than the politicians, the stakes of policy change are concrete and easily measured in terms of status, prestige, working conditions, and the like. Although the preferences of the public may at times coincide with those of the politicians and/or the professionals, conflict is much more likely, given the sharply different perspectives on criminal process.

The police subculture has a distinctly punitive bias. Insofar as police policies are concerned, therefore, the politics of law and order might seem rather like carrying coals to Newcastle. Indeed, rank-and-file associations, the International Association of Chiefs of Police, and individual police chiefs as well frequently play an advocacy role in behalf of the politics of law and order. But the total picture is more complex. While traditional police values are in basic harmony with the politics of law and order, those traditional values are under some pressure, and the situation is further complicated by organizational and political accommodations.

In all police departments there is certain to be tension between managerial and rank-and-file priorities. Despite shared values, the organizational interests of managers and the rank-and-file diverge rather sharply, leading to contrasting perspectives on operative policy. The rank-and-file, consistent with subcultural values, have traditionally preferred discretionary and confrontive policing. The new-style police manager tends to be uncomfortable with this policing, which is inconsistent with effective control of the police organization. Whether managers are able, or even willing, to do anything about this depends on the organizational and political circumstances.

The key to a police style, according to Wilson, is the political setting.[3] In machine cities, police chiefs are more inclined to think of themselves as agents of the machine than as managers. Accordingly, discretion and confrontation are likely to be acceptable, perhaps even encouraged, as long as influential politicians, their cronies, and important constituency groups are handled with kid gloves. Reform cities insulate the police from politics, and it is expected that law enforcement will be characterized by uniformity and civility. If these standards are not met, the chief's position will be in some jeopardy.

More idiosyncratic factors also shape police style. Progressive chiefs, who are most likely to appear in reform cities, may steer a department away from confrontive policing. But whether such reforms are effective depends very much on the persuasive power and managerial capabilities of the chief. A particularly gifted and progressive chief may even learn to live with team policing if his reforms lead to a well-trained and enlightened rank-and-file that can exercise discretion in a responsible fashion. Conversely, a militant and cohesive rank-and-file can make things difficult for even a determined and politically secure reformer, as Muir has shown.[4] {228} Even a poorly organized rank-and-file is difficult to influence because police officers, like other street-level bureaucrats, operate so much on their own and because police work often requires quick decisions under unpredictable circumstances.[5]

Obviously, policing practices differ widely from city to city, but there is uniformity as well as diversity in police policy making. Policy is invariably based, in the first place, on a delicate multilateral balance struck among the essentially parochial and competing concerns of politicians, police managers, and rank-and-file officers. It would be wrong to think of any department's policy as the product of a concerted response to the problems of crime control and social disorganization. Second, despite considerable variation in police styles, there is an underlying predisposition in virtually all departments toward discretionary and confrontive policing. These biases are rooted in the police subculture and the protean circumstances of street-level policing. Finally, regardless of how the final balance is struck among politicians, police managers, and rank-and-file officers, there is considerable reluctance to upset hard-won political and organizational accommodations—meaning that police departments are very resistant to change of any sort.

The implications for the politics of law and order are clear enough. In some cities, the politics of law and order will indeed amount to little more than carrying coals to Newcastle. That will be the case where confrontive and discretionary policing already prevails. Under these circumstances, the politics of law and order will simply work against any incipient forces of reform. In other cities, the politics of law and order may well undermine established reforms and breathe new life into the self-defeating priorities of traditional policing. In neither case, however, will the politics of law and order be likely to be a decisive determinant of police policy. That will happen only in the unlikely event that the pressures generated by the politics of law and order are sufficiently intense and sustained to transform a city's political culture. Absent pressures of these dimensions, politicians will probably combine ringing symbolic endorsements of vigorous crime control with actual acceptance of prevailing policy accommodations.

The criminal courts present a surprisingly different picture. Policy making in criminal courts, it is true, is based on political and organizational accommodations analogous to those that determine police policy. Within criminal courts, however, these accommodations are not rooted in a punitive subculture; nor does there seem to be all that much variation from city to city in the basic forms of bureaucratic justice. Finally, criminal courts, for all their purported legal autonomy, are not particularly resistant to the politics of law and order.

There is a tripartite division of labor within the criminal courts. Prosecutors, judges, and defense counsel have different responsibilities and are socialized into distinctive roles. Defense attorneys may be more or less aggressive on behalf of their clients, but their job satisfaction and, to a {229} significant extent, their career prospects are linked to the defendants' interests. Prosecutors, in contrast, tend to identify more closely with the police, upon whom they depend for evidence and, indeed, for cases. Judges, for their part, have responsibility for managing conflict and maintaining the flow of cases. If they are to be effective, judges must maintain their impartiality and their detachment from the issues dividing the defense and the prosecution.

Despite this division of labor, the level of conflict within the criminal courts is really very moderate. Defense attorneys, prosecutors, and judges are all lawyers; they have been trained to routinize and depersonalize conflict so as to keep it within manageable bounds. They work together on a daily basis and find it easy to communicate with one another. It is also true that they all have a stake in making the criminal courts function as smoothly as possible. Finally, they all partake of the same legal culture, which means that they see pretty much eye to eye on the correct procedures for processing cases. For all these reasons, it is relatively easy to compose the differences engendered by the division of labor within the criminal courts.

The legal subculture plays a somewhat anomalous role in all this, but the net effect is to make the criminal courts more orderly and equitable than they might otherwise be. Taken at face value, it might seem that the legal sub-culture would nurture the unremitting and time-consuming conflict of ad-versary justice. Insofar as cases go to trial, this is precisely what does occur. Nevertheless, the legal subculture also provides the mutual confidence and shared values, which allow the vast majority of cases to be settled without formal trials. Defense attorneys, prosecutors, and judges are all concerned with the factual accuracy of criminal court proceedings; all accept the importance of dealing with defendants in a reasonably respectful fashion; and all agree that sentences must be fair and consistent. Moreover, the legal subculture makes it likely that these standards will be interpreted in pretty much the same way by all criminal court professionals, regardless of role or locale.

The result is a consensus within and among jurisdictions on the two principles of bureaucratic justice: the presumption of guilt and the operational morality of fairness. There is, first, widespread agreement that it is all right to rely on the facts as ascertained by the police and monitored by the pros-ecutors. Thus, cases may be processed in an orderly and expeditious fashion. Second, fairness is protected by a sentencing process directed at giving defendants their due—as measured by the offense they have committed and the kind of people they are. Whether codified in determinate sentencing plans, which are currently fashionable, or more informally incorporated in criminal court norms, the operational morality of fairness provides a desert-based and reasonably consistent sentencing process.

Despite widespread consensus on bureaucratic justice, there is still {230} considerable sentencing disparity from place to place and from time to time. The legal subculture nurtures agreement on how to process cases, what crimes are the most serious, and which defendants merit harsh sentences. It is, however, one thing to agree on what and who is to be sentenced severely and another to agree on how severe that penalty should be. At this point, conflicts over the purposes of sentencing intrude, and these conflicts are rooted in political and social, rather than legal, values. Prosecutors and judges are elected to office and, broadly speaking, they sort out the competing claims of deterrence, rehabilitation, and so on according to prevailing community values, which may vary significantly across the country.[6] This variation ac-counts for much of the sentencing disparity of which critics have complained. Disparity is, then, a direct consequence of the political accommodations of criminal courts to their respective local settings, not a reflection of irrational practices, as the critics contend.

Clearly, criminal courts are politically permeable and are likely, therefore, to be responsive to the politics of law and order. There are, however, two parts to the law-and-order critique of criminal courts: that the courts are unjust and that they are permissive. As to the first charge, the politics of law and order has probably not changed things much. The basic principles of bureaucratic justice—the presumption of guilt and the operational morality of fairness—are too well entrenched and serve too many organizational purposes to have been significantly undermined by the symbolic and somewhat transient pressures generated by the politics of law and order. On the other hand, as the political climate became more punitive, so too did the legislators who prescribe criminal penalties and the prosecutors and judges who apply them. It is hardly surprising, then, that jails and prisons have been filling and in fact overflowing at an alarming rate, even though the basic forms of bureaucratic justice have probably not changed very much.

In any case, the policy consequences of the politics of law and order turn out, once again, to be problematic. Insofar as penalties have increased for the relatively few predatory strangers caught and convicted, the incapacitative purposes of sentencing may well have been served. Deterrence has probably not been increased, however, since there is no reason to believe that predatory strangers are being caught and convicted more frequently. Since certainty of punishment is more important to deterrence than severity, stiffer sentences without more reliable apprehension are not particularly helpful. Moreover, the incarceration of less dangerous offenders who have probably been made scapegoats by the more punitive sentencing tendencies of recent years is bound to be self-defeating. These relatively harmless criminals ordinarily emerge from brutal and overcrowded prisons as hardened predators.

The silver lining in all this is that the public is showing signs that it is {231} unwilling to foot the bill for housing ever increasing numbers of prisoners. The Reagan administration and other conservatives have until recently beaten the drums in behalf of prison construction.[7] The public is not enthusiastic, and the resultant fiscal backlash may be leading the administration to rethink its position. The attorney general has recently recommended that nonviolent offenders not be incarcerated.[8] This proposal is not necessarily inconsistent with the earlier plan to lock up violent offenders, but it could be a significant departure from the President's belief that criminals, in general, should pay heavily for the crimes they commit.[9] More concretely, early release plans have recently surfaced as a way of relieving prison overcrowding, and parole provides a covert means to the same end.

These tendencies suggest that the law-and-order tide may be turning, but for pragmatic rather than principled reasons. It certainly would be unrealistic, at least in the short run, to expect any change in the punitive policy preferences of the general public. If, however, it becomes increasingly less attractive, even for fiscal reasons, to campaign on get-tough anticrime platforms, the political climate may cool significantly. The ensuing depoliticization of crime will put policy back into the hands of the criminal process professionals. Without the intense public scrutiny that has characterized the last twenty years, the professionals can be expected to lead a retreat from the punitive drift of recent years. The prospects for more thoroughgoing reforms, whether along the lines of neighborhood justice considered in the previous chapter or in some other direction, are less promising. The vested interests that must be overcome are much too strong to allow for anything but incremental adjustments in established practices.

NOTES

1. See, generally, Anne Heinz, Herbert Jacob, and Robert L. Lineberry, eds., *Crime in City Politics* (New York: Longman, 1983).

2. Ibid.

3. James Q. Wilson, *Varieties of Police Behavior: The Management of Law and Order in Eight Communities* (New York: Atheneum, 1970).

4. William K. Muir, Jr., *Police: Streetcorner Politicians* (Chicago: University of Chicago Press, 1977).

5. Michael Lipsky, *Street-Level Bureaucracy: Dilemmas of the Individual in Public Service* (New York: Russell Sage, 1980).

6. Martin A. Levin, *Urban Politics and the Criminal Courts* (Chicago: University of Chicago Press, 1977).

7. See editorial comment in the *New York Times* on the report of the Attorney General's Task Force on Violent Crime, 20 August 1981. Chief Justice Burger has also argued for more and better prisons. See *New York Times*, 9 February 1981.   {232}

8. *New York Times*, 4 March 1983.

9. See the report of President Reagan's speech to the International Association of Chiefs of Police, *New York Times*, 29 September 1981.

Index

*[Page numbers refer to the original edition's pagination.
The original page numbers are inserted into text
in the present edition by using brackets.]*

A

Addonizio, Hugh, 78

Attorneys, *see* Legal

B

Balbus, Isaac, 20n, 188–190

Baldwin, James, 117

Bayley, David, 97

Belief system, 59, *see also* Public

Bennett, W. Lance, 76

Berger, Peter, and Neuhaus, Richard, 209–210

Berkow, Ira, 26–27

Blumberg, Abraham, 99, 105, 153–155, 175

Bordenkircher v. *Hayes*, 149n

Braverman, Harry, 15

Brereton, David, and Casper, Jonathan D., 155

Brown, Michael K., 146n66, 222n41

Bureaucrats, street-level, 111

C

California Determinate Sentencing Law, 187

Cambridge-Sommerville study, 8

Campaigns, political, *see* Politicians

Capital punishment, 45–46, 212, *see also* Punishment

Capitalism, 15

    crime as adaptation to, 15

    as criminogenic, 15, 20, 52

Capitalist

    class, crimes committed by, 16

    worker relationship, 14–15

Carr, Craig, 222n43

Carranza, Daniel, 122–123

Casper, Jonathan D., 168

Class

    antagonism and crime, 14

    conflict, 14–15

    division, 13, 19–20

    interests and values, 14

    relationships, 13–14

Cloward, Richard A., and Ohlin, Lloyd E., 8

Cole, George F., 221n11

Coles, Robert, 25

Communication

    neighborhood networks, 42–43

    social, 219

Community, *see also* Neighborhood justice, Reform

    development, 6, 208–211

    flight to suburbs, 7, 21

    human infrastructure, 7

    outreach programs, 206–207

    reaffirmation of, 71–75

Community-based corrections

Conflict

    class, 14–15, 203

    crime and politics, 19–29

interest, 224

political definition of, 22

and politics, 203–204

theory, 5, 19, 21, 24, 27–29, 204, 224–225

Conservative

hard-line, 9–11, 181

moderate, 6–9, 182–183, 185, 187

viewpoint, 4–5, 72, 181–182, 185

Corruption, civil, 26, see also Police

Courts, criminal, 148–197, 228–229, see also Legal; Plea bargaining, Punishment; Sentencing

bias, 167

bureaucratic justice, 157–169

coercion, 153–156, 158, 228–229

defendant's character, 173

docket congestion, 151–152

equity in, 148–169

ideology and policy, 180F

job perspective, 175–176

jury system, 186

legal principles vs. principles of exchange, 149

misperceptions of, 148–157

mistakes, 164

penalties in sentencing, 174

permissiveness of, 47, 151–153

professionals, role of, 160, 165, 175

reform, 173–197

screening of cases, 160

victims' unwillingness to prosecute, 153

Crime, see also Crime, types; Politicization

as adaptation to capitalism, 15

attack strategy, 118–119, 129–137, 139

and blacks, 26, 42, 48, 50, 109, 117, 126, 156, 191

capitalism as cause of, 20

causal analysis of, 7–8

and common sense, 3–5

and conflict, 19–29

consequences of, 17–19

control, 6, 13, 28, 48, 65–68, 84, 88, 95, 111, 192–195

control objectives of police, 129

cost to criminal, 8, 192–193

cost to society, 17

and culture, 64–75

economic, 16

and elderly, 42–43, 50

images of, 51

nature of, 5–17

and politics, 16, 19–29, 79–88

predatory, 6–7

and punishment, myth of, 59–64, 86–87, 204

rate, 19, 49, 54–55, 140, 151, 203

rules, 4–5, 11, 153

social, 16

social factors, relevance of, 19

state committed, 16

and women, 42–43, 48, 50, 63

Crime, types

of accommodation, 16

assault, 24, 60, 80, 207, 218

automobile theft, 6

burglary, 6, 23

drug dealing, 16

felonies, prior relationship, 152–153, 157, 207

inside, 121

larceny, 6, 207

mugging, 41

murder, 20, 23, 60, 80, 218

neighborhood, 39–42

outside, 121

personal, 16

predatory, 6, 16

and punishment, myth of, 59–64, 204

rape, 20, 41, 60, 80

robbery, 6, 20, 23, 26, 41, 60, 80, 152

street, 3, 6

vandalism, 207

Crime Control and Safe Streets Act, 84–85

Criminal code, 14

Criminal justice, 203–231

Criminal process, 95–197, 224–231

Criminals, *see also* Defendants; Strangers

and behavior modification, 8

rights of, 9, 84

street, 12

as victims of circumstance, 184–185

Criminology, conflict theory, 19, 21, 23–24, 27–29

Cultural diversity, 212

Cultural perspective of crime, 75

Cultural presence, 62–64

Cultural roots, 61–62

Cultural seduction, 54–57

Currie, Elliot, 197

D

Defendant, *see also* Criminals; Guilt; Poverty

character of, 155

financial resources of, 164, 167, 183

moral career of, 154

role of, 155

Delinquency, 43

causes of, 8

prevention program, 206

Democracy, 37, 49–51

Deterrence, 8, 10, 84, 174, 180, 182–183, 187

Discretion, 211, 214, 216, 217, 219

in criminal courts, 150, 168

of police, 112, 227

DuBow, Fred, McCabe, Edward, and Kaplan, Gail, 51

Due process, 13, 64, 174, 181, 183, 185, 187

Durkheim, Emile, 71–72, 86

E

Edelman, Murray, 76

Ehrlich, Isaac, 194

Eisenhower, Dwight D., 78

Eisenstein, James, and Jacob, Herbert, 155, 157, 159, 163–164, 190

Enforcement, 5, 24

Equality

before the law, 181, 183, 215

formal, 214–215, 218–219

F

Fairness, *see also* Sentencing

in criminal process, 229–230

operational morality of, 161–164, 166–167

Fear of crime, 7, 28, 37–43, 50, 104

Feeley, Malcolm, and Sarat, Austin, 85

Feeley, Malcolm, and Tomasic, Roman, 205

Fishman, Mark, 58n42, 81

Flanagan, Timothy J., *et al.*, 46–47

Force, 9, 102 *see also* Violence

and police, 101–104

professionalization of, 102, 111–112

Friedman, Bruce Jay, 68–71

Friendly, Officer, 111

Fuller, Lon, 182

G

Gaylin, Willard, 162–163

Gerbner, George, and Gross, Larry, 42, 62–64

Gibson, James L. 172n79

Goffman, Erving, 154

Golding, Martin, 184

Goldstein, Herman, 124

Goldwater, Barry, 77–78

Gorz, Andre, 17, 53

Greenberg, David F. 20n

Guilt, 10

    factual versus legal, 181–182

    presumption of, 154–155, 158–161, 165, 167

H

Halpern, Stephen C., 147n83

Heumann, Milton, 196

Hogarth, John, 198n15

Humphrey, Hubert, 79

I

Ideology, 53

    and sentencing, 180–186

Incapacitation, 174, 180–182, 193

Individual goal choices, 21

Individual responsibility, American ideal of, 62

Insanity defense, 186

Insecurities of society, 68–71

Interests, 203, 214

    class, 14

    conflicts, 224

J

Jacob, Herbert, and Lineberry, Robert L., 191

Jacob, Herbert, and Rich, Michael J., 132

Johnson, Lyndon B., 11, 52

Jury system, 186

Justice, 215–219, *see also* Neighborhood justice

    bureaucratic, 157–169, 195

    discretionary, 173, 219

K

Kansas City Preventive Patrol experiment, 121–122

Kirkham, George, 99

Knapp Commission, 125

L

Labor, 13

Laconia police force, 112, 141

Lasswell, Harold, 68–71, 86

Law

    autonomous, 211

    enforcement, 83–84, 86

    repressive, 211–212

    responsive, 211–213

    Law and order, *see also* Discretion

    accountability, 211–212

    attitudes, 38–49

    political candidates, 55

    politics, 28, 75–88, 113, 113–119, 137–143, 187–195, 213

    values, 54

Law Enforcement Assistance Administration (LEAA), 83–86

Legal, 83–86

    authority inversion, 159

    criminal courts, 176

defense counsel, 154, 228–229

    expertise, 165–166

    subculture, 229

Leniency, 13, 153, 189

Levi, Margaret, 145n39

Levin, Martin, 188, 190–191, 216–217

Liability, distinction between civil and criminal, 23, 218

Liberal perspectives, 4–5, 11–13, 71, 183–185, 187

Lindsay, John, 79, 140

Lipsky, Michael, 98, 111

Littrell, W. Boyd, 154, 158–160, 162–163, 196

Locke, Hubert G., 114n11, 144n31, 145n44

M

Manning, Peter K., 102, 104–105

Marxist perspectives, 4–5, 13–20, 28, 37, 51–54, 81, 87, 162–173, *see also* Capitalism; Capitalist; Class; Conflict; Quinney

Mather, Lynn M., 167

Maynard, Douglass W., 164

McCord and McCord, 8

Media, 55–56, 62–63, 76, 80–82, 197

Merry, Sally, 207

Miranda decision, 84

Moderate political viewpoint, 5

Moral judgments, 25

Morality

    and criminality, 24–27

    social, 216–220

Muir, William K., 97–98, 103, 111–112, 120, 133, 227

Murphy, Patrick V., 127, 129

N

Neighborhood, 39, 42

    dispute resolution, 207

Neighborhood justice, 204–220, *see also* Police, Policing

    accountability, 211–212

    citizen participation, 206–207

    community-based corrections, 208

    community development, 206, 208–211

    decentralization, 204–209

    institutions, responsive, 211–213

    mediating structures, 209, 211–213

Nightingale, Florence, 111

Nixon, Richard M., 78

Nonet, Philippe, and Selznick, Philip, 211–213, 219

P

Packer, Herbert, 54, 158–159

Parisi, Nicolette, et al., 48

Particularization, 174, 215

Penalties, *see also* Punishment, Sentencing

    as crime deterrent, 10

    social purposes served by, 174

Phillips, Steven, 176–180

Plea bargaining, 149, 159, 163

Police, 95–143, 227, *see also* Crime; Discretion; Force; Policing; Reform; Value; Violence

    accommodation, political, 108–111

    arrest practices, 195

    chiefs, role of, 109–113, 128, 141, 227

    and community relations, 110, 123–127, 130–137, 142

    continuity of policy, 137–139

    corruption and misbehavior, 109, 123–127, 141

    as crime fighters, 105, 120

crime prevention capacity, 10

crime solutions, 107–108

cynicism of, 101, 120

danger, 111

fears, 104–105

and guilty pleas, 159

homogeneity of, 97–98

identifying criminals, 101

informants, 107, 122–123

managers, 96, 108, 113, 118, 127–128, 133, 135, 225, 227–228

organizational tensions, 106–110

professionalization of, 127

rank and file influence, 96, 113, 121–123, 127–130, 133–135, 139–140, 225, 227–228

reform, 95, 117–147, 196

response time, 130

social isolation of, 98–100

subculture, 96–106, 125, 228

values, 100–106

as victims, 104–105

working conditions, 97–99

Police Foundation, the, 128

Policing, 228

assignment practices, 126

patrolling, 106–107, 121, 129

progressive, 127–137

punitive, 140–142

styles of, 119

community service, 133–137

legalistic, 106, 110–111, 131

team, 133–136, 204–205, 207, 220

watchman, 106, 109, 119–126, 131

traditional, 95–113

Political authority, 13

Political conflict, 22

Political salience, 43–45

Politicians, 26, 38, 54–55, 59, 75–79, 82, 87, 110, 195, 226

Politics

"caretaker," 109

cities, machine versus reform, 188–196

and criminal process, 224–231

and policy, 28, 83–86

Politicization

of crime, 22, 37–38, 49–57, 191–192, 226

police policies, 138–139

of social conflict, 19, 21–24, 28–29, 218

Population, 18

Poverty, 11, 21, 25–27

bias against, 167

and crime, 12

material deprivation, 12

"War on," 11

Profit, 14

Public, 37–88, see also Conservative; Fear; Moderate; Liberal; Marxist attitudes and responses of, 4–5, 28, 37–38, 43–49, 51, 53, 59, 68–71, 78–81, 97, 225–226, 231

Punishment, 6, 8, 60–61, 72, 74, 181, 184, 194–196, 226, 230, see also Sentencing

capital, 45–46, 212

crime and, myth of, 59–65, 75, 86–87, 204

Punitive policies, 66, 204

Punitive sentencing, 181–182, 185, 195

Punitive values, 45–19

Q

Quinney, Richard, 14–20, 22, 49, 51–53, 81, 83

R

Racial bias, 126, 156

Ravitz, Judge Justin, 162

Reagan, Ronald, 77, 79, 81

Redemption, 65–66

Reform, *see also* Courts; Police;
Sentencing

    community service strategy, 118

    crime-attack strategy, 118–119,
129–137, 139

    criminal courts, 150, 173–197

    institutional, 11–12

    organizational barriers to, 96

    politics of, 110, 117–143, 173–197

    prison, early, 12

    social, 6, 11–12

Rehabilitation, 11–12, 65–66, 174, 180, 183–
185, 187

Reiman, Jeffrey, 23

Reiss, Albert, 104, 123–124, 126

Repression, 53

Repressive manipulation, 51–54

Retribution, 174, 180, 184–185

Rich, Michael J., Lineberry, Robert L.,
and Jacob, Herbert, 138

Rizzo, Frank, 78

Role models, 25

Rubenstein, Jonathan, 102, 104, 107, 120–
122

Rural hunting culture, 48

Rural residents, 50

S

Schaar, John, 198n17

Scheingold, Stuart A., 64, 171n65

Schumer, Charles E., 80

Sentencing, 10, 150, 162–169, 173–174, 196–
197, 229–230, *see also* Deterrence;
Plea bargaining; Punishment

    dilemmas of, 175–187

    disparities, 156, 163, 230

    due process, 187

    fairness, 161, 181, 229

    and ideology, 180–186

    incapacitation, 181–185

    insanity defense, 186

    insiders' rules and views, 164,
186

    interpersonal dimensions, 176–
180

    job perspectives, 175–176

    law and order, 187–195

    and legal values, 182

    leniency, 189

    and politics, 180–185, 188–189

    punitive viewpoint, 181–182, 185

    and race, 191

    responsiveness to legal values,
182

    retribution, 184

Silberman, Charles, 25–26, 101, 107, 132,
134–135, 152–153, 163, 193–194, 206

Skogan, Wesley G., and Maxfield,
Michael G., 41–42, 50, 56, 66

Skolnick, Jerome, 122, 165

Smith, William French, 81

Social communication, 219

Social contract, 4

Social disorganization, 52

Social inequity, 13

Social morality, 216–220

Social order, 13

Social programs, 12, 53

Social stratification, 23

Spohn, Cassia, Gruhl, John, and Welch,
Susan, 156

Stark, Rodney, 103

Stein, Sol, 72–74

Stenvig, Charles, 78

Stinchcombe, Arthur L., 47–48

Strangers, predatory, 6, 60, 66, 87, 122,
193, 195, 197

Subculture, 225
  legal, 229
  police, 96–106, 125, 228
Sudnow, David, 158, 161, 167
Supreme Court, 9–10, 65, 149
Symbol, 68, 75–76, 87, 186, 226
  crime as, 75
  politics, 85

T

Television, 62–64
Thomas, Isiah, 26–27
Tomasic, Roman, and Feeley, Malcolm, 205
Tracy, Dick, 111
Tumulty, Brendan, 122–123
Turk, Austin, 24–25, 23n62

U

Unemployment, 18, 44
Unger, Roberto, 222n42

V

Values
  class, 14, 203, 209–210, 214
  conflict, 28–29, 224
  legal, 182

police, 96–106, 112–133, 119
political, 180–185
societal, 214
van den Haag, Ernest, 11, 151, 193
Victimization, 40–43, 50, 73–78, 80, 105, 154–155, 203
Vigilantism, 61
Villmoare, Adelaide, 90n55, 91n64
Violence, 26, 62–63, 102–104, 141

W

Walker, Samuel, 97, 127, 140
Wallace, George, 78
Wambaugh, Joseph, 99–101, 105
Warren, Chief Justice Earl, 9
Warren Court, 9, 65
Whitaker, Gordon P., *et al.*, 145n54, 145n57
Wilson, James Q., 5–13, 21, 49, 52–53, 84, 97, 106–110, 118, 126, 131, 137, 139, 150–152, 175, 189, 193–196, 227
Wilson, James Q., and Boland, Barbara, 129, 131
Woodson, Robert, 209–210
Working class, 13–15
Wright, Richard, 17n
Wylie, Martha, 208

Part of the *Classics of Law & Society Series* from Quid Pro Books. Available in ebook formats. Please see other works from Dr. Scheingold, and all our titles, at *www.quidprobooks.com*.

www.ingramcontent.com/pod-product-compliance
Lightning Source LLC
Chambersburg PA
CBHW031532260326
41914CB00026B/1667